China Tourism: Cross-cultural Studies

Deriving from a special issue on "China Watching" (*Journal of China Tourism Research*), this book presents the readers with a collection of seven independent research reports that adopt cross-cultural communication and cultural studies approaches to China tourism. Topics covered include the authenticity in cultural diffusion, the articulation of China through tourism, cross-cultural comparison of vacation consumption interpretation, the Chinese gaze of Europe, influence of globalization and localization on the development of tourism, behavioral implications of Chinese outbound tourism, and citing behaviors of Chinese tourism researchers from foreign language sources.

The book will be of great interest to academic researchers, graduate students, policy makers, and destination managers who are interested in China tourism. The varied aspects covered, together with the engaging writing style, makes the text a pleasure to read.

This book was published as a special issue of the *Journal of China Tourism Research*.

Honggen Xiao, PhD., is Assistant Professor in the School of Hotel and Tourism Management at The Hong Kong Polytechnic University. His research interests include knowledge development, leisure and society, and tourism and culture.

Mimi Li, PhD., is Assistant Professor in the School of Hotel and Tourism Management at The Hong Kong Polytechnic University. Her research interests include tourism planning, destination marketing, consumer behaviour in hospitality and tourism, and China tourism.

China Tourism:
Cross-cultural Studies

Edited by
Honggen Xiao and Mimi Li

Routledge
Taylor & Francis Group

LONDON AND NEW YORK

First published 2015
by Routledge
2 Park Square, Milton Park, Abingdon, Oxon, OX14 4RN, UK

and by Routledge
711 Third Avenue, New York, NY 10017, USA

Routledge is an imprint of the Taylor & Francis Group, an informa business

© 2015 Taylor & Francis

British Library Cataloguing in Publication Data
A catalogue record for this book is available from the British Library

ISBN13: 978-1-138-80754-9

Typeset in Times New Roman
by RefineCatch Limited, Bungay, Suffolk

Publisher's Note
The publisher accepts responsibility for any inconsistencies that may have
arisen during the conversion of this book from journal articles to book chapters,
namely the possible inclusion of journal terminology.

Disclaimer
Every effort has been made to contact copyright holders for their permission to
reprint material in this book. The publishers would be grateful to hear from any
copyright holder who is not here acknowledged and will undertake to rectify
any errors or omissions in future editions of this book.

Contents

Citation Information

The chapters in this book were originally published in the *Journal of China Tourism Research*, volume 8, issue 3 (August 2012). When citing this material, please use the original page numbering for each article, as follows:

Chapter 7
Culture-Based Interpretation of Vacation Consumption
Xiaoxiao Fu, Xinran Y. Lehto, and Liping A. Cai
Journal of China Tourism Research, volume 8, issue 3 (August 2012) pp. 320–333

Chapter 8
The Behavior of Citing: A Perspective on Science Communication Across Languages
Honggen Xiao, Qu Xiao, and Mimi Li
Journal of China Tourism Research, volume 8, issue 3 (August 2012) pp. 334–356

Please direct any queries you may have about the citations to
clsuk.permissions@cengage.com

Guest Editors' Note

This special issue publishes research on tourism to (and from) China and its associated policy, development, and business practices from cross-cultural communication and cultural studies perspectives. Theoretically, the (re)presentation and interpretation of culture are often characteristic of an incommensurability and at times contradictions in ideology and values, which often result in discourse that does not share cultural and rhetorical traditions. Liu (1999), in argumentation studies, alluded to such cross-cultural, typically East–West, interlocutions as the justification of one's position in another's terms, in which he observed "non-Western interlocutors in general are willing to debate cross-cultural issues in Western terms, whereas Western interlocutors are also increasingly seeking to justify their positions in non-Western terms" (p. 297). Contextually it is within the same complexity that this special issue on "China watching" is conceived.

For discourse analysts, the (re)presentation and interpretation of cultural Others have remained a key concern in tourism (Caton & Santos, 2009). In this regard, for more than half a century, China has been both changing and changed in her journey toward modernization and growth, which is typical of a mass-mediated process of global–local interactions (Teo, 2003) and mutual gaze (Maoz, 2006). As a cultural encounter, tourism to and from this emerging world-leading destination and origin serves as an ideal magnet for a cross-cultural scrutiny of the politics, art, and even beauty of China watching (Xiao & Mair, 2006). As such, it provides a culturally distinct and rich context to bring into play the perspectives of cultural studies, media and communication studies, journalism, and Chinese and Asian studies for the interpretation of cultural (re)presentation in relation to tourism and leisure.

This special issue features seven articles that adopt cross-cultural approaches to China tourism. In terms of perspectives on research collaboration, four articles were written by coauthorships of both Chinese and Anglo-European origins. Keith Hollinshead and Chun Xiao Hou provocatively discuss China tourism capitalizing on a (the) "soft power" derived from traditional Chinese philosophies and Confucian thoughts, as a subtle authority and undersuspected agency that the nation deploys, through its government projection, in alignment with its economic strength and international strategies. Jundan (Jasmine) Zhang and Eric J. Shelton address authenticity in cultural diffusion through their reflection, and occasionally eulogy, of the construction (or reproduction) of a Chinese garden in New Zealand. Nicolette de Sausmarez, Huiqing Tao, and Peter McGrath report on the cultural differences and behavioral implications of Chinese outbound tourists to the United Kingdom, whereas Julio Aramberri and Chunmei Liang take a reverse track of the "gaze" by analyzing how Chinese travel magazines portray Europe to their potential tourist audiences.

In addition, three articles were produced by authors of Chinese origin, who nevertheless are Western educated and consequently are conversant in Western rhetoric and capable of understanding, communicating with, and even debating on tourism issues from cross-cultural perspectives. Yujie Zhu, taking *Naxi Ancient Music*, *Lijiang Impression*, and *Naxi Marriage Courtyard* in southwest China's Yunnan Province as examples, explores how globalization influences the three cultural performances as an external force (e.g., catering to Western tourists) and how these performances as a form of cultural capital are internally interpreted, imagined, and transformed by the local/domestic tourist market. Xiaoxiao Fu, Xinran Y. Lehto (half Chinese by name), and Liping A. Cai investigate cultural and behavioral differences in Chinese versus American vacation experiences and find that divergences in values are instigated by unique cultural dispositions. The last article in this collection, by Honggen Xiao, Qu Xiao, and Mimi Li, looks at power relationships that govern the perceptions and behavior of Chinese tourism researchers citing foreign-language sources in contemporary social science communication.

We wish to thank our panel of referees for their time and expertise. Candy Li, editorial assistant of *Journal of China Tourism Research*, has been very helpful in coordinating anonymous reviews of these manuscripts. Without their commitments and inputs, this special issue would not have been possible. Notwithstanding the scope of China watching, articles in this collection are complementary in approaches and perspectives; it is our hope that this special issue will trigger interest in, and in a way point out directions for, future undertakings on China tourism from cross-cultural perspectives.

Honggen Xiao
Mimi Li
Guest Editors

References

Caton, K., & Santos, C. (2009). Images of the Other: Selling study abroad in a postcolonial world. *Journal of Travel Research, 48*(2), 191–204.

Liu, Y. (1999). Justifying *my* position in *your* terms: Cross-cultural argumentation in a globalized world. *Argumentation, 13*(3), 297–315.

Maoz, D. (2006). The mutual gaze. *Annals of Tourism Research, 33*(1), 221–239.

Teo, P. (2003). Global and local interactions in tourism. *Annals of Tourism Research, 30*(2), 287–306.

Xiao, H., & Mair, H. (2006). "A paradox of images": Representation of China as a tourist destination. *Journal of Travel and Tourism Marketing, 20*(2), 1–14.

The Seductions of "Soft Power": The Call for Multifronted Research Into the Articulative Reach of Tourism in China

'软实力'的诱惑 — 以中国旅游为例

KEITH HOLLINSHEAD
CHUN XIAO HOU

In recent years, tourism has been increasingly posited as not just that set of ordinary promotional processes by which destinations are projected to visitors from afar (and by which those holiday-makers/trippers are managed there) but also as that mix of political and aspirational activities through which institutions and interest groups variously collaborate and contend to solidify particular visions of their supposed culture, heritage, and nature for not only distant/external others but for their own proximal/internal selves. Working from these later/broader perspectives, this article calls for a much richer critique of the ways in which China itself is articulated. Drawing particularly from Bell's (2008) scrutiny of Confucian orientations to the world and from Nyíri's (2006) examination of declarative agency of and over tourism, this article calls for deeper and more sustained critique of the conceivable "soft power" normalizations of China through tourism today.

Introduction: The Power of Representation in Tourism

Recently, the subject of *representation*—that is, the production of meaning through language, discourse, and image (S. Hall, 1997)—has won a pivotal position in contemporary investigations of culture. And recently, tourism has been found to play a prominent role as a producer and communicator of such sorts of representational meaning (Selwyn, 1996; Rothman, 1998). This investigation of and about China proposes to examine the role and function of tourism as a representational system through which the meaning of and about peoples, places, and pasts is made and exchanged; that is, made and exchanged via the everyday institutional and corporate interactions (and the social and personal interactions) of international tourism/global travel. To this end, the study proposes to follow the lead of tourism studies researchers such as Buck (1993), Lidchi (1997), Kirshenblatt-Gimblett (1998), and Hollinshead (2007) and explore the ordinary and the special fashions by which tourism:

- expressively articulates populations and places;
- creatively images populations and places; and
- performatively manufactures/demanufactures/remanufactures populations and places.

In this way, this study of China as an imaginal realm proposes to probe the manner in which cultural, ethnic, regional, and other differences about peoples and nations are nowadays signified through tourism in China; that is, how the government (at various levels) and the tourism industry construct (or rather coconstruct) particular local visions and national versions of identity as particular places/particular pasts/particular presents are opened up, exhibited, and/or promoted. Consequently, the investigation (Hou, 2010) upon which this article is largely based positions tourism as a rich narrative arena of representation in which concrete practices of signification and received or established interpretations may be discerned to define what given nations, or given cities, or given cultural spaces are and thereby who rightly belongs or rules there and also who is being excluded from such representations or otherwise denied/delimited by them.

Before attention is turned in this article to the more concrete matters of signification and symbolism that Bell (2008) and Nyíri (2006) specifically addressed in and around "soft power" and declarative articulations of China, respectively, attention will be given here to explain how representation is generally a critical matter to explore in terms of the subjects it makes and the silences it deals in or engenders. This is a must for this study: this critique in *Journal of China Tourism Research* is premised on the view that the Eurocentric held truths that are conveyed through representational practices have become a powerful force to undersuspectingly dominate the rest of the world. But during the 21st century, other outlooks—particularly those reflective of the BRIC nations of Brazil, Russia, India, and of China, itself—will come to challenge (and already are challenging) that symbolic/significatory hegemony. And tourism certainly will increasingly matter in terms of such replacement knowledge production, such corrective place creation, and such realigned interpretation of history and geography.

To Gandhi (1998), it is highly important that considerable attention is made to who encodes and who decodes what, where, and when if the power of the representational talk and deeds of governments and corporations are to be decently understood and effectively monitored. To her, we all increasingly live in an age of constant cultural/ political projection and ethnic/national articulation—an age of coercion and seduction. As Said (1994) informed us, while the world quickly globalizes or quickly glocalizes, it is vital for many populations and governments that the representational violence of imperialism of the last two centuries (and more!) are recognized and that the touchy significations of knowing the self and knowing the other are closely tracked. And it is crucial (in fields like tourism management and tourism studies) that the fresh representational counternarratives of colonized populations (or formerly colonized populations) are closely identified. Such—in tourism management and tourism studies—is the new and expansive discursive cartography of tourism in response to its old universalizing representational geography. Such is the new symbolic sensorium of (especially) the self-representation of peoples/places/pasts and thereby the new and previously unimaginable or impossible representational utterances of tourism and related fields (Venn, 2006). Such is the power of tourism and related fields in matters of being and becoming and thereby in the new strategic rhetorics of futurity (Agathangelou & Ling, 2009).

Background: Soft Power Articulation and Understanding

Having introduced the general and incremental importance of representational activity today, a short opening comment will be given as to the representational repertoires (after S. Hall, 1997) that exist in China today that the tourism state of China can and does draw upon. It will be carried out via an explanation of what soft power and declarative agency are in terms of the general articulation of cultures/places/nations through tourism. (For an explanation of the dynamisms and mobilizations of the tourism state, see McKay [1994], originally speaking of Nova Scotia, and refer to Hollinshead [2009b] for further critique of the emergent declarative role of the state in tourism.)

The Basis of Soft Power

In general terms, *soft power* is the capacity of populations, governments, or nations to achieve what they want to attain through influence and understanding rather than through the hard power techniques of coercion or economic force (Nye, 2004). Hence, soft power's effectiveness tends to arise from the strategically exhibited or the tactically communicated attractiveness of the culture of a people or a country and from the understood appeal of its customary practices, its political ideas, and thereby its contemporary policies. Accordingly, when the customs and policies of a population/government/nation are appreciated in their own light and deemed acceptable and/or legitimate, the soft power influence of that people, that authority, or that country is accentuated or enhanced. In this sense, in contrast to *hard power* (which tends to rely on such things as military force and financial inducements), soft power tends to help instrumentalities and nations obtain what they seek through understanding, through conveyed or revealed attractivity, and through cooption.

Theorists maintain that the concept of soft power works through the successful encoding and decoding of peaceful and attractive and otherwise alluring images of a place, notably in terms of the felt brilliance of its history and the believed genius of its contemporaneity. That attractivity is used by governing bodies to alter or manipulate the styles of thinking or the preferences of "other (target) peoples" and, indeed, that very soft power agency may be used inwardly among populations *within nations* and not just outwardly to other peoples *between nations*. Commonly associated with the imaging or reimaging of the intangible assets of a culture, soft power communication tends to seek the spread of esteemed value or cherished inheritance and it is deployed (often quietly and unsuspectingly or undersuspectingly) in order to stimulate that target internal population or that target external people to engage with that very value or to internalize that very signified inheritance.

Though the principal currency of soft power is culture itself (Zheng, 2008), its use is primarily a matter of relationship building, where "seduction is almost always more effective than coercion" (Nye, 2004, p. x). In international affairs, the use of soft power may constitute part of a nation's grand strategy "charm-offensive" policy and it may range over many or all continents in many industries. Soft power may thus also be used locally and incidentally to help educate or indoctrinate a specific external population (or, to repeat the point, even to inform or persuade a specific domestic one) about a particular doxa, a held truth, or a cultural warrant. At the macrolevel of international affairs, then, a nation like China may, for instance, want to use soft power's influence to promote Chinese socialist values as an alternative to Western values, or it may be used locally or internally to build up "the spiritual civilization" of a or the people there (Glaser & Murphy, 2008, p.15). Although in China the Chinese approach to soft power has been interpreted as being holistic and organic (embracing both macrolevel/foreign policy strategies and microlevel matters of homeland culture/spiritual reform), the nation of China is yet to develop a comprehensive and coherent national soft power strategy (Glaser & Murphy). No nation on earth is actually known to have yet or ever developed a thorough and integrated *de fond en comble* (top-to-bottom/all-embracing and exhaustive) approach to soft power through political action, though.

The problem for all governments and instrumentalities that wish to engage in soft power is that the gain of cultural influence takes much time, much perseverance, and much controlled constancy to message (Tuke, 2009). But the capacity of a country to influence specific external or internal others through attraction and persuasion (rather than force) may be achieved (or, at least, approached) through a variety of "appeal arenas." For instance, during the opening years of the 21st century, the Beijing Olympic Games presented China with an immense opportunity to mark the end of its supposed "century of humiliation" (notably after the Opium Wars of the 19th century; Tuke). Likewise, the exhibitional march of the First Emperor's Terracotta Army to the distant British Museum (and to numerous other places around the globe) enabled much to be articulated about the longtime brilliance of the ancient Chinese inheritance (*Daily Telegraph*, 2008), and the recent ordered expansion of Confucian Institutes around the world (increasing from 120 in May 2007 to 307 eighteen months later, spread across 78 countries) constituted a very important diplomatic tool through which Chinese language and culture could be readily promoted (Tuke).

It is important, therefore, to examine how, where, and when tourism is deployed as a key tool in China's soft power diplomacy or its charm-offensive toolbox. China is indeed believed to be the lead exponent of soft power fantasmatics (Nye, 2004). (For an explanation of *fantasmatics* itself, please refer to Hollinshead [1998a, 1998b, 2004].)

Of course, one may justifiably enquire why it is necessary to work with a new concept like soft power when there are so many existing other concepts (especially in Western continental philosophy about ideology and hegemony) that could conceivably already do the job. Such Doubting Thomases could no doubt insist that the consolidating field of cultural studies is replete with concepts about signification, rational action, and the relationships between nations and culture. But do the existing notions of the governance and the governmentality of things really suit the matters of seductive articulation being covered in this article? For instance, Barker (2002) strongly argued that culture and knowledge are very difficult entities to treat universally. To him, it is unwise (within the arena of cultural studies and related fields) to try and understand theories of governance and hegemony as grand world-relevant narratives but rather as *local tools* that describe specific aspects of the circumscribed parish or the provincial realms of the particular defined "we." As such, to him, cultural studies (and related fields) currently lacks (lack) a singular and universal unit of analysis about the legitimations of absolutism, fundamentalism, and nationalism that can be operationalized on a global scale across nations and ultimately across continents (Barker).

In extending Barker's (2002) point, one could bring in any number of European/ continental/other theorists of power at work, but each might come freighted with emphases and orientations that limit their fit for the understanding of soft power dynamics at play, notably in the particular sphere of Asian/East Asian history and contemporaneity. One could bring in existing Marxist or neo-Marxist treatments of ideology, but thinkers of and about representation have generally found them to be distinctly inadequate in terms of their capacity to gauge kaleidoscopic questions of subjectivity, non-economic meaning, and aspirational cultural politics (Barker). One could bring in the more flexible existing Gramscian notions of ideological hegemony, but his conceptions of hegemonic power at play are more suited to spheres of activity where popular culture is itself a site of ideological struggle where that ideology acts as a glue that binds quite a range of diverse social groups together en bloc (Bennett, Mercer, & Wollacott, 1981) rather than national populations. They are more fitting to scenarios where an undergirding multiplicity of diverse wills and heterogenous aims (rather than a single national fellowship) are welded together by the temporary social authority and leadership of that hegemonizing ideology (Gramsci, 1971).

One could bring in Foucault's vast existing conceptual lexicon on the power/ knowledge dimensions of normalizing discourse (via, for example, capillary power, petty power, biopower, etc.), but to him the truths conveyed through that discursivity are inevitably discontinuous, being marked by pungent historical ruptures of understanding where the particular social world "is no longer perceived, classified and known in the same [dominant] way" (Barker, 2002, p. 47). Thus, Foucault's (1980) constructions of capillary truth do not lie comfortably with nationalistic ideas of being and becoming that are proto-metaphysical and proto-transcendental in the degree of their almost blanket or totalized nationalism. Foucault's sustained work on counterconduct (see Prado, 2000) may be very useful for those who want to explore how soft power articulations are seemingly resisted here and there, but (as for Gramsci) his developed analytics of *a* or *the dispositif* works more tellingly where there are multidimensional (contesting) possibilities of being and becoming or otherwise plural zones of power functioning rather than ultra-strong but contained authoritarian styles of governance (Dean, 2010). Foucauldian Kant-inspired notions of power/knowledge work best where an irreducible multiplicity of power relations conceivably exists and where truth concepts are never fixed or pre-fixed (as under the 40 centuries of the Chinese inheritance they are commonly taken to be) but are sagitally related to—that is, structurally conditioned by or within—the teeming present (Foucault, 1986).

And one could bring in yet further existing constructions from other philosophers or cultural studies theorists to challenge the utility of soft power notions of articulation. Perhaps such rival constructions will indeed appear in a future issue of *Journal of China Tourism Research* to punctuate or replace soft power syntax. But in order to replace these advocated soft power understandings, they must be flexible in their explanatory authority to account for not only how lived worldviews thrive as values but how they are constructed and articulated within closed/partially closed rather than in open, plural, and ascendant spheres of statist articulation.

Focus on China: Regimes of Representation in and Through Tourism

This critique of soft power and declarative agency in *Journal of China Tourism Research* comprises the critical investigation of tourism as a powerful creator and producer of social knowledge or held truths as to what China is (or has become) within and through national and international tourism. Hou's (2010) investigations upon which much of this article is based explore how regimes of representation work in tourism (at the general level) and situate that insight within discursive understandings of and about China to ascertain who is authorizing which visions of Chinese identity and heritage (in collaboration with whom), at the expense of which other contesting versions of what China is (or should be) today. Throughout those platform studies, a strong effort is made to explore the manner and fashions by which—in tourism—China has been contained within longstanding Western visions of what it is as a land, a nation, a culture, and a people, where that Western imaginal is not conceivably congruent within the visions of land-hood, nation-hood, culture-hood, and people-hood that tend to arise within China itself.

To that end, Hou's (2010) study that prompted this article was itself posited as:

- *a Foucault-inspired inspection* of the inventive politics and fabricative poetics of place-making;
- *an interpretivist study* predicated on the view that contemporary visions of peoples, places, and pasts commonly result from longheld cultural, social, nationalistic, and other notions of identity and of difference that may not necessarily be held consciously by those vision-holders;
- *an open-ended inquiry* into the need for the cultivation and development of improved dialogic understandings (in tourism, as elsewhere) as to the communicated or apparent distinctiveness of places.

Please refer to Hou (2012) for fuller background insight on China as an imaginal realm; on the representation and misrepresentation of China, today; and on dominant constructions of nationalism in China. Much of Hou's (2012) critical inspection of the cultural grammar of vision-making in China stems from her informed synthesis of Unger's (1996) edited portrayal of the contestations between traditional and emergent constructions of "Chineseness." Hou's (2010) work does not seek to secure congruence or closure on what Chineseness actually or currently is. It seeks, instead, to draw due attention to the weight of the importance of Chineseness within performative industries and declarative spheres of cultural production like tourism in order to engender much more informed and mature reflexive and seasoned critique in tourism studies of those meaning making issues notably where old and new Eastern cosmologies rub up against received and efflorescent Western certitudes.

Having clarified the subject-making potency of declarative forms of representation in general and drawn attention to the common pungency of orientalist discourse in Eurocentric knowledge in particular, this study advances with the understanding that scrutiny of the productive representational power of meaning-making should occupy a central place in contemporary analysis of culture and place projection in tourism (i.e., in tourism studies). Hereafter, therefore, this study proceeds by targeting the representations of China in the international tourism marketplace. It especially inspects how the language, the discourse, and the images that are current in contemporary significations of and about China indeed work as a system of representation actively making, de-making, and remaking what is there to be seen in the history, the heritage, and the culture of what many regard as both the world's largest national territory and the world's most populous nation. In this regard, the study works from the view that is now prevalent in much cultural studies work that meaning is inherent in things in the world but is constructed by particular people in particular contexts in capillary fashion (S. Hall, 1997), something that Platenkamp (2007) has written most insightfully about in the twin domains of tourism studies/leisure studies. Hence, this unfolding inquiry will broadly operate from the Foucauldian understanding (after Foucault, 1970, 1980) that the relations of meaning that constitute the representation of a people or a place are actually relations of power or, rather, of power-knowledge in tandem (Hollinshead, 1999).

The authors of this article therefore seek to explore in China how the relations of power, which are transmitted through tourism (as a representational system), help manufacture—or indeed manufacture, per se—China as a realm of held social knowledge. In a nutshell, the authors (as researchers of soft power and of declarative authority) seek to pry into the ways in which China (as a subject in the language, the discourse, and the images for tourism) is signified (and thereby produced). The synthesis produced focuses upon what in China is signified and who is doing that signification about China. In the Foucauldian sense (Hollinshead, 1999; Prado, 2000), this study is part of a larger ongoing multistudy research agenda in which the authors seek (in various administrative and promotional settings) to delve into the following productive sites/processes/channels where versions and visions of China are regularly produced and normalized:

- the government approaches in the production of Chinese national tourism;
- the corporate regimes-of-truth about what the nation (of China) is;
- the discursive statements (about Chinese history/heritage/culture) that are mainstreamed—that is, normalized and in strong administrative and representational vogue;
- the particular nationalistic narratives myths, storylines, and themes (of and about China/Chineseness) that are routinely emploted and that do systemically circulate and–in comparison, to explore which alternative narratives tend to be bypassed or ignored and which thereby do not get emploted for circulation.

Clearly, as the authors' overall research agenda unfolds, it will hopefully be possible over the coming years to study these items in a large variety of interpretive place-making contexts and in a broad mix of different promotion-regulating settings within which particular forms of soft power seductions are suspected of being exercised.

Soft Power Articulations: The Declarative Reach of Tourism in China

Having introduced the concept of soft power and explained its general applicability to the development and management of tourism in China, an attempt will now be made to detail the alluring authority and the arrestive agency of tourism in the making of peoples, places, pasts, and presents in China through distillation of two recent commentaries on contemporary representational activity in China. The first piece of critique involves scrutiny of the work of Bell (2008), who generated the aforesaid host of interpretations about the value and relevance of Confucian meanings of soft power for the people of China (and for the East and, indeed, for the world) today. The second piece of critique involves an examination of Nyíri's (2006) study of the so-called famous *scenic spots* for tourism and travel in China tourism, and thereby of the state program-approved representation of the viewable mytho-history and the visitable cultural-geography of China.

The Confucian Concept of Soft Power: Bell's Commentary on Its Role and Function in China Today

Here, an attempt is made to look at the sorts of contemporary values in China that affect the ways in which Chinese people view themselves and their extremely long historical (or national) inheritances. This inspection is carried out per medium of a short critique of the writings of Confucius on life and the world. The critique focuses upon the observations that Bell (2008) recently made about the great philosopher Confucius, for although Bell himself is not Chinese, his works sell extremely well in China. The key element for this scrutiny of applied Confucian thought, then, is the distillation on and about the concept of soft power, as given in Table 1.

Daniel Bell is a professor of political philosophy at Tsinghua University in Beijing. A Westerner who lives in China, who speaks Chinese, and who teaches at a foremost Chinese institution, Bell writes about his adopted country with large doses of both appreciation and critical distance. In his illuminating coverage of the politics of banal life in the changing society of China, Bell draws our attention to what in the West is the undersuspected open political future that lies ahead for China. To him, China is not as totalitarian as many Western observers axiomatically seem to assume, and he writes about everyday life and political action in China in order to reveal not so much the innate political conservatism of the country but its teeming progressivism. Bell is able to approach this task by examining the Confucian values that infuse Chinese politics and the daily lives of its people. In drawing attention to these contemporary manifestations of Confucian thought, Bell seeks to portray the New Confucianism of China not as a mere redecoration of narrow forms of old nationalism but as a rich mode of utopian cosmopolitanism—that is, as an action-based kind of ethics in which many populations (and not just the Chinese) can indeed participate. Table 1 provides a distillation of what Bell (2008) conceivably put forward in his recent Princeton University book. In this work—an extension of many other Bell treatises on Confucius—Bell attempted to engage the reader in dialogue about the immense new possibilities that are currently presented to the people and nation of China as it moves center stage to become a leading player in world affairs. He advocates the view that China can now become a new power but one rather different from the old Western Empires that conceivably ruled so much of the world in the 19th and 20th centuries—that is, a nation driven by a leadership that is founded on the role of New Confucianism as "a compelling alternative to Western liberalism" (Bell, back cover). Table 1 is itself taken from Hou's (2010) recent study of symbolic power in the representational repertoires of tourism bodies in China.

In his book, Bell (2008) covered the sorts of important host nation perspectives that this study in *Journal of China Tourism Research* (of the internal and external seductions of soft power) is centrally targeting. Moreover, as Table 1 seeks to reveal, Bell scrutinized the possibilities that exist as particular Chinese values can now spread more readily across the world as the 21st century runs its globally connected Information Age course. In this late work, he showed China to be a nation whose leaders crave stability among all things and where so many areas of present life are unified into and within the received national inheritance. Thus, even Chinese adherents of Marxism may be seen to be an extension of Confucianism (Bell). In this effort to condemn the crude stereotypes that exist of and about China in the West, Bell repeatedly examined matters of

Table 1. China in and Across the World:
The Function of Confucian Thought as Soft Power, According to Daniel Bell (2008).

- *Bell's Clarifications of the Meaning of Soft Power:*
  - Soft power is that subtle authority and undersuspected agency that a nation deploys (in alignment with a strength of position in economic and other strategic matters) to use particular values and favoured practises to win over the hearts and minds of foreigners.
  - Soft power is that authority or power to act that is used to invoke centuries old thoughtlines and longstanding ways of seeking and knowing the world. It is the quiet forethought through which (in the current context) China creatively adapts and translates understanding about its inheritances and its sacred/secular preferences for digestion by others.
  - Much of the context of current soft power projection by governments of China is based on the thinking of the Chinese intellectual Kang Xiaoguang and the longstanding interpretations of Mencius.
  - One of the lead rhetorical claims of Confucianism—as projected through its soft power channels—is that not only individuals but also peoples and nations should seek to engender harmony within themselves and among each other.
  - In this light—through the broader population-based/nation-based mediations of soft power—Confucianism is a philosophy of life in which the world beyond China can fully engage.

- *Bell's Clarifications of the Value of Confucian Thought*
  - Many Chinese people feel that Confucianism "is in our blood" (p. 12; based upon a statement from Eva Wang, a leading trainer in Confucian methods).
  - When exercised through soft power mechanisms, Confucianism can become a double-edged sword: it can serve as a positive alternative to Western liberalism, but it can also become confused with Chinese administrative forms of legalism and be condemned by outsiders (beyond China) as a mere justificatory source of authoritarian nationalism.
  - Fundamentally, Confucianism and New Confucianism are ethical philosophies (though) and as such are views of the world that are not containable within language or ethnic groupings.
  - Participation in New Confucianism is a never-ending process, a matter of becoming and not of being; engagement in New Confucianism constitutes a personal attitude toward modesty, tolerance, and a willingness to learn and is not a matter of political commitment.

- *Bell's Observations on the Soft Power Potential of Confucian Thought Applied to Tourism: Tourism as althe Declarative Agency*
  - Like other domains and arenas tourism can serve as a teacher to individuals and to the world—a source of intellectual wisdom and a model of ethical living.
  - Just as athletics and athletes have been used in soft power fashion by the state of China to score political points projections about moral and intellectual development, so the work of cultural tourism managers, heritage tourism developers, and nature tourism programmers can be used to advance particular world—declarative or worldmaking visions of and about China;

(Continued)

Table 1. Continued.

- Though the staging of the Beijing Olympics may have served as a vital opportunity for the promotion of *aoyun liyi* (Olympic civility) within and beyond China, the presentation and projection of particular lead tourism sites in China may be used by the state to advance selected notions of inheritance and preferred notions of well-being.
- Tourism settings and storylines can serve as an important resource by and through which the people of China and the people beyond China can learn about life and existence from past thinkers and exemplary rulers (in the received Confucian tradition): tourism sites and themes can thereby serve as a new and catalysing font for this high esteem for learning.
- Because many tourist sites are axiomatically situated within everyday social settings and communal locales, they may be readily harnessed to draw graphic attention to not just arcane forms of learning but to "lived life"; as such, there may be (in tourism) ample scope to help individuals not just talk the talk in terms of Confucian values but to see how to walk the walk.
- Because many tourist sites are readily accessible and viewable, the field of tourism provides considerable opportunity for New Confucianism (as, indeed, for other philosophical/cosmologies/ethical ways of living) to be popularized and projected beyond academic circles.

Source. Hou (2010), derived mainly from Bell (2008).

legitimacy in China and noted how it is regularly woven from three cardinal sources—from (firstly) "sacred texts," from (secondly) "the sanction of historical continuity," and from (thirdly) "the tacit acceptance by the people of the day" (p. 179). What thereby fascinates Bell is how the teaching of Confucius pungently reflects all three of these cardinal sources. It is contained in sacred sources and longstanding interpretations. Its quest for harmony (not mere conformity) is a recurring facet of the historically continuous essence of Chineseness. And its contemporary popularity among the people of China—as attested to by sales of Yu's (2006a, 2006b) popular recent treatment(s) of Confucius—speaks to the undoubted tacit acceptance of Confucian thought among current people of China, north, south, east, and west.

As this inspection of Bell's (2008) examination of Confucian thought provided in Table 1 suggests, New Confucianism is thus a vital part of the efforts of present-day government of China to not only consolidate received Chinese culture and the ancient Middle Kingdom inheritance in the banality of day-to-day life in China, but it stands as a main means by which so-called Eastern ways of living are explained and substantiated elsewhere in the world. Though large Chinese corporations may use New Confucianism to fortify the loyalty of their workers within China, it is the government of China that is taking those aforesaid active steps to establish Confucian institutes in strategic locales around the world beyond China for soft power influence (Bell).

But we must give richer special attention to the specific matter of soft power per se. Table 1 has been provided to illuminate what is meant by *Confucian soft power*—a construct that must be understood by those who seek to appreciate what tourism conceivably authorizes and conceivably legitimizes in China. Table 1 thereby frames the concept of soft power in terms of its capacity to articulate the values of New Confucianism, and tourism is then introduced into this table as an arena in which such forms of Confucian soft power may be readily exercised. Though Bell himself clearly writes about soft power and Confucius, the third leg of the table (the coverage of tourism, ipso facto) is an effort by Hou (2010), herself, to translate Bell's (2008) work on Confucian soft power to the context of representational activity in and of tourism. Hou indeed maintained that the term New Confucianism acutely captures much of what is going on today in the projection of China, Chinese ways, and Chinese being to other populations abroad. She therefore joined Bell in the force of his relativist views of the Chinese cultural poetic today: "[While] Westerners want to marketize everything, the Chinese value relationships based on care and emotion" (Bell, p. 82).

The Chinese Concept of Scenic Spots: Nyíri's Commentary on the State Legitimation of Place-Making Today

The material for this second part of the critique constitutes a distillation of the commentary of Nyíri (2006) on the role of both tradition and the agency of the state (in China) in exerting cultural authority over what is deemed to be properly viewable and decently visitable within and across the nation. Nyíri's work is a very readable Western interpretation of what is seen to be supportable in terms of the duteously visited cultural and natural heritage of China, although he argues frequently that the Chinese have little concern for the distinct Western notion of authenticity per se. In clarifying that, he introduces and explains many of the distinct Chinese constructions that relate pointedly to China's own visions of its heroic past and thereby to preferred visions of its contemporary present. His *Scenic Spots* account is indeed a very rare and valuable attempt of an outsider to describe the state's ultimate responsibility to determine the meaning of special landscape and revered locality within and across China.

Much of Nyíri's (2006) inspection is tailored to his view that in China tourism development has been heavily orchestrated by the state, where special/registered scenic spots (*jingdian*) and approved theme parks are strategically harnessed and pointedly promoted as both instruments of patriotic education and national modernisation. Nyíri, a Hungarian researcher currently based at an Australian University, terms this utilitarian outlook on tourism in China as "indoctritainment" (Nyíri, 2006, p. 76). Thus, in his view, tourism sites in China tend to be regarded as an important product that has to be made orthodox—and thereby be bounded, approved, rated, and consumed in the appropriate and reverentially observed fashion.

Table 2 is now offered to distill some of the key ways in which "ortholalia" takes place—where ortholalia is Nyíri's borrowed term for the manner through which the scenic spots (*jingdian*) are thus represented, emploted, and carefully programmed according to Nyíri's assessment of the found statist normalization or naturalization of the historical, heritage, or environmental phenomenon at hand.

Nyíri's (2006) work provides a penetrating but accessible deconstruction of cultural authority at work in China. It offers an informed coverage of the manner in which scenic spots, theme parks, and literary sites have been discursively normalized (historically), though Nyíri did temper his findings about the totalization of site regulation by showing how in the last decade or so, new sorts of differentiation and certain instances of resistance have occurred in terms of the way antiquity and esteemed landscape beauty have been codified in China. Nyíri's work will thus be a central plank of the ongoing umbrella research agenda of the authors of this article as they thus conduct their own ongoing program of integrated studies into the cultural grammar involved in the normalization of place and the naturalization of space in China over the coming decade.

Table 2. The Programmed Representation of China:
State Ortholalia in and Through Tourism, According to Nyíri (2006).

Some findings on the governing reach of the state: Instances of cultural authority in the tourism of China

- The experiences Chinese people pursue at special tourism sites are largely shaped by the state (promotional flier for scenic spots, issued 2006).
- ◆ "Tourism in China is understood by its managers as the consumption of bounded and controlled zones" (p. 7).

- In China, tourism development at important scenic spots and theme parks is not only "guided by state" (Nyiri, 2006, p. 7), but is used pointedly as a form of indoctritainment to demonstrate China's heroic past and as an indexing tool to service patriotic education and modernization.
- ◆ Drawing from Wang (2001, p. 49)—"[under] the liberating potential of Chinese tourism, despite its regimented nature . . . whether we define the people as agent or dupes, the issue of PLEASURE is critical."

- Because the development of lead tourist sites in China is heavily uniform and encased, the business of tourism and travel is one of the least free sectors of the retail economy there.
- ◆ "Most tourism development projects are joint ventures between state actors (governments, tourism corporations, or state enterprises) and private investors, in which the state party interests invest no cash but hold veto power" (p. 72).

- In China, the narrative uniformity that is enforced upon and over lead tourist sites constitutes a form of cultural grammar by and through which the state defines travel itineraries and controls the meaning held over landscape, space, and place.
- ◆ "While the state rarely intervenes directly in the details of development, it sponsors a discursive regime in which scenic spots and their state-endorsed hierarchy are tools of patriotic education and modernization" (p. 75).

- Although the state closely regulates what it is possible to stage or project at important scenic spots and theme parks in China, such entities are managed and developed through an undisguised heavily commercialised approach (promotional flier for scenic spots, issued 2006).
- ◆ "Commercialisation is not only rapid and uniform . . . but also striking overt. Unlike tourism development in the West, no attempts are made to disguise commercialisation through clever design, use of materials, or sales behaviour" (p. 54).

- Following Diller and Scofidio (1994) Nyíri maintains that, in China, a tacit pact of semi-fiction exists at lead tourist sites between the sightmakers and the sightseers that blurs the distinction between the real and the counterfeit.
- ◆ "Western tourists [who visit China] desirous of an 'authentic' or 'picturesque' shot, purified of blatant signs of tourist activity, look around in desperation. The result of each uniform and self-conscious commercialisation is the erasure of differences between tourist practices that, in the West, are perceived as distinct, such as ecotourism versus sightseeing" (p. 54).

Table 2. Continued.

- The development and projection of lead tourism sites in China is managed to help honor the population's special feeling of Chineseness and to empower Chinese people to know and appreciate their roots in received versions of national culture.
◆ "Tourism is an arena in which the production of cultural discourse penetrates everyday consumption . . . [and] is a key sphere in which the reinvention of the Chinese subject takes place, and consequently an important area for the state to control" (p. 97).

- Just as the state in China plays a highly selective and controlling role in determining what ought to be done at or said about important scenic spots and theme parks, so it plays a large mediating role in influencing the decontextualisation and/or recontextualisation of tourist sites abroad for the due knowledge of Chinese people.
◆ "The Chinese state is attempting to influence . . . representations [of foreign tourist sites]. Remarkably, the first large-scale study of internet filtering in China found tourism to other countries—along with such other topics as . . . political issues, religion, and health—to be one of the topics which the Chinese government regularly blocked web access" (p. 107).

- In China, the lead tourism sites of other countries are taken from the local tourist canon in those nations but are articulated and managed in terms of the official (Chinese statist) history of the day.
◆ "Unlike Western city guidebooks, these [Chinese guidebooks] present no walks, neighbourhoods, or atmospheric descriptions, let alone 'off the beaten track' tips. . . . Similar to the touristic representations of 'minorities' in China, festivals such as the German Mardi Gras are represented as activities in which all members of the nation participate" (pp. 105–106).

- Though the state remains the ultimate authority determining the values and meaning of scenic spots and theme parks, significant evidence exists that the state is slowly/steadily withdrawing its stranglehold on the development and promotion of such tourism sites.
◆ "Even though the tourism business is generally [and increasingly] market-driven, consumer-oriented, and by nature global, the presence of the state [in China] informs the transmissions between the cultural and the economic that have shaped the directions of tourism's development [there]" (p. 98).

Note. ◆ = example of a relevant direct statement from Nyíri (2006).
Source. Hou (2010): these issues have been synthesized from Nyíri (2006).

In sum, Nyíri's (2006) *Scenic Spots* study is a valuable primer for those who require a grounding in the governance of official tourism sites and settings in China. It constitutes an insight-loaded inspection of the principal matters of *orthopraxy*—where orthopraxy is Nyíri's favored concept to describe approved or designated action in terms of what the state deems ought to be undertaken to facilitate the due celebration of China—and what is thereby of rendered properly viewable or visitable in terms of specific scenes, locations, and storylines.

It is important to emphasize Nyíri's maintained point that these matters of ortho-praxy are heavily nationalized forms of propriety as expressed in and through tourism. They comprise key ways in which tourism to and within China and China itself should be staged, according to Beijing authorities. They are manifest acts of meaning-making in and for China that speak to what Hollinshead (2007, 2009a, 2009c) has called the worldmaking role and function of tourism. (Please refer to Hollinshead, Ateljevic, & Ali [2009] for a short and generalized explanation of the ubiquitous but undersuspected worldmaking power and reach of tourism in all of its local, regional, national, and supranational dimensions.)

Recently, Hou (2010), the originator of Table 2, has painstakingly distilled the following acts of meaning making in China from Nyíri's commentary. Here is an encapsulation of Hou's close scrutiny of Nyíri to that end, where the following are an extension of the material presented in Table 2:

- **The sovereignty of state-produced representations:** Participation in tourism (by Chinese people in China) is seen to be a state-sponsored practice of shared ritualism (Nyíri, 2006): these rules of propriety (i.e., these forms of national orthopraxy) are initially inculcated through the provision of the state production line of official brochures and registered catalogues of sites and places (Nyíri). Accordingly, in recent years (in the view of Nyíri), China has only been understood and celebrated through a limited numbers of approved ways of seeing (Nyíri).
- **The force of state theming:** In China, sanctioned tourist activities are generally established or created (whether displays, shows, or visitable sites) via controlled theming (Nyíri): the designated tourist product might (for instance) be constituted within a designated "golden week," on a designated "golden route," or otherwise classified with the same sort of rigor that has been (and is still) used to classify sacred temples (Nyíri) in religious or philosophical life.
- **The additive vision of the unified nationscape:** In China, when sites are given a or the correct representation or classification, that signification helps fortify preferred visions of the nationscape (Nyíri) and is seen as helping to bolster the precious historical unity of the nation (Nyíri). Much of the accent and strength of these national classifications stems from the literati tradition from which they are pre-dominantly derived in China (Nyíri).
- **The affinitous engagement of tourists in national myth making:** The national feelings that the designated sites/activities/experiences are intended to engender tend to be affinitous rather that introspective (Nyíri): the state authorities thereby generally seek to promote participation rather than the sorts of contemplation commonly enabled or targeted at heritage tourism sites in the West. The Chinese state autho-rities pointedly seek to promote and articulate aspects of the national sublime, not cultivate freshly derived or individually inspired in situ reflection (Nyíri)—and especially so from and by dutiful domestic tourists in China.
- **Empowerment through statist classification systems:** In many instances, in Nyíri's estimation, when the state awards a classification of some sort to an important local tourism site or valued setting, it generally does so without the provision of accom-panying development funds (Nyíri): the local authorities and community groups revere the designated status, itself, and it is that which subsequently generates the income they themselves crave. Though the awarding state bodies may play no day-to-day active role in the management/development of the designated sites, they do

generally retain a right of veto over the range of activities permissible at such locations (Nyíri).

- **The multiplied reach of state-controlled classification—across the industry:** In China, the media and the market have historically played a matching (complementary) role with government in supporting the statist articulation of what is deemed to be right and proper at and for significant tourist sites (Nyíri). Though most tourism development projects are collaborative ventures between state instrumentalities and private interests, the state works through its veto power and its serialized forms of guided influence. Individual managers at tourist sites fundamentally act as contractors of state agencies (conducting their own business in return for the supply to the state of an agreed profit share quota). These managers have to work with tour routes formally sanctioned by the state and they are expected (for instance) to promote ethnic tourist villages approved by it (Nyíri, drawing from Oakes, 1998).
- **The almost unquestioned literary and then industrialized consecration of Chineseness:** The level of information exchange at or about lead tourism sites in China tends to be poor (Nyíri): what tends to count locally and nationally there is not (unlike in the West) what is authentic at that site or setting but actually how it has been nationally enshrined (Nyíri). Quite frequently, this enshrinement comprises a kind of semiotic overdetermination where the Chinese exalt in their received literary history to an intense degree (Nyíri).
- **The internal exoticization of minority populations through tourism in China:** Throughout China, the projection of tourist places and spaces is constructed and delivered in a manner that sustains the imaginal of a rich multicultural national community (Nyíri). In Nyíri's view, in building up such a vision of simple and blissful existence (i.e., coexistence), much of this representational activity tends to infantilize minority groups (Nyíri), all too often presenting them as "happily backward and fixed populations" (Nyíri, p. 29)—or, rather, presenting them as a heavily essentialized and othered folk (Nyíri). Thus, Nyíri instances Tibetan traditions that have readily been appropriated in ritualized fashion and ethnic tourist villages that have been contextually themed via national outlooks (where the locals are fossilized and rendered immobile, accordingly living within enclaves cut off from wider society "unrelated to the vernacular constructions of the society that surrounds them" (Nyíri, p. 55, drawing from Edensor, 1998; see also Nyíri, p. 74, drawing from Oakes, 1998). Nyíri (following Oakes) suggested that one of the functions of the strong performative presentation of ethnic villages is to reveal the primitive "against which the urban [Chinese] tourist can define his or her [own] modernity" (p. 50).
- **The continuing efforts to check what is projected of/about China as the representational system further technologises:** So important is the creation of the national/the literary/ the multicultural myth of a cohesive China that state authorities devote considerable time and effort to Internet filtering to control what foreign and other/outside voices say about tourism sites and travel experiences (Nyíri).
- **The late rise of nonstatist and external sorts of representational scripting:** In recent years, there is evidence that certain travel markets in China (even for the traveling domestic Chinese) are beginning to rely upon nonstatist authorizations of place and of quality—such as *The Lonely Planet* (guidebook) listings (Nyíri)—at the expense of received, official, or closed national classifications. The backpacker market has been of primary effect in this sort of casual but incremental disregard for established statist

or heavily nationalist forms of propriety and orthopraxy (Nyíri). Accordingly, many nonnational sites of significance are now emerging (Nyíri).

Such is Hou's (2010) penetrative probe into Nyíri's (2006) recent judgments of the role of Chinese authorities in worldmaking in the industrial scripting of tourism and in essentializing ploys concerning the general or permissible representation of China—though Nyíri himself does not explicitly use the term *worldmaking* per se. It was incumbent upon Hou (and now upon Hou and Hollinshead, in tandem, in their ongoing research agenda on the normalization and naturalization of things) and also on other researchers in tourism studies/tourism management and beyond in their own research bailliwicks to pry further into matters of emplotment and signification in China to see whether Nyíri's (2006) judgments are indeed supportable assessments. It is important that such critical forms of monitoring now take place across a multifronted range of individually conducted and collectively orchestrated investigations across a plethora of geographical settings and representational contexts to determine whether any other symbolic and significatory activities are actually at work as China itself globalizes/glocalizes and as each city and province conceivably develops its own confident and perhaps somewhat independent imaginal profile (possibly thereby acting incrementally a little more freely from the established eye of authority in Beijing). The merit of Nyíri's judgments must be tested and assessed via a range of fresh contexts.

Though Nyíri's points made above are not each primarily and directly illustrative of soft power approaches per se, they do attest to the force of the state as a controlling guardian of the selection of sites, settings, and storylines that ought to constitute the viewable gene bank of the national cultural/heritage and the visitable national natural inheritances. Before promotional soft power noise can be made about the manifest virtues and the visitable draw cards of a territory, it would be advantageous if coherent control were exerted upon the proper ranking and labeling of the candidate sites, settings, and storylines. In this sense, the scenic and literary *jingdian* of China have to be selected and regulated if that soft power coherency is to be maintained. As Langley (2007) stated in a profile of the captivating and seductive use of terracotta warriors of Xian, for 2,000 years the manifold ranks of clay soldiers have protected the necropolis of the Emperor Qin Shihuang, but now these brilliantly sculptured military men work on further state/national duty as they freshly act as leading figures in soft power articulation of and about China.

But Nyíri's (2006) work suggests that it is difficult for the state or for authorities in Beijing to maintain their authority over such classificatory activity against the rising cacophony of other voices that increasingly appear to have an effect across China. Nyíri's work on orthopraxy and indoctritainment must therefore be repeated or, rather, reapplied in a teeming variety of other interpreted settings and locales across China. Is the supposed received literary character of lead sites and storylines still relevant? Are particular and fresh narratives of place and space emerging locally and regionally in China that are nowadays rather too numerous and varied for Beijing instrumentalities to corral together these days? Is the representational repertoire of China not so much imploding but fast diversifying and otherwise slowly fragmenting? Such are some of the cardinal queries that it is now timely and opportune to inquire into on a mutifronted research basis if the declarative/articulated agency and reach of tourism is to be substantively assessed.

Prospect: The Serious and Sustained Ongoing Examination of Soft Power and Declarative Authority in China

This article has sought to introduce those who work in tourism studies/tourism management to the myriad ways in which China as an imaginal realm is currently being addressed through the projective and performative reach of tourism. In providing something of a primer on soft power (viz. notably regarding New Confucian forms of soft power) and on declarative authority, for those who work in research or in operational practice in tourism, the article has sought to not only gauge the discursive cartography of tourism but to also draw attention to its commonly undersuspected power and governance in the making, remaking, and de-making of places and in persuasive worldmaking education about culture and inheritance. But examinations of diplomatic or indoctritaining soft power are rare in tourism studies. Much more frequent examinations of the cultural selection processes and the cultural production procedures through which national and other myths are articulated are decidedly needed, within each and every country (C. M. Hall, 1994; Meethan, 2001). And they are particularly needed in China, the nation that will receive the most tourist visitations in the world by the middle to the end of the current decade.

Though Hou is already engaged on her own ongoing research agenda on the articulative reach of tourism in China (as evidenced by Hou, 2012), other researchers from within and beyond the field of tourism studies/tourism management per se, are hereby encouraged to develop their own substantive and long-term investigations of imaginal realms, of declarative authority, and of fantasmatics as they are crafted through the prevailing discourse and praxis tourism and its collaborative industries in China. The following startup questions are thereby provided to catalyze that required individual and collaborative scrutiny:

Ongoing Investigative Issue on the Normalization/Naturalization of China

1. **The impact of Confucian thought today.** Where the exercise of soft power is found or suspected in China through tourism practices, how genuinely Confucian is it?
2. **The complementary or conflictual character of Confucian influence.** Where the exercise of soft power is found or suspected in China, do any of its possible/conceivable Confucian elements significantly conflict with any other communistic, capitalistic, or other tacit (but ultra-strong) notions of selfhood for China/for the Chinese people?
3. **The felt presence of New Confucianism through tourism practices in China.** What is New Confucianism in terms of tourism, ipso facto, and are there any prime/well-suspected/effective explicit projections of New Confucianism in the emergent representational repertoires of institutions and organizations responsible for the development of tourism in China?
4. **The found vehicles for the articulation of soft power.** Which lead festivals/events/sites/settings have been appropriated as, coopted for, or developed to serve as lead instruments of soft power in the development and promotion of national gene bank of heritage tourism/cultural tourism/literary tourism in China?
5. **State classificatory and developmental control in tourism.** Does the national government of China still exercise full control/predominant development/controlled projection of the lead tourism sites of China—or is that sanctioning centralized

authority waning along trajectories identified by Nyíri (2006) or otherwise along other trajectories not actually recognized by Nyíri?

6. **Comparative messaging of and for the fantasmatics China within and across other industries.** Where the exercise of soft power—or of some other distinctly programmed nationalist/provincialist/regionalist form of fantasmatics—has been uncovered within the representational repertoire of contemporary tourism production and promotion in China, does that found soft power projection (that found fantasmatic emplotment) tally precisely with the represented projections uncovered within parallel performative industries such as the film, theater, and museum exhibits (in their own respective declarations about China)—or is there evidence of new/fresh/specialist seductive persuasion in the distinct attractivity of tourism alone?

7. **The osmotic effects of foreign travelers on the exhibited fantasmatics of China.** Is the local/national canon of what constitutes important places to see and experience in China changing in significant ways because of the increased presence of foreign visitors in China during the 21st century—and, if so, what are those novel or emergent ways (in terms of the visited or favored sites/scenes/storylines)?

8. **Independent or differential messaging across China—by place and space.** Is there significant conflict between the ways in which (or the themes by which) particular cities/provinces/populations in China now promote or project themselves vis-à-vis the ways in which (or the themes by which) central state authorities in Beijing project those said cities/provinces/populations—and, if so, what are those indicative contesting differences of projection?

9. **Differential decoding of the inheritances of China by visiting oversea tourists.** In which significant ways do substantive numbers of foreign tourists in China appear to fail to register/understand/appreciate the sanctioned narratives or the emploted fantasmatics that are regularly offered to them/for them at lead sites/settings/themes and through which the selected inheritances of China are currently projected—if any?

10. **Responsiveness to unexpected foreign visitor interpretations of Chineseness.** Is there evidence that substantial numbers of foreign tourists to China wish to visit/experience/engage in Chinese cultural, national, or spiritual (in the widest sense) activities that are not currently readily facilitated or generally empowered by official tourism authorities in China—and, thereby, what are these principal externally sought appeals or externally favored unserved/underserviced activities?

Hopefully, over the next decade, these questions can generate a diverse and penetrative multifronted mix of investigations from a panoply of informed researchers into the declarative reach of tourism in China. Hopefully, these questions can prime the pump and catalyze the development of a new-fashioned portfolio of investigations into the conceivable soft power and worldmaking characters of what tourism helps profess and promulgate in and about China. Thereby, hopefully, these matters can serve as cornerstone lines of inquiry to throw considerable light (soft light) on these pressing questions and dynamic challenges about seductive normalization and seductive naturalization. Ateljevic, Pritchard, and Morgan (2007) is just one of several recent sets of commentators on international tourism which has shown how tourism studies is systemically still a widely noncritical domain of understanding. Yet tourism is a, or even the, prime vehicle today by and through which the longstanding legacies of history, culture, and presence are articulated.

In the People's Republic of China, we are now very fortunate to have Bell's (2008) promptings about the Confucian impulses that energize the people today, but in tourism studies we do need specific and penetrative critical interrogation of the ways in which those Confucian cosmological hues and those long-wrought Middle Kingdom narratives are deployed to characterize and/or buttress the approved projection of Chineseness today. And in the Peoples' Republic, we are very fortunate to have Nyíri's (2006) external view of cultural selection and cultural production at work in the projection of Chinese fantasmatics, but it remains merely one observer's beyond-the-boundary assessment of worldmaking governance at work in the country. In China, we simply need many more informed research agendas established, working on what Buck (1993) called the mytho-politics of place and space and the mythopoesis of received/lived heritage if those who work in tourism studies are to cumulatively get anywhere near interpretive sufficiency on these symbolic issues and governing (but dynamic and changeable) practices. Tourism studies yet remains a field of rather raw and unseasoned analysis in China—as is the case elsewhere (Meethan, 2001)—in these vital society-sustaining and society-projecting concerns of local, regional, and national collective fantasy. Tourism can make, remake, and de-make peoples, places, and pasts—but in China (again, as elsewhere) do enough researchers spend committed time critically examining that creative authority and communicative genius that is routinely or strategically being exercised each month and each year over those society-sustaining matters of fact and fantasy? Do enough critical studies interpretive researchers watch over those who proudly and honorably (one may presume) staff the worldmaking watchtower of declarative authority in the tourism development and promotion bodies of the People's Republic of China? And is there much informed dialogue (about the identification and representation of what constitutes the national "gene bank" of culture/nature/inheritance) within tourism management circles between these interpretive researchers and the governing adminis-trators of people-making, place-making, and past-making in China? Or is this form and level of critical dialogue about inscriptive and performative agency something to be freshly and creatively engendered over the immediate decade(s) ahead for China, which is conceivably the nation (of all nations) with the richest mix of historical sites and cultural stories to select from?

References

Agathangelou, A. M., & Ling, L. H. M. (2009). *Transforming world politics: From empire to multiple worlds*. London, England: Routledge.

Ateljevic, I., Pritchard, A., & Morgan, N. (Eds.). (2007). *The critical turn in tourism studies: Innovative research methodologies*. Amsterdam, The Netherlands: Elsevier.

Barker, C. (2002). *Making sense of cultural studies: Central problems and critical debates*. London, England: Sage.

Bell, D. (2008). *China's new Confucianism: Politics and everyday life in a changing society*. Princeton, NJ: Princeton University Press.

Bennett, T., Mercer, C., & Wollacott, J. (Eds.). (1981). *Popular television and film*. London, England: British Film Industry.

Buck, E. (1993). *Paradise remade: The politics of culture and history in Hawaii*. Philadelphia, PA: Temple University Press.

Daily Telegraph. (2008). Tomb raiders. *Telegraph Magazine*, 46–50.

Dean, M. (2010). *Governmentality: Power and rule in modern society*. Los Angeles, CA: Sage.

Diller, E., & Scofido, R. (1994). Suitcase studies: The production of a national past. In E. Diller & R. Scofidio (Eds.), *Back to the front: Tourisms of war* (pp. 32–107). New York, NY: Princeton Architectural Press.

Edensor, T. (1998). *Tourists at the Taj: Performance and meaning at a symbolic site*. London, England: Routledge.

Foucault, M. (1970). *The order of things*. London, England: Tavistok.

Foucault, M. (1980). *Power/knowledge: Selected interviews and other writing*. New York, NY: Pantheon.

Foucault, M. (1986). Kant on revolution and enlightenment. *Economy and Society*, *15*(1), 88–96.

Gandhi, L. (1998). *Postcolonial theory: A critical introduction*. St. Leonards, Australia: Allen & Unwin.

Glaser, B. S., & Murphy, M. E. (2008). Soft power with Chinese characteristics. In C. McGiffert (Ed.), *Chinese soft power and its implications for the United States: A report of the CSIS smart power initiative* (pp. 10–26). Washington, DC: Center for Strategic and International Studies.

Gramsci, A. (1971). *Selections from the prison notebooks* (Q. Hoare & G. Nowell-Smith, Eds.). London, England: Lawrence and Wishart.

Hall, C. M. (1994). *Tourism and politics: Policy, power, and place*. London, England: Belhaven.

Hall, S. (Ed.). (1997). *Representation: Cultural representation and signifying practices*. London, England: Sage.

Hollinshead, K. (1998a). Disney and commodity aesthetics: A critique of Fjjellman's analysis of "Distory" and the "Historicide" of the past. *Current Issues in Tourism*, *1*(1), 58–119.

Hollinshead, K. (1998b). Tourism and the restless peoples: A dialectical inspection of Bhabha's halfway populations. *Tourism, Culture and Communication*, *1*(1), 49–77.

Hollinshead, K. (1999). Surveillance of the world of tourism: Foucault and the eye-of-power. *Tourism Management*, *20*(1), 7–23.

Hollinshead, K. (2004). Tourism and third space populations: The restless motion of diasporic peoples. In T. Coles & D. J. Timothy (Eds.), *Tourism, diasporas and space* (pp. 33–49). London, England: Routledge.

Hollinshead, K. (2007). "Worldmaking" and the transformation of place and culture: The enlargement of Meethan's analysis of tourism and global change. In I. Ateljevic, A. Pritchard, & N. Morgan (Eds.), *The critical turn in tourism studies: Innovative research methodologies* (pp. 165–193). Amsterdam, The Netherlands: Elsevier.

Hollinshead, K. (2009a). Tourism and the social production of culture and place: Critical conceptualizations on the projection of location. *Tourism Analysis*, *13*(5–6), 639–660.

Hollinshead, K. (2009b). "Tourism state" cultural production: The remaking of Nova Scotia. *Tourism Geographies*, *11*(4), 526–545.

Hollinshead, K. (2009c). The "worldmaking" prodigy of tourism: The reach and power of tourism in the dynamics of change and transformation. *Tourism Analysis*, *14*(1), 139–152.

Hollinshead, K., Ateljevic, I., & Ali, N. (2009). Worldmaking agency—Worldmaking authority: The sovereign constitutive role of tourism. *Tourism Geographies*, *11*(4), 427–443.

Hou, C. X. (2010). *China as an imaginal realm: A study of the representational framing of a nation in tourism* (Unpublished doctoral dissertation). The University of Bedfordshire, Luton, England.

Hou, C. X. (2012). China and deep-rooted vision: Cultural grammar in contest in tourism, today. *Tourism Analysis*, *17*.

Kirshenblatt-Gimblett, B. (1998). *Destination culture: Tourism, museums, and heritage*. Berkeley, CA: University of California Press.

Langley, W. (2007, August 26). Feat of clay: Profile—The terracotta warriors. *Sunday Telegraph*.

Lidchi, H. (1997). The poetics and politics of exhibiting other cultures. In S. Hall (Ed.), *Representation: Cultural representations and signifying practices* (pp. 151–208). London, England: Sage.

McKay, I. (1994). *Quest for the folk*. Montreal, Canada: McGill and Queens University Press.

Meethan, K. (2001). *Tourism in global society: Place, culture, and consumption*. Basingstoke, England: Palgrave.

Nye, J. S., Jr. (2004). *Soft power: The means to success in world politics*. New York, NY: Public Affairs.

Nyíri, P. (2006). *Scenic spots: Chinese tourism, the state, and cultural authority.* Seattle, WA: University of Washington Press.

Oakes, T. (1998). *Tourism and modernity in China.* London, England: Routledge.

Platenkamp, V. (2007). *Contexts in tourism and leisure studies: A cross-cultural contribution to the production of knowledge.* Wageningen, The Netherlands: University of Wageningen.

Prado, C. G. (2000). *Starting with Foucault: An introduction to genealogy.* Boulder, CO: Westview Press.

Rothman, H. K. (1998). *Devil's bargains: Tourism in the twentieth-century American West.* Lawrence, KS: University Press of Kansas.

Said, E. (1994). *Culture and imperialism.* London, England: Vintage Books.

Selwyn, T. (Ed.). (1996). *The tourist image: Myths and mythmaking in tourism.* Chichester, England: John Wiley & Sons.

Tuke, V. (2009, Summer). Confucian values: China's search for soft power. *China Ethics,* 46–47.

Unger, T. (Ed.). (1996). *Chinese nationalism.* Armonk, NY: M. E. Sharpe.

Venn, C. (2006). *The postcolonial challenge: Towards alternative worlds.* London, England: Sage.

Wang, J. (2001). The state question in Chinese popular studies. *Inter-Asia Cultural Studies, 2*(1), 35–52.

Yu, D. (2006a). *Confucius from the heart: Ancient wisdom for today's world.* London, England: Macmillan.

Yu, D. (2006b). *Professor Yu Dan explains the analects of Confucius.* Beijing, China: Zonghua Book Co.

Zheng, D. E. (2008). China's use of soft power in the developing world. In C. McGiffert (Ed.), *Chinese soft power and its implications for the United States: A report of the CSIS smart power initiative* (pp. 1–9). Washington, DC: Center for Strategic and International Studies.

Authentic Antipodean Chineseness? A Scholar's Garden in Aotearoa/New Zealand

大洋彼岸真实的中国特色？新西兰的中国古典私家园林

JUNDAN (JASMINE) ZHANG
ERIC J. SHELTON

"Chineseness" may be linked to the Chinese garden and ancient Chinese poetry. This article presents a study set in a Chinese garden in Dunedin, New Zealand. This scholar's garden is marketed as being authentic in that it was designed in China, constructed using traditional materials imported from China, and built according to traditional principles by Chinese artisans. In this article we critique the use of the term authentic in this setting and argue that it is the visitors' experiences of the garden that act to authenticate authenticity, or otherwise, depending on their personal characteristics. In addition, we argue that ancient Chinese poetry is a suitable and important medium through which to offer visitors opportunities to engage with the garden and with Chineseness.

The art of the Chinese garden emphasizes the portrayal of a mood, so that the hills, waters, plants, and buildings as well as their spatial relationship are not just a mere materialistic environment but also evoke a spiritual atmosphere. The builder of the garden, through symbolism and allegories, the search for a poetic mood, the gathering of relics from all over, and the building of temples, streets and even taverns, strives to reach a realm that is natural yet elegant, combining the art of the garden with classical Chinese literature, painting and theatre, where in the true essence of traditional culture lies.

Qingxi Lou (2003, p.3)
"Chinese Gardens" From the Cultural China Series

The development of Chinese gardens in New Zealand testifies to their importance in reinforcing various aspects of "Chineseness" in New Zealand. To long-established members of the Chinese New Zealand community in Dunedin, its Chinese garden offers both a tangible connection to their forebears and to the culture that sustained such "classical" garden culture, but also a basis for the development of future relationships with this region.

James Beattie (2007, p.58)
Growing Chinese Influences in New Zealand: Chinese Gardens,
Identity and Meaning

In 2003, the Cultural China Series, comprising nine volumes, was published and made available online at the Website of the Ministry of Foreign Affairs of the People's Republic of China.[1] The first quote above, from the "Chinese Gardens" section of the series, provides a glimpse of the tenor of the series. Subtly illustrated is the willingness to share the art and poetic mood that are embedded within the "essence of traditional culture" (Lou, 2003, p. 3). However, what do the recipients, from both China and other countries, think is "Chinese culture"? Literature and public media reports suggest that, for Chinese college students, the most common icons of Chinese culture are Confucius, traditional Chinese medicine, and Chairman Mao (Q. Li, 2011), whereas Chinese cultural development, soft power, and "Chineseness" are the sources of recent excitement and enthusiasm in Western media (Gill & Huang, 2006; Paradise, 2009; W. Zhang, 2010). Indeed, interest in the notion of cultural China and Chineseness is growing, not only in the Chinese domestic regions and communities but also in the rest of the world (Wu, 2008). One of the most significant phenomena is China's outbound tourism, whose strong growth has been recognized as a tourism manifestation of "the imagined community of 'Chineseness'" (Arlt, 2006, p. 199). The question arises: How do these different understandings of Chineseness affect visitor experiences?

After considering "Chinese Gardens" as presented in the "Cultural China Series," this article shifts the geographical focus to antipodean New Zealand and focuses attention on a Chinese scholar's garden there. Existing as a local tourism attraction and as part of Chinese heritage, this Chinese garden was constructed in 2008 in Dunedin, a sister city of Shanghai. Beattie's quote above suggests that the Dunedin Chinese Garden reinforces various aspects of Chineseness in New Zealand (Beattie, 2007). In this article, we explore the tensions between the Dunedin Chinese Garden functioning as a tourism attraction and the notion of authentic Chineseness and inquire about how visitors to an overseas Chinese garden perceive it and how these perceptions interact with this notion of authentic Chineseness.

This article presents the findings of a qualitative study conducted in the Dunedin Chinese Garden and integrates academic literature with original material from on-site communication with, and observation of, local, domestic, and international visitors. Setting such a current inquiry alongside a historical understanding of Chinese Gardens in China allows visitors' comments about the Dunedin Chinese Garden to illustrate different approaches on how to experience the garden, specifically by utilizing either a cultural approach or by utilizing a touristic approach. That the garden may be viewed as an immersive cultural landscape suggests that we should take a different perspective from the conventional dichotomy of the visitor and the visited, and from this insight emerge implications for tourism operation and management based on the idea of authenticity.

Historical Background: Understanding the Chinese Garden

Presently, often the original function or intention of building Chinese gardens is only partially understood by the public who visit them. Misinterpretation or inaccurate messages in public media is one of the reasons. For example, a garden writer for the *Otago Daily Times*, the local newspaper for Dunedin, summarized that "[t]he inspiration for the traditional Chinese Garden came from Taoist hermits 2000 years ago" and "[p]rivate gardens emerged during the late Han Dynasty (about AD 200) as a completely separate style from the earlier great hunting parks of the emperors" (Madgin, 2008, ¶4 and ¶11). These claims are presented as authoritative but are in fact inaccurate.

The earliest and original shape of a Chinese Garden—*Tai*—appeared before the Zhou Dynasty (mid-11th century BC to 258 BC) and fulfilled mainly religious and ritualistic functions; human pleasure was not predominant until the Eastern Zhou Dynasty (770–256 BC) when the gardens started to function as places of entertainment. Since the Western Zhou Dynasty (1046–771 BC), scholars had escaped from social and political chaos to reclusion and such movement became intertwined with garden culture during the late period of the Han Dynasty and the Three Kingdoms Period (AD 220–265). For example, the hermit-poet Ji Kang (AD 223–262) retired to his home with flourishing willow trees, surrounded by rushing water, very pure and cool in the summer, beneath which he could always disport himself proudly (Y. Wang, 2004).

Understanding the pre-Han historiography of the Chinese Garden is important because the society's perceptions of wilderness were transformed from animist worship to romanticized escape[2] and this transformation was manifest in the changing functions and forms of the Chinese garden. The academic literature has overly emphasized the close connection between the individual's requirement for natural surroundings and his respectable virtue (Y. Wang, 2004), as in Confucius's famous dictum that: the man of knowledge delights in water, and the man of goodness delights in mountains (智者乐山，仁者乐水).

People's changing perceptions of wilderness led to the further evolution of the Chinese garden, which moved its location from rural settings to urban areas. This move reflects the changing views of scholars about the meaning of virtue-maintain (养德) and escape-to-nature, and again this originated during a period of socio-historical adjustment. In the Wei and Jin dynasties (AD 265–420) the garden was built far away from the city in order to be near the wilderness; physical withdrawal was the basic form of reclusion. Since the Tang dynasty (AD 618–907) the gardens began to be constructed on the principle of "a world of teapot"[3] and, in cities, private scholars' gardens emerged.

Rather than simplifying a Chinese garden's aesthetics at this period to only one type of spirituality (e.g., Daoism or Confucianism), they may better be understood through theories of poetry; for example, the poems of Bai Juyi (白居易), who was known for his *xianshi shi* (poetry about enjoying idleness, 闲适诗) and his theory of "Hermit in Between"[4] (中隐). This poet, both in poetry and theory, expressed a passive character of scholars' ethics—*dushan* (preserving one's own integrity, 独善). A scholar is able to preserve his integrity by means of an idle and indolent mood, a mind of emptiness and stillness (Xiao, 2001).[5] If Bai represents Daoism, then another scholar of the late Tang Dynasty, Sikong Tu (司空图), may represent Confucius. Sikong withdrew from the city and committed suicide at the end of the Tang Dynasty, after years of reclusion in his rural private garden. Both men owned their private gardens but had different political attitudes. The physical detachment and reclusion of the scholars is not easily explained either by Confucianism or Daoism. Nevertheless, Sikong Tu and Bai Juyi both were representative of the ancient China scholars, for both attempted strenuously to achieve some degree of autonomous rights and self-reflection which they presented in their poetry and garden design.

"Hermit in Between" caused a transformation from retreating to wilderness to residence in an ambience of man-made hills and waters, which began to be considered as an ideal environment for withdrawal from the world and which then developed into a technique of landscape. Therefore, the Chinese garden, since the Tang Dynasty, gradually went from being an unsophisticated space to being a place of sophisticated exquisiteness. The mid-Tang Dynasty period was the time the Chinese garden reached its peak and retained intimate interactions with other forms of art such as painting, literature and music. Contemporaneously, these art forms also were flourishing in their golden age. It is important to note that the glory of each art form, including garden design, was inseparable from political stability and economic strength.

Despite increasing exquisiteness, the Chinese garden did not follow a linear development but rather a parabolic trajectory. The development of the Chinese garden was marked by other alterations during the Northern and Southern Song dynasties (AD 960–1279) with the rise of neo-Confucianism. Due to the more crowded cities, the garden became smaller and therefore the landscape layout required a more compact design to achieve limitlessness in a limited place. Later, in Ming and Qing Chinese Gardens, garden-design reached a stage whose style can be summarized in the phrase "a mustard seed containing Mount Sumeru"[6] (Schmidt, 2003, p. 499). From then until the Qing Dynasty (AD 1644–1908) artificial elements came to play an increasingly important role in the garden. The highly exquisite spatial division of the landscape ceased having any practical function after moving from an original role of worship to being a place for entertaining, the reclusion of hermits, and socializing among scholars and their artistic friends. The Ming and Qing dynasties' Chinese gardens developed into an artifice and a symbol of social status (Cheng, 1998). Wilderness no longer embraced everyone but became a decorative element in the man-made landscape.

Following this tendency, the development of the Chinese garden in the last decades of the Qing Dynasty was limited within the "mustard seed containing Mount Sumeru" model, instead of improvising and recreating. The increasing congestion and pretention thus indicated the depletion of the art of the Chinese garden. It has been argued by historians that the decay resulted from the nature of feudal society and the circumscribed nature and frequent antinomy involved in neo-Confucian thought (Y. Wang, 2004). Noticeably, this notion was also implied in a famous Chinese literary masterpiece *The Story of the Stone* (or *The Dream of the Red Chamber*) in which the novelist Cao Xueqin (曹雪芹) told stories set in the "Grand-view Garden." Cao described the conflict between the neo-Confucianist canon and Daoist thought through the characters' attitudes and understanding of the grand-view garden (Jencks, 2003), further indicating, through the tragic ending of the characters who live there, the attrition of feudalism (Xiao, 2001). Coincidently, in history, the catastrophe of the burning down of Yuan Ming Yuan (Summer Palace or Garden of Perfect Brightness) has been interpreted as a sign of the decline and fall of the Qing dynasty and so also for the Chinese garden as a form of art (Y. Wang).

The newspaper report in the *Otago Daily Times* (Madgin, 2008) neglects the history of gardens before the Han Dynasty and the Dunedin garden's connection with later styles. In addition, this inaccurate description reveals a lapse in consideration of the transformation of scholars' (not hermits initially) attitudes toward changes in their inner and outer worlds. Such an example leads us to think of why an accurate historical perspective of representing Chinese gardens is missing, and to what extent does such misinterpretation contribute to or detract from the notion of Chineseness? Currently, places like the Dunedin Chinese Garden enable visitors to experience a Chinese garden outside of China. What role might such a garden serve in matching visitors' images of China and Chinese culture and how might such experiences affect the evolving notion of Chineseness when, for the majority of visitors, the historical perspective is absent? The hybrid and complex nature of the Dunedin Chinese Garden makes it an ideal site within which to situate an enquiry into these questions.

Understanding the Dunedin Chinese Garden

Our study comprised critically reading and analyzing public media's reporting of the garden, relevant academic literature, and qualitative, interpretivist on-site fieldwork. One of the authors (Jasmine Zhang) was involved with the garden as a volunteer tour guide, allowing for semistructured interviews and participant observation while guiding. There was no charge for the guiding of visitors and the guide usually was easily approachable. Therefore, interactions between all the participants in the study occurred in a relatively natural setting (Willis, Jost, & Nilakanta, 2007). Part of the guiding involved introducing to visitors the Dunedin Chinese Garden's social background and explaining how the reports presented in the public media explain the stories of how the Dunedin Chinese Garden came to be a tourism attraction.

Dunedin Chinese Garden: Social Background

In 1998 the local Chinese community decided that constructing a Chinese garden in Dunedin was an appropriate commemoration of the Chinese contribution to Dunedin's development since the 1860s. The proposal and its rationale were well covered by the local newspaper. Since the gold rush of 1861, Chinese migrants had worked as gold miners in central Otago and by 1865 their population had reached 4,000. Many stayed after the gold rush and continued contributing to New Zealand society through small businesses such as fruit and vegetable gardens, markets, shops, restaurants, and laundries and through public involvement such as military service (Agnew, 2011). In a video made specifically for the Dunedin Chinese Garden (Orton, 2007), local historian Jim Ng explained his concern about the lack of recognition in New Zealand of those individuals who comprised the Chinese diaspora. His concern reflects that of Chinese intellectuals in New Zealand who have sought to remind people that Maori (the indigenous people) and Pakeha (Europeans) were not the only people to make the history of this country (Moloughney & Stenhouse, 1999). This commemoration, therefore, was intended to provide a voice and a focal place for the local Chinese community.

In addition to the historical diasporic significance, another purpose for building the garden was as a gift given by Dunedin's sister city Shanghai. Mackenzie's (2008) newspaper report "Garden—And China ties—Blooming" described the garden as a sign of the blossoming friendly relationship between New Zealand and China. The public focus on financial issues of building and operating the garden and the donations the project received indicated that the function of the garden as a gift was controversial (*Otago Daily Times*, 2008a, 2008b). Such controversy may be attributed to the Chineseness of the Dunedin Chinese Garden raising public concern about who would benefit from the gift. Therefore, in our study, local residents who visited the completed garden received special attention and were asked specifically how they felt about the garden being intended to be a profitable tourist attraction. An older couple said:

> It is a good thing we have this garden here in Dunedin, but we are really worried about how could Chinese people want to come here to see something they have at home. (Dunedin residents, April 3, 2011)

When the newspaper reported that the visitor number of the Dunedin Chinese Garden dropped again in 2011 and the city council was seeking a solution for the garden, one local resident said:

> I find it disturbing. People paid tax for this but it is not really needed.

There was a similar case in Birmingham, England. A Chinese pagoda was donated to the city as a gift from a successful Chinese immigrant (Chan, 2004). The materials and main parts were made in China and transported to Birmingham. The pagoda suffered extensive criticisms and disrespectful behavior from some members of the local community. Chan pointed out that when a city's multicultural urban-regeneration strategy is examined there is always a dominant understanding of the public cultural item (in Birmingham the pagoda and in Dunedin the Chinese garden) that "involves an attempt to situate the origins of particular developments within particular ethnicities" (p. 15). This kind of popular and dominant understanding will thus affirm the cultural item's status as a marginalized coexisting figure. The story of the dominant understanding of the Dunedin Chinese Garden as a marginalized cultural item was, and continues to be, presented in the local public media; for example, feature articles and letters to the editor in the regional daily newspaper, the *Otago Daily Times*.

Such public media played an important role in reporting the process of lobbying for, and the construction of, the garden. The *Otago Daily Times* has reported on the garden on various topics since early 2008, the year the garden opened. The original rationale for building the garden was emphasized repeatedly in the newspaper and an image of an authentic Chinese garden was portrayed on the garden's brochure and Website, promising "the only authentic Chinese Garden in New Zealand. . . . It is one of only a handful outside of China" (Dunedin City Council, 2011) and, as a result, was "the first garden of this size to be wholly designed and built in China with its structures shipped out to New Zealand and reassembled by Chinese craftspeople" (Beattie, 2007, p. 62). On June 10, 2008, the blessing of the garden got under way for its opening on July 8 (Harvey, 2008).

From the beginning of discussions about establishing the garden, it was intended to function not only as a local cultural object but also as a tourist attraction. The Dunedin City Council promoted the Dunedin Chinese Garden at the annual Tourism Rendezvous New Zealand (TRENZ) gathering, a forum for marketing tourist products internationally. It was anticipated that large numbers of Chinese tourists would be attracted to the Dunedin Chinese Garden and thus to the other tourist attractions of Dunedin (McNeilly, 2008). However, there was little attention paid to the wider notion of Chinese gardens as tourist products either within, or outside of, China.

Chinese Gardens as Tourism Products

In mainstream media, the phrase "Chinese garden" is portrayed in a way that evokes a timeless and classic oriental image (Tredici & Yu, 1993; Yan & Santos, 2009). Such imagery is widely used in China's tourism marketing strategy as an icon of Chineseness, but how well the Chinese garden has been understood through this written and visual representation remains to be explored. This is not to say that the literature on visitors' perceptions of visiting Chinese gardens is exceptionally sparse but only that it is limited in its scope and depth of analysis. Here, we focus on how, in various locations, Chinese gardens are produced and operated as tourism products. The conversations with tourists in the Dunedin Chinese Garden highlight the fact that, when viewing the garden as a tourist product, local, domestic, and international visitors focus on different elements. Our position is that for overseas Chinese gardens it is problematic to discuss simply how authentic these gardens are; the concept of authenticity itself is too problematic to be used in this way. Rather, following Bendix (1997) and Rickly-Boyd (2012), we suggest that inquiry into the gardens' authenticity discourse may more profitably consider what work the concept of authenticity does in these settings and how the term has been used.

Gradually, since China's first tourism development in the late 1970s, it has become the norm for cities in China to be accessible and to have become tourist destinations (Ryan & Gu, 2009). The tourism infrastructure has changed considerably and a wide range of cultural and natural heritage has been promoted as tourist products. The Classical Gardens of Suzhou and the Summer Palace in the Imperial Garden in Beijing were listed as Cultural World Heritage Sites in 1997 and 1998, respectively, and soon became popular scenic spots for domestic and international tourists (G. Zhang, 2003). Chinese tourism scholars have commented on the critical issues that emerged from this process of making touristic place, and some of these issues apply to Chinese gardens. In addition, concerns about commodification, standardization, and serialization were expressed (Nyíri, 2007). Mao and Zhou (2006) contended that currently the Chinese gardens, especially the scholars' gardens in the southern part of China (Jiangnan Yuanlin), are facing a crucial situation in that their function as a tourist product is decaying. Though the total number of visitors is growing, the rate of growth is slowing. Overcrowding and poor facilities in the gardens now fail to satisfy visitors' expectations and thus the gardens cannot achieve sustainable development as tourist attractions. Additionally, researchers argue that the background knowledge and essence of these Chinese gardens are no longer familiar to Chinese audiences because their consumer behavior is rapidly changing and with it what used to be regarded as universal cultural knowledge (Mao & Zhou). S. Lu, Zhang, and Gan (1999) suggested that even though the original functions of Chinese gardens have been lost, promoting the gardens as tourism products may revive their cultural aspects.

The first descriptions of Chinese gardens reached Paris in 1749, where the spatial irregularity and the philosophical basis of Chinese gardens soon became a significant part of the fashion of "Chinoiserie" (Keswick, Jencks, & Hardie, 2003, p. 24). Not until China opened her door to the world in the late 1970s did Westerners see Chinese gardens with their own eyes. Greater mobility allowed Western gardeners, by gaining firsthand impressions and transporting original Chinese plants, furnishings, and paintings home, to shape their own gardens, following the ideas of Chinese gardens (Chasse, 2010). Until the end of the 20th century, a number of facsimile Chinese gardens were built overseas, designed by professional architects and craftsmen in China and the building materials assembled and shipped to the host countries (Chasse, 2010). The first overseas Chinese garden was created for the Metropolitan Museum of Art in New York City in 1981 (Hammer, 2003). Chasse (2010) noted that since then several dozen gardens have been constructed throughout the world, many of them as a cultural exchange or symbol of friendship, sometimes as a direct result of a sister city relationship with a Chinese municipality. Some were constructed as a cultural asset for a local community of Chinese immigrants, as occurred in Seattle, Washington. Other overseas Chinese gardens were constructed in Canada, Germany, and the United States. Within Asia, Chinese gardens can be found in Singapore, Japan, and other Pacific nations (Rössler, 2006). By 2007, there were 35 Chinese gardens built overseas (Beattie, 2007).

The Dunedin Chinese Garden is described by its advocates as an authentic Chinese cultural heritage item in that it was designed in China, constructed using traditional materials imported from China, and built according to traditional principles by Chinese artisans specially brought over from China. In the public media, this authenticity of the Dunedin Chinese Garden is emphasized as a selling point in that it is "New Zealand's first authentic Chinese Garden—only the third outside of China and the first in the southern hemisphere" (Tourism New Zealand, 2008, 1).

What the Dunedin Chinese Garden is publicizing is the idea of objective authenticity, which is believed to be achieved through fulfilling a set of standardized categories. However, there are several reasons for rejecting this claim. Since MacCannell (1976) introduced the concept of authenticity, its ambiguity and limitations have been critiqued continuously by scholars from within the tourism field. Speculating on the museum-linked usage of authenticity and its extension to tourism, N. Wang (1999) suggested two different issues of authenticity in tourism: that of tourist experiences, and toured objects. N. Wang fitted the complex nature of authenticity in tourism into three categories, namely, objective, constructive, and existential. Furthermore, to elucidate the experience-oriented and thus ever-changing existential authenticity, N. Wang noted that *intrapersonal* and *interpersonal* are two aspects of existential authenticity. These understandings of authenticity have a profound effect in moving away from the traditional singular way of looking at tourist experience and thus tourist attractions. As Reisinger and Steiner (2006) pointed out, objective authenticity is irrelevant to many tourists. The authenticity of a site can be evaluated categorically but it is often separated from the authenticity of tourists' experiences.

The first reason for rejecting Dunedin's claim is that Chinese gardens are historically and culturally defined. Beattie (2008) noted that there has never been one orthodox Chinese garden style that prevailed in the great variety of gardens developed in different regions throughout Chinese history. Most of the overseas Chinese gardens followed the style of a scholar's garden in southern China, particularly the Suzhou Garden, but it has been argued whether or not the Suzhou Garden can be representative of a Chinese garden or even Chinese culture as a whole. To use the term Chinese garden may depend on how Western visitors perceive it in terms of their own needs (Clunas, 1996). In addition, from a historical perspective, Chinese gardens that are still surviving today have been extensively altered and redesigned by their various historical owners. These alterations have intertwined relationships with social structures and the cultural transformations of China's history (Y. Wang, 2004) described above. The point is that such complexities and ambiguities involved in Chinese gardens serve as resources that allow different groups to tell their own stories, believing them to be authentic. In other words, there is no standard category for objectively evaluating an authentic Chinese garden.

The interpretation panels and normal guided tour commentary in the Dunedin Chinese Garden do not engage with or elaborate on the issue of what is an authentic scholar's garden, other than simply to state that the garden is authentic. When the author of this article guided visitors, they often asked questions such as "Do the gardens in China really look like this?" and "Have the Chinese gardens always been like this?" Such visitors' curiosity indicates that the current interpretation and commentary could be expanded to engage critically with the topic of authenticity. Clearly, in this garden, the function of the concept of authenticity, in terms of Rickly-Boyd's (2012, p. 270) focus on "what does authenticity do," is to provide a "point of difference," however spurious.

Second, the authenticity of the notion of Chineseness that is attached to Dunedin's Chinese Garden also is arguable. Tu's (2005) project on "Cultural China" is an intellectual effort to break the rigid and stereotypical definitions of Chineseness, which include being of Han ethnicity, being born in China proper, speaking Mandarin, and observing the patriotic code of ethics. Tu perceived Chineseness as a discursive discourse that fluidly challenges the cultural authority of geopolitical leadership. Such a discursive approach destabilizes the authentic Chineseness claimed for those gardens located in China. Though the Dunedin Chinese Garden is marketed as a tourist attraction and was intended to appeal to Chinese tourists from Mainland China, it is inevitable that there will be Chinese visitors from other parts of the world or the New Zealand Chinese diasporic community. It is the same for other similar overseas Chinese gardens around the world; there is no unified understanding of Chineseness that can be used to target a single Chinese market.

More important, the theoretical and practical debates around the term *authenticity* should carefully be considered in the case of the Dunedin Chinese Garden. If the term objective authenticity does not apply to it, how should we position the visitor experience the garden offers? N. Wang's (1999) existential authenticity is useful here in allowing consideration of individual experiences of the authentic. The phenomenon of constructing Chinese gardens overseas provides a rewarding opportunity for understanding authenticity in its different aspects. The singularly authentic object must be experienced in place and space (Crouch, 2000), where a sense of place may operate inside or outside a tourism location, and focuses on the "relationship between object and experience as one that is integrally woven into a physical and cultural matrix" (Jamal & Hill, 2004, p. 356).

The visitors interviewed were domestic tourists, international tourists from the United Kingdom, Australians, a number of Chinese tourists from China and other Asian countries, and Chinese immigrants living in New Zealand. Collectively, visitors had different reactions to the dominant interpretive narrative of the Dunedin Chinese Garden and expressed very different perceptions of their visits. Interestingly, several visitors reported being very influenced by the on-site interpretive material and the public media they had experienced before their visit. For example, a couple from Australia said:

> We went to the Chinese Garden in Vancouver and Sydney before. This one (Dunedin's) is very authentic because obviously it is completely made in China, except the plants.

Similarly, a couple who live in Dunedin said:

> Me and my wife come here very regularly. I think it is a blessing that Dunedin has one of only three authentic Chinese Gardens out of China,

and I wish it to be good. I am quite upset when I read the newspaper and listen to the people's criticisms. They are just the loud and negative minorities and they really should come even once by themselves.

In contrast, a Chinese guy from a southeast Asian country said:

There is so little fish swimming in the pond. It is not authentic at all. Only foreigners could be coaxed because they never saw a real one in China. I haven't been to China and never saw a Chinese Garden there but I am a Chinese. The one we have in Malaysia is much better than this.

A young couple traveling from Mainland China commented that

It's nice, but it is too small, comparing with the Gardens in China!

We argue that these visitors' comments highlight the relationships between place, identity, and tourism (Lasansky & McLaren, 2004; White & White, 2004). The Chinese garden has been recognized as being transformative of identity in some older Chinese immigrants in New Zealand as they recount activities such as gardening as a means of forging a new sense of self and place in their adoptive country (W. Li, Hodgetts, & Ho, 2010). Place, as Crouch (2000) noted, is negotiated socially—people define identities, friendships, and cultural relationships through embodied encounters with other people and objects that then become places of memory and knowledge. For each of these visitors, in different ways, Chineseness is closely attached to such memories and knowledge. The different reactions toward authenticity from visitors who have different social and cultural backgrounds indicate that the concept of authenticity is constructed, utilized, and challenged by different individuals and, in such situations, the perception of Chineseness is easily essentialized and politicized.

Recently, tourism scholars have suggested that even objective and existential authenticity have their own approaches to constructing the concept. Thus, it is crucial to keep asking, "What does authenticity do in this setting?" rather than to ask, "What is authenticity?" (Rickly-Boyd, 2012). This new focus is consistent with a trend or shift away from authenticity to an emphasis on processes of authentication (Ateljevic & Doorne, 2005; Cohen & Cohen, 2012; Rickly-Boyd; Xie, 2011). It is then possible to view the claim of having an authentic Chinese garden as a claim of having the resources to offer a visitor experience that will authenticate the concept of authenticity. Authenticating authenticity now becomes an integral part of the product and is no longer based solely on the object. Though the claim of objective authenticity is delivered through on-site interpretation and public media, the authentication of authenticity is constructed through individual visitors' experiences. There is an inherent tension between these two processes of delivery and construction, and the authentication of Chineseness as part of the product must be situated somewhere within this tension.

Chinese Gardens as Cultural Landscape

Typically, after visiting a tourist attraction, visitors with different social and cultural backgrounds actively create their memories and reproduce their knowledge of the attraction (Bendix, 1997). The garden, though, is not best suited to be considered as a conventional tourist product. The usual binary divisions between the visitors and the visited and the ordinary and the extraordinary neglect the relationship between the visitors and the images they hold toward the places they are visiting. MacCannell (2011) pointed out that it is the first task of tourism researchers to explain how the tourist imaginary is positioned between tourists and the objects of their gaze (Urry, 1990). This insight applies to interpreting Chinese gardens as cultural landscapes, because visitors construct and interpose their own understandings of the garden as such a cultural landscape. In an overseas Chinese garden the visitors' cultural narratives are important in mediating their touristic subjectivity because, while they visit, they construct their own sense of authenticity and, within this, the nature and role of authentic Chineseness.

Cultural landscapes are defined as being "at the interface between nature and culture, tangible and intangible, biological and cultural diversity—they represent a closely woven net of relationships, the essence of culture and people's identity" (Rössler, 2006, p. 334). Thus, the visitors' different approaches to perceiving the Dunedin Chinese Garden relates to how they position themselves in this net of relationships of nature, culture, and personal identity. The comments of visitors to the Dunedin garden demonstrated two different approaches within viewing the garden as a cultural landscape, namely, a touristic approach and a truly cultural approach.

One illustration of these two approaches is an *Otago Daily Times* article about an Austrian backpacker visiting the garden before it was officially opened because "the garden was on his list of 'must-see' attractions during his three-day visit to Dunedin," and after visiting he noted "this is one of the top 10. . . . It is so beautiful and tranquil" (Lewis, 2008, ¶5 and ¶7). This comment implies that the Austrian backpacker positioned himself as being on the outside, who may cast a touristic gaze upon the Dunedin Chinese Garden. Similar responses were elicited from those domestic tourists and international tourists who were interviewed.

> We only have two days to stay here and we think this is a good place to visit. Last time when we came the Garden was not here yet. It is nice to have something new to see. (Couple from the United Kingdom)

The newspaper report and these visitors' comments indicate a touristic approach to constructing the garden's cultural landscape. Urry (2002, p. 3) argued that

> the tourist gaze is directed to features of landscape and townscape which separate them off from everyday experience. . . . The viewing of such tourist sights often involves different forms of social patterning, with a much greater sensitivity to visual elements of landscape or townscape than normally found in everyday life.

Interestingly, some domestic tourists' comments exposed the social ideologies they were influenced by. For example, a tourist from Auckland said:

> This place is like an oasis in the middle of the town. However, I found the chimney and the western style buildings outside of the wall very incompatible with the atmosphere of the Garden. They are a bit disturbing actually.

Commenting on the same scene, while being inside the garden looking outside, a tourist from Wellington said:

> I find this place very exotic, I like the spot on top of the rocks, where you can see the combination of the East and the West.

It is interesting that these visitors held such opposite opinions about the mixed architecture of East and West. Similar comments emerged several times and often visitors compared the Dunedin Chinese Garden to other Chinese gardens in Sydney and Vancouver. Particularly, they emphasized those gardens being located in a context of a Chinatown. Recognizing and commenting primarily on the difference in architectural styles indicates that the visitors are constantly observing this aspect of their surroundings and are thus positioning themselves outside of the cultural landscape. These visitors are viewing the garden within the conventional notion of Chineseness and with multiple and contesting senses of place (Chang, 2000).

A woman from Dunedin illustrated a truly cultural approach when she reacted differently and claimed that she was not coming to visit or watch anything:

> I feel relaxed by just being here, sometimes doing nothing, sometimes reading or thinking. It is a place to calm down and contemplate.

Also, another domestic tourist said:

> I think it is amazing how balanced the nature and artificial structures are and how embraced I feel to be here.

In comparison with the visitors who gazed at the garden, these other visitors positioned themselves within the garden. Both groups were Westerners and this raises questions about whether cultural background and historical knowledge really are important in being able to feel completely inside a Chinese garden. Researchers ranging from environmental historians to urban planners have discerned that the Chinese garden is an aesthetic space that exceeds the status of being significant for only a certain ethnic group (Jacques, 1990; Yang, 2003; Y. Zhang, 2007). This universality suggests that there is widely accessible textual signification through which the architecture of the Chinese garden is made available to its visitors, regardless of the visitors' ethnicity. In New Zealand, the Chinese garden has been positioned within Chineseness but it has been argued that the elements of Chineseness are "now part of the cultural repertoire of a large number of New Zealanders, only some of whom are of ethnic Chinese extraction" (Moloughney, 2005, p. 400), due to the long local history of the Chinese diaspora. Such a finding indicates that an appreciation of Chineseness is widely available.

The dominant narratives above on how to understand the garden ignore the individual connections between the objects and experiences. Deciding to visit an overseas Chinese garden reflects the visitor's self-positioning in the cultural landscape and their personal understanding of the regeneration of urban areas and the relation of such regeneration to Chineseness. For example, a couple from Auckland reflected that:

> We are from Auckland and we come to Dunedin for nostalgia reason—my wife was growing up here and we once lived here. I feel so proud of Dunedin for having this Garden as if we are the citizens of Dunedin. The things are changing so quickly, in Auckland we have a lot of Chinese neighbors and they are very nice even if at times we can't communicate with them. But I feel glad to see my grandchildren grow up in a more multicultural environment.

The Dunedin Chinese Garden elucidates a cosmopolitan potential in a global context and the visitors' personal understandings of the garden are intimately influenced by its available symbolic meanings. Such symbolic representation of a place is connected also with visitors' self-reflections, as shown in an Irish visitor's comment:

> Today is my last day in New Zealand of my world trip and next stop is China. It is interesting to be in a Chinese Garden in New Zealand and I love it. It reminds me of my hometown in Ireland. Actually this trip makes me grow and think about myself, I never thought I would miss home before this. Everything green reminds me of the mountains there. I know this is a Chinese Garden but I feel at home, I like the rocks most and the reflections on the water just look so amazing. The more places I go, the more similarities I find of each places with my home.

Here, the visitor's interpretation of the garden certainly is influenced by the garden's architecture but more in an experiential way. Architecture scholars argue that in a Chinese garden, the viewer's experience is that he or she is open to other senses and that the scenery is a continuum of the self and the garden space (A. Lu, 2011). The Dunedin Chinese Garden is built in the style of a scholar's garden in southern China, particularly the Suzhou Garden (Cao, Chen, & Tan, 2008), which normally generates idealized images conceived in Chinese ancient paintings and poetry (Petersen, 1995). However, A. Lu contended that a Chinese garden is different from picturesque gardens because the idea of realm in Chinese poetic theory reveals the interdependence between the self and the space. Hinton (2005) further explained that in Chinese rivers-and-mountains poetry, the nondualistic Chinese wilderness discloses a cosmology that is different from either a dichotomy between human and nature or a picturesque realm seen from a spectator's distance. Han (2012) indicated that meanings of Chinese landscape are closely associated with subjective recognition of the values of nature. The visitors' telling about their experiences in the garden resonates from such association; for example, a Dunedin local resident reported that:

> I once was arguing with my mother when we talked about the (Dunedin) Chinese Garden; she said she thought this place is too artificial, not natural at all. I think it the opposite, I don't feel close to nature in a wild mountain, I feel I am in nature here—everything is so balanced.

For this visitor, being in the garden was a way of perceiving nature that is different from the Western aestheticization, transforming natural features into wilderness, which, without exception, must be situated within either a Burkean or Kantian concept of the Romantic sublime. Typical Western perceptions of landscape are thus divergent from the "pre-existing common knowledge of the Chinese subject" (Petersen, 1995, p. 142). This visitor's mother, who thought the Chinese garden was artificial, was negatively influenced by this preexisting common knowledge of Chineseness, and this led to a disappointing misinterpretation of the official symbolism of the Chinese garden. The current on-site interpretation in the Dunedin Chinese Garden describes the garden as a social structure that merely imitates nature. One interpretation panel stated:

> The Lan Yuan[7] is a man-made landscape. Its designers have replicated all of nature's basic features (i.e. mountains, waters, grass, trees, sunshine) in

miniature on flat ground. Since it is impossible to move mountains, an artificial mountain was built to complete a natural environment. The Chinese word for landscape, shan shui, literally means "mountains and waters" while a common phrase for making a garden means "digging ponds and piling mountains" . . .

This simplification limits the visitors to viewing the garden from a Western perception of nature and does not guide the visitors to a better understanding of their own experiences.

Artistic and aesthetic ways of seeing landscape in association with tourism consumption have been explored (Aitchison, MacLeod, & Shaw, 2000). However, key words such as *picturesque*, *sublime*, and *imagery* remain the focus of the popular gaze, both for tourists and researchers alike. Indeed, the Romantic aesthetic and its attendant ecological subject continue to dominate Western ideas of nature (Cronon, 1996; Morton, 2010).

The transformation of the Chinese garden in Chinese history and its interrelation with Chinese poetry and the cosmology it illustrates led to Han's (2012) observation that

> China's highly developed landscape languages with symbolic and metapho-rical allusions could contribute to the encoding and interpretation of the meanings of landscape and values of nature and also help to understand authenticity as a living and evolving concept and in a culturally diverse context. (p. 104)

Western researchers in tourism studies have examined the relationship between litera-ture and tourism (Squire, 1994). In addition, recent research discusses the potential relationship between the culture of tourism and interpretation of ancient Chinese poetry (Gu & Kang, 2010). There is not yet an integrative view of the poetics of garden literature that creates the sense of place and also creates the landscape that produces coherent stories. The landscape of the Chinese garden and its complicated social attributes display an interesting relationship between tourism and poetry.

Typically, any tensions around how a visitor should position herself in the garden would involve the conventional dichotomies of the visitor and the visited. The pre-sentation of the garden as a cultural landscape and its poetic language that visitors experience act together to produce an embodiment of poetic place. Ateljevic, Morgan, and Pritchard (2007) argued that in such positioning it is not an "either/or" situation, rather it is a "both/and" option for inclusion (p. 3). In an overseas Chinese garden, the poetics is generated through the activities of different narrators, not only the public media and the interpretation panel but also the visitors and the garden itself. The poetic atmosphere of the place produced through the provision of poetry therefore functions as an abstract and open narrative, allowing, encouraging, and facilitating individual agents to tell their own stories.

Furthermore, the fluidity of poetry helps both the tourism operators and the garden managers to administer the garden beyond its being a traditional tourist product. It is important to involve local residents and to listen to their and visitors' perceptions so that the meaning of the garden is not limited, which will be the case unless it can reach out to all of its communities. In addition, formulating the garden in this way, as an embodiment of poetry, supports the evolving understanding of authenticity discussed above, that the aura of a contextualized product can engage better with visitors' subjectivity and their own understandings of authenticity (Rickly-Boyd, 2012).

Conclusion

In this article we have offered both theoretical and practical insights into Chinese gardens. Recently, there has been a request for a more critical awareness in tourism research, an awareness that can provide an integrated theoretical framework within which research can be conceptualized and contextualized (Jamal & Lelo, 2010). Here, we have attempted to contribute to such integrative awareness by presenting a Chinese garden constructed in 2008 in Dunedin, New Zealand, and its interaction with the notions of authentic Chineseness. Even though the literature on the Chinese garden's history and sociocultural background is relatively rich, there has been little study done on Chinese gardens constructed overseas. In addition, there has been scant research done on visitors' perceptions of their experiences when visiting an overseas Chinese garden.

We claim that the public media, both Chinese and Western, albeit unknowingly, misrepresents Chinese gardens' histories. We have argued here that it is important to understand the social and cultural transformations over Chinese history in order to understand the poetic realm the Chinese garden is designed to present and also the cosmology informing its own landscape language. The social background of the Dunedin Chinese Garden involves its role as a commemoration of nostalgia for those of the Chinese diaspora in New Zealand, an illustration of friendship between Dunedin and Shanghai, and therefore between New Zealand and China, and a representation of authentic Cultural China. The Dunedin Chinese Garden is promoted as a tourism attraction, intended to provide domestic and international tourists with a multicultural experience.

Although it is not novel to build Chinese gardens outside of China, within tourism studies there has been little critique of these; the complications and implications of such projects are not yet clearly formulated. The current literature focuses on the oriental and dream-like image the Chinese gardens create, but it has been argued within China that the Chinese gardens have lost their touristic potential due to the changing patterns of consumption of Chinese tourists. The overseas Chinese gardens allegedly represent China's growing influences and a transformation of the notion of Chineseness. The emphasis on authenticity of such overseas Chinese gardens raises questions of what an authentic Chinese Garden is and what authentic Chineseness is. We have argued that this promotion of authenticity is problematic. The Dunedin Chinese Garden illustrates how objective authenticity is constructed by public media to become a dominant understanding of the garden but the existential authenticity that visitors expressed was constructed through their own experiences and reflections. We found that different groups of visitors experienced the garden differently. Some visitors perceived the garden from a touristic perspective, influenced by the dominant understanding of the garden. These visitors cast a touristic gaze upon the garden, whereas others embodied the tourist subject, individually positioning themselves in this tourist environment while being unaware of the deeper and more nuanced historically and politically determined elements of Chineseness available.

For others, the relationship between Chinese gardens and Chinese poetry theories, their personal interpretations of this poesis, and how then they disport within the garden suggest that, for them, a cultural approach to viewing is available.

For gardens both overseas and in China, to assist visitors in understanding their cognitive and affective responses and also to deconstruct an ethnically essentialized Chineseness, we suggest an emphasis on culturally and historically contexualized interpretation. Visitors' telling of their feelings of home, embodiment, and being close to nature indicates that there is a cosmopolitan potential for the Chinese garden and that well-contextualized interpretation will enhance such potential. This is not to say the current interpretation offered at, for example, the Dunedin Chinese Garden is somehow wrong but, rather, it is to encourage a recognition of new interpretive opportunities available through embracing a broader context.

Consequently, current marketing strategies may repay being reviewed. Selling or promoting the exotic appeal of a Chinese garden only in a tourism context risks modifying the Chineseness or Chinese culture aspects of the historical, sociocultural, and politically sensitive positions the gardens represent. Furthermore, if the selling point of a garden as a tourism product is based primarily on the authenticity of its Chineseness, then the opportunity for broader contextualized meaning-making is lost.

We conclude that, within a Chinese garden, the performance of tourism is available as a mechanism for communicating meaning. Such a performance facilitates communication between the various roles available, especially communication where the text involves a poetics that goes beyond verbal or written language while still linking the garden and the visitor. This idea that ancient Chinese poetry can be narrated through landscape is an alternative perspective on interpretation. However, within tourism studies, a sophisticated analysis is required in order to identify the particular performances being produced and how to analyze and develop these.

The fact that the garden is built overseas, within Western surroundings, further increases the potential communicative function. Ang Lee said that in order to be more Chinese one has to be Westernized (Chan, 2004). Nevertheless, there is a risk of oversimplification of the opposition between the local and the global (Brooker & Thacker, 2005). When we allow Chinese poetry to represent a more fluid Chineseness, we need to keep in mind that the very action of decentering could lead to the centering of another, conventional Chineseness (Ien, 1998; Jameson & Miyoshi, 1998). Petersen (1995) raised a similar caution that the need for visitors to have prior knowledge of Chinese landscape as poetry and painting has become such a serious problem for Chinese tourism that the decision makers should be careful with such a cultural demand. These concerns would repay analysis from a postcolonial frame of reference.

Simply translating Chineseness into other languages is inadequate. To properly interpret the text of a Chinese garden or help visitors understand the narratives of that textual element is a constant process of negotiating landscapes. These landscapes may be internal, affective, cognitive, and external; that is, the negotiation is of the material production of culture that the garden embodies. In the story of the Dunedin Chinese Garden, we see an opportunity for Dunedin City and its visitors to engage with and understand a poetic place. More important, the garden can stimulate and inspire the visitor to create a new story for herself, the garden, and the city. In this way, the garden becomes more than an amenity for the diasporic Chinese community, or merely a tourist product but, with the laying down of each story, acts as an urban palimpsest, an integral element of a poetics of place.

Notes

1. Access to the index of the nine volumes can be found at: http://www.fmprc.gov.cn/ eng/swzl/rwzg/index.htm
2. An article discussing the origin of Romanticism in the Chinese garden (Lovejoy, 1933) offers some interesting insights that may connect intercultural understanding with Romanticism in Western philosophy.
3. The expression is from a story that a Daoist magician who sold medicine in the market retired each evening to rest inside a pot he had hung up by his shop.
4. In some translations it is also read as "Middling Hermit."
5. This quality is reminiscent of Sontag's remark on Benjamin in *Under the Sign of Saturn*, "The more lifeless things are, the more potent and ingenious can be the mind which contemplates them" (Sontag, 2002, p. 120).
6. This expression comes from a passage in the Vimalakirti Sutra, describing how the Buddha "contained the height and breadth of Mount Sumeru inside a mustard seed without any increase or decrease in its size" (Schmidt, 2003, p. 499).
7. The Dunedin Chinese Garden is named *Lan Yuan*.

References

Agnew, T. (2011, April 23). Brothers in arms. *Otago Daily Times*, p. 55.

Aitchison, C., MacLeod, N. E., & Shaw, S. J. (2000). *Leisure and tourism landscapes: Social and cultural geographies*. London, England: Routledge.

Arlt, W. G. (2006). *China's outbound tourism*. Abingdon, England: Routledge.

Ateljevic, I., & Doorne, S. (2005). Dialectics of authentication: Performing "exotic otherness" in a backpacker enclave of Dali, China. *Journal of Tourism and Cultural Change*, *3*(1), 1–17.

Ateljevic, I., Morgan, N., & Pritchard, A. (2007). Editors' introduction: Promoting an academy of hope in tourism enquiry. In I. Ateljevic, A. Pritchard, & N. Morgan (Eds.), *The critical turn in tourism studies* (pp. 1–10). Amsterdam, The Netherlands: Elsevier.

Beattie, J. (2007). Growing Chinese influences in New Zealand: Chinese gardens, identity and meaning. *New Zealand Journal of Asian Studies*, *9*(1), 38–61.

Beattie, J. (2008). Gardens of southern China. In J. Beattie, & D. C. G. Trust (Eds.), *Lan Yuan: The garden of enlightenment: Essays on the intellectual, cultural and architectural background to the Dunedin Chinese Garden* (pp. 61–89). Dunedin, New Zealand: Dunedin Chinese Gardens Trust.

Bendix, R. (1997). *In search of authenticity: The formation of folklore studies*. Madison, WI: University of Wisconsin Press.

Brooker, P., & Thacker, A. (2005). *Geographies of modernism: Literatures, cultures, spaces*. Abingdon, England: Routledge.

Cao, X. (2002). *A dream of red mansions*. Beijing, China: People's Literature Press.

Cao, Y., Chen, L., & Tan, Y. (2008). A garden of distant longing: The Dunedin Chinese Garden. In J. Beattie & D. C. G. Trust (Eds.), *Lan Yuan: The garden of enlightenment: Essays on the intellectual, cultural and architectural background to the Dunedin Chinese Garden* (pp. 45–60). Dunedin, New Zealand: Dunedin Chinese Gardens Trust.

Chan, K. (2004, Summer). The global return of the *wu xia pian* (Chinese sword-fighting movie): Ang Lee's *Crouching Tiger, Hidden Dragon*. *Cinema Journal*, *43*, 3–17.

Chang, T. C. (2000). Singapore's little India: A tourist attraction as a contested landscape. *Urban Studies*, *37*(2), 343–366.

Chasse, P. (2010). Chinese gardens abroad. *Perspectives in Landscape Design and History*, *25*(1), 1–4.

Cheng, L. (1998). *Ancient Chinese architecture: Private gardens*. Wien, NY: Springer.

Clunas, C. (1996). *Fruitful sites: Garden culture in Ming dynasty China*. Durham, NC: Duke University Press.

Cohen, E., & Cohen, S. A. (2012). Authentication: Hot and cool. *Annals of Tourism Research*. doi:10.1016/j.annals.2012.03.004

Confucius, The analects of Confucius (Lun Yu), translated by Arthur Waley. Retrieved from http://myweb.cableone.net/subru/Confucianism.html

Cronon, W. (1996). The trouble with wilderness; or, getting back to the wrong nature. In W. Cronon (Ed.), *Uncommon ground: Rethinking the human place in nature* (pp. 69–90). New York, NY: W. W. Norton & Company.

Crouch, D. (2000). Places around us: Embodied lay geographies in leisure and tourism. *Leisure Studies, 19*(2), 63–76.

Dunedin City Council. (2011). *History of Dunedin Chinese Garden*. Retrieved from http://www.dunedin.govt.nz/facilities/dunedin-chinese-garden/history-of-the-chinese-garden

Gill, B., & Huang, Y. (2006). Sources and limits of Chinese "soft power." *Survival, 48*(2), 17–36.

Gu, Z. Y., & Kang, T. J. (2010). 古诗词英译中的旅游文化 [The culture of the tourism in the translation of ancient Chinese poetry]. *Journal of Chonqing Technology and Business University, 27*(5), 126–131.

Hammer, E. (2003). *Nature within walls: The Chinese Garden Court at the Metropolitan Museum of Art*. New York, NY: The Metropolitan Museum of Art.

Han, F. (2012). Cultural landscape: A Chinese way of seeing nature. In K. Taylor & J. L. Lennon (Eds.), *Managing cultural landscape* (pp. 90–108). London, England: Routledge.

Harvey, S. (2008). *Perfect start as doors to Chinese garden open*. Retrieved from http://www.odt.co.nz/news/dunedin/12621/perfect-start-doors-chinese-garden-open

Hinton, D. (2005). *Mountain home: The wilderness poetry of ancient China*. New York, NY: New Directions Publishing.

Ien, A. (1998). Can one say no to Chineseness? Pushing the limits of the diasporic paradigm. *Boundary 2, 25*(3), 223–242.

Jacques, D. (1990). On the supposed Chineseness of the English landscape garden. *Garden History, 18*(2), 180–191.

Jamal, T., & Hill, S. (2004). Developing a framework for indicators of authenticity: The place and space of cultural and heritage tourism. *Asia Pacific Journal of Toutism Research, 9*(4), 353–371.

Jamal, T., & Lelo, L. (2010). Exploring the conceptual and analytical framing of dark tourism: From darkness to intentionality. In R. Sharpley & P. R. Stone (Eds.), *Tourist experience: Contemporary perspectives* (pp. 29–42). London, England: Taylor & Francis.

Jameson, F., & Miyoshi, M. (1998). *The cultures of globalization*. Durham, NC: Duke University Press.

Jencks, C. (2003). Meanings of the Chinese Garden. In M. Keswick, C. Jencks, & A. Hardie (Eds.), *The Chinese garden: History, art and architecture* (pp. 209–217). Cambridge, MA: Harvard University Press.

Keswick, M., Jencks, C., & Hardie, A. (2003). *The Chinese garden: History, art and architecture*. Cambridge, MA: Harvard University Press.

Lasansky, D., & McLaren, B. (2004). *Architecture and tourism: Perception, performance and place*. New York, NY: Berg.

Lewis, J. (2008). *Tourist rates garden highly*. Retrieved from http://www.odt.co.nz/news/dunedin/6182/tourist-rates-garden-highly

Li, Q. (2011). *Confucius, TCM best represent Chinese culture*. Retrieved from http://www.chinadaily.com.cn/china/2011-01/04/content_11793518.htm

Li, W., Hodgetts, D., & Ho, E. (2010). Gardens, transitions and identity reconstruction among older Chinese immigrants to New Zealand. *Journal of Health Psychology, 15*(5), 786–796.

Lou, Q. (2003). *Chinese gardens* (L. Zhang & H. Yu, Trans.). Beijing, China: China Intercontinental Press.

Lovejoy, A. O. (1933). The Chinese origin of a Romanticism. *The Journal of English and Germanic Philology, 32*(1), 1–20.

Lu, A. (2011). Lost in translation: Modernist interpretation of the Chinese garden as experiential space and its assumptions. *The Journal of Architecture*, *16*(4), 499–527.

Lu, S., Zhang, J., & Gan, M. (1999). 城市古典园林原始功能老化的初步研究 [Aging of classic garden in city-concept model and case study]. *Economic Geography*, *1999*(5), 85–90.

MacCannell, D. (1976). *The tourist: A new theory of the leisure class*. London, England: University of California Press.

MacCannell, D. (2011). *The Ethics of Sightseeing*. London, England: University of California Press.

Mackenzie, D. (2008). Garden—And China ties—Blooming. Retrieved from http://www.odt.co.nz/news/dunedin/9153/garden-and-ties-china-blooming

Madgin, D. (2008). *Form follows feng shui*. Retrieved from http://www.odt.co.nz/lifestyle/magazine/3473/form-follows-feng-shui

Mao, H., & Zhou, W. (2006, September). 江南古典园林旅游功能缺失研究 [Study on the lack of tourism function of Chinese classic gardens]. Paper presented at Cultural Heritage Conservation and Tourism Development International Symposium, Nanjing, China.

McNeilly, H. (2008). *DCC to promote garden*. Retrieved from http://www.odt.co.nz/news/dunedin/4837/dcc-promote-garden

Moloughney, B. (2005). Translating culture: Rethinking New Zealand's Chineseness. In C. Ferrall, P. Millar, & K. Smith (Eds.), *East by South: China in the Australasian imagination* (pp. 389–404). Wellington, New Zealand: Victoria University Press.

Moloughney, B., & Stenhouse, J. (1999). "Drug-besotten, sinbegotten fiends of filth": New Zealanders and the oriental other, 1850–1920. *New Zealand Journal of History*, *33*(1), 43–64.

Morton, T. (2010). Ecology as text, text as Ecology. *The Oxford Literary Review*, *32*(1), 1–17.

Nyíri, P. (2007). *Scenic Spots: Chinese tourism, the state, and cultural authority*. Seattle, WA: University of Washington Press.

Orton, M. (2007). Dunedin Chinese Garden [video file]. Retrieved from http://www.youtube.com/watch?v=waM5QK4KN2Q

Otago Daily Times. (2008a, May 31). $200,000 boost for Chinese garden. Retrieved from http://www.odt.co.nz/news/dunedin/7995/200000-boost-chinese-garden

Otago Daily Times. (2008b, May 28). Glimpse at Chinese Garden. Retrieved from http://www.odt.co.nz/news/dunedin/7462/eleven-year-wait-chinese-garden

Paradise, J. F. (2009). China and international harmony: The role of Confucius institutes in bolstering Beijing's soft power. *Asian Survey*, *2009*(49), 647–669.

Petersen, Y. Y. (1995). The Chinese landscape as a tourist attraction: Image and reality. In A. Lew & L. Yu (Eds.), *Tourism in China: Geographic, political and economic perspectives* (pp. 141–154). Boulder, CO: Westview Press.

Reisinger, Y., & Steiner, C. (2006). Reconceptualizing object authenticity. *Annals of Tourism Research*, *33*(1), 65–86.

Rickly-Boyd, J. M. (2012). Authenticity & aura: A Benjaminian approach to tourism. *Annals of Tourism Research*, *39*(1), 269–289.

Rössler, M. (2006). World heritage cultural landscapes; a UNESCO flagship programme 1992–2006. *Landscape Research*, *31*(4), 333–353.

Ryan, C., & Gu, H. (2009). Introduction: The growth and context of tourism in China. In C. Ryan & H. Gu (Eds.), *Tourism in China: Destination, cultures and communities* (pp. 1–10). New York, NY: Routledge.

Schmidt, J. (2003). *Harmony garden: The life, literary criticism, and poetry of Yuan Mei (1716–1799)*. London, England: RoutledgeCurzon.

Sontag, S. (2002). *Under the sign of Saturn*. New York, NY: Picador USA.

Squire, S. J. (1994). The cultural values of literary tourism. *Annals of Tourism Research*, *21*(1), 103–120.

Tourism New Zealand. (2008). *Dunedin opens authentic Chinese garden*. Retrieved from http://www.newzealand.com/travel/media/press-releases/2008/6/culture_dunedin-chinese-garden_press-release.cfm

Tredici, P. D., & Yu, K. J. (1993). Infinity in a bottle gourd: Understanding the Chinese garden. *Arnoldia*, *53*(1), 2–7.

Tu, W. (2005). Cultural China: The periphery as the center. *Daedalus*, *134*(4), 145–167.

Urry, J. (1990). *The tourist gaze: Leisure and travel in contemporary societies*. London, England: Sage Publications.

Urry, J. (2002). *The tourist gaze*. London, UK: Sage.

Wang, N. (1999). Rethinking authenticity in tourism experience. *Annals of Tourism Research*, *26*(2), 349–370.

Wang, Y. (2004). 中国园林文化史 [China landscape cultural history] (J. Zhang, Trans.). Shanghai, China: Shanghai People's Publishing House.

White, N. R., & White, P. B. (2004). Travel as transition: Identity and place. *Annals of Tourism Research*, *31*(1), 200–218.

Willis, J. W., Jost, M., & Nilakanta, R. (2007). *Foundations of qualitative research: Interpretive and critical approaches*. Thousand Oaks, CA: Sage Publications.

Wu, D. D. (2008). *Discourses of cultural China in the globalizing age*. Hong Kong, China: Hong Kong University Press.

Xiao, C. (2001). *The Chinese garden as lyric enclave: A generic study of the Story of the Stone*. Ann Arbor: Center for Chinese Studies Publications, University of Michigan.

Xie, P. F. (2011). *Authenticating ethnic tourism*. Bristol, UK: Channel View Publications.

Yan, G., & Santos, C. A. (2009). "China, forever" tourism discourse and self-orientalism. *Annals of Tourism Research*, *36*(2), 295–315.

Yang, X. (2003). *Metamorphosis of the private sphere: Gardens and objects in Tang-Song poetry*. Cambridge, MA: Harvard University Asia Center.

Zhang, G. (2003). China's tourism since 1978: Policies, experiences, and lessons learned. In A. A. Lew (Ed.), *Tourism in China* (pp. 13–34). New York, NY: Haworth Hospitality Press.

Zhang, W. (2010). China's cultural future: From soft power to comprehensive national power. *International Journal of Cultural Policy*, *16*(4), 383–402.

Zhang, Y. (2007). Discussion on the philosophical meaning of the classical garden in China. *Modern Gardens*, *2007*(3), 25–28.

Chinese Outbound Tourism to the United Kingdom: Issues for Chinese and British Tour Operators

中国公民到英国旅游 — 探讨两地旅游经营商面对的问题

NICOLETTE DE SAUSMAREZ
HUIQING TAO
PETER MCGRATH

This study explores the developing relationship between British inbound tour operators and their Chinese counterparts since 2005, when Britain acquired Approved Destination Status. Empirical data were collected from tour operators in both China and Great Britain between 2006 and 2011. The findings suggest that many British tour operators consider that the profit from the Chinese inbound market is not worth the work involved. Differing cultural expectations are identified as the main source of difficulty in respect of accommodation and food; the cost and difficulty in obtaining a visa for the UK is considered the main obstacle to the growth of this important market segment.

Introduction

International tourism has shown spectacular growth since the 1950s and now contributes substantially to the economies of both developed and developing countries. It is viewed in the developed world principally as a means of achieving socioeconomic goals, such as regional development and increased employment, especially in the low-skill sectors; additionally, in less economically developed economies tourism is an important source of stable foreign exchange and often a means of diversifying a narrow resource-based economy. However, implicit in the concept of international tourism is the movement of people from one culture to another and this will inevitably engender some degree of conflict at times. Tour operators act as brokers in the tourism industry and are located in both the generating and destination countries; therefore, it is important that successful and harmonious working relationships are developed between them in order to ensure that business performance is optimized.

The global economic recession since 2008 and the subsequent crisis in the Euro zone have affected many European countries, and international tourism offers a means of stimulating the economy and generating jobs. As a result, there is fierce competition between the United Kingdom and other traditional European destinations for new tourist-generating markets, and China offers enormous potential in this regard. Because tour operators play such a pivotal role in international tourism and in view of the considerable disparity between the two cultures, the purpose of this study is to explore the early stages of the relationship between the Chinese and British intermediaries and to identify any issues arising that need to be addressed.

The Growth of Chinese Tourism

Since the opening up of China to Western trade and investment in the late 1970s and the concomitant domestic agricultural reforms, the Chinese economy has shown rapid and consistent growth, averaging 9.11% per year (United Nations Statistics Division, 2011). A consequence of this is that many Chinese now have the means to travel both at home and abroad, and tourism is fast becoming a major factor in the growth of the Chinese economy. In 2007, there were 1.61 billion domestic visits, with revenue of CNY (Chinese Yuan) 777.1 billion (US\$121.8 billion), an increase of 15.5 and 24.7%, respectively, over 2006 (China National Tourism Administration [CNTA], 2011a). The total contribution of travel and tourism to the gross domestic product was estimated by the World Travel and Tourism Council (WTTC) to be 8.6% in 2011 (WTTC, 2011). International tourism is a significant source of foreign exchange. According to the United Nations World Tourism Organization (UNWTO), in 2010 international arrivals reached 55.7 million, with receipts of US\$45.8 billion, a 9.4 and 15.5% increase over the previous year, respectively (UNWTO, 2011c). It is predicted that arrivals will reach 84.389 million by 2021, representing growth of 4% per annum (WTTC).

Recognizing the economic benefits associated with domestic tourism, over the years the Chinese government has adopted a variety of measures to stimulate demand, such as the introduction in 1999 of three public holidays, or Golden Weeks, to celebrate Chinese New Year, May Day, and National Day in October. In 2008, not only was the number of national holidays increased from 10 to 11 days to allow more time for travel but employees are also now entitled to 5 to 15 days paid annual leave, depending on length of service (Lehman, Lee, & Xu Law Firm, 2011). This has not only had a positive impact on domestic tourism, but it has also given people more time to travel abroad.

Although Chinese outbound tourism is a relatively recent phenomenon, growth here is strong, too. According to the China Outbound Tourism Research Institute (COTRI), the number of Chinese traveling abroad in 2010 reached a figure of 57.4 million, an increase of more than 20% over the previous year (COTRI, 2011). In 1995, the UNWTO forecast that by 2020 China would be the fourth largest generating country in the world, with a 6.4% market share and 100 million Chinese outbound tourists (UNWTO, 2003). However, in light of current trends, it is now considered likely that this figure will be reached earlier (UNWTO, 2011a). There is great potential for countries attracting Chinese outbound tourists, because the Chinese market is considered to be very lucrative; from expenditure of US$470 million in 1990 (UNWTO, 2011b), in just 20 years the Chinese have risen to third place in the 2010 UNWTO ranking of the world's top tourism spenders, accounting for US$54.9 billion (UNWTO, 2011c).

There are, however, some restrictions on outbound travel. Outbound tourists have to be part of a tour group, which has to be organized by an agency authorized by the China Tourism Bureau to arrange tours and to submit tour group applications for visas. This measure both controls the number of outbound independent tourists and assists the development of outbound travel businesses, although it inevitably favors the larger, better-known travel companies (Pan & Laws, 2001). No distinction is made in China between the roles of tour operators and retail travel agents (Haden, 2011) and for the purposes of this study, they will all be referred to as tour operators.

Unique to China is the approved destination status (ADS) arrangement, a bilateral agreement between the Chinese government and another country or region, whereby Chinese tourists are permitted to undertake leisure travel in groups to that destination. By April 2011, 140 countries and/or regions had been approved, with 110 of them officially open to Chinese tourists (CNTA, 2011c). Though a substantial proportion of Chinese outbound tourists travel to destinations in the East Asia Pacific region, the number traveling further afield is also increasing, with Russia, Australia, and the United States ranked sixth, eighth, and ninth most popular destinations in 2009, respectively (CNTA, 2011b). The primary purpose of 70% of international trips in 2009 was for leisure and the remainder for business purposes (Uren, 2009). Chinese outbound tourists make up only 3.6% of the total population and those visiting European destinations are typically affluent, urban-based, young and middle-aged working professionals, and they travel during Chinese official holidays (Haden, 2011).

The UK as an Approved Destination

At the time of writing, there were over 60 travel agencies in China accredited to submit approved destination scheme visa applications to the UK Border Agency through nominated visa application centres, based in 12 principle cities. Visas are valid for a month and require successful applicants to enter, travel within the territory of the United Kingdom, and leave as a member of a tour group (UK Border Agency, 2011a). To be eligible for a visa, the British government stipulates that prospective visitors should have a good visa record and evidence that they have been financially solvent for at least 6 months (UK Border Agency, 2011b).

Since the millennium, international tourism growth has suffered a number of far-reaching setbacks, with terrorist attacks in many generating and receiving countries, natural disasters such as severe acute respiratory syndrome (SARS), and the Indian Ocean tsunami in 2004 and currently the world economic recession. The United Kingdom has had its share of difficulties and the potential economic benefit of the Chinese inbound market is recognized as being substantial. ADS was agreed between the British and Chinese governments in 2005. Initially, the UK was braced for an influx of tourists from China resulting from successful familiarization trips for Chinese sales personnel that year and the announcement of an increase in the number of flights from

China to the United Kingdom, although it was accepted that there would not be substantial growth in arrivals in the short term (Jinman & Pai, 2005). However, between 2005 and 2010 the United Kingdom lost market share to other destinations, most notably France and the United States, and efforts are being made to rectify this situation (VisitBritain, 2011). It is hoped that this research will make a positive contribution in this regard by identifying issues that need to be addressed in order for the market to develop further and for the industry players to maximize their performance.

Research Context

Research into Chinese outbound tourism is proliferating as the sector becomes more established and that with the greatest relevance to this study can be considered within four broad areas: Chinese motivation for outbound tourism, the economic benefits to the destinations, tour operator relations, and cross-cultural business practice.

Chinese Motivations for Outbound Tourism

Investigating the growth of Chinese outbound tourism from Mainland China to Hong Kong prior to its return to China in 1997, Qu and Lam (1997) suggested that disposable income and more relaxed visa requirements were the only two significant determinants of tourism demand. As might be expected, the preferences and expectations of the Chinese as international travelers tend toward shopping, because they attach considerable importance to buying gifts for parents and elders as a mark of respect for age and authority (Mok & DeFranco, 2000). This was also the case with Chinese travelers visiting the United States (Jang, Yu, & Pearson, 2003), where the main attraction was shopping, although dining in restaurants, visiting historical places, and sightseeing in cities were also popular. In contrast, Ryan and Mo (2002) found that in the case of visitors to New Zealand, although shopping was considered important, the tourists gained more satisfaction from experiencing the natural environment. Clearly, the appeal of New Zealand as a destination lies in its stunning scenery and opportunities for outdoor activities.

The Economic Benefits to the Destinations

There has been some research quantifying the benefits that ADS can bring to China's outbound destinations. Australia and New Zealand were granted ADS in April 1999, becoming the first Western countries that the Chinese government allowed its citizens to visit. Lim and Wang (2005) suggested that this gave both countries a short-term competitive edge over other long-haul destinations. Pan (2003) and Pan, Scott, and Laws (2006), researching Australia's inbound Chinese arrivals, found that in the first year after ADS was granted there was a 34.2% increase in Chinese arrivals.

Similarly, Tretheway and Mak (2006) illustrated the extent of tourism growth by means of the number of visas issued to Chinese citizens; in the 5-year period from 1997–1998 to 2002–2003 the number of Australian visitor visas issued to Chinese citizens increased by 130%. To contextualize this finding in current terms, data collected by Tourism Australia (2011) indicate that China is now Australia's third largest tourist market, with 519,200 tourist arrivals in the year ending September 2011, an increase of 20.6% over the previous year. Tretheway and Mak's research has been corroborated more recently by Arita, Edmonds, La Croix, and Mak (2011), who analyzed data from 61 destinations for the period 1995–2005 and showed that there was an increase in visitor arrivals averaging 25–52% three years after achieving ADS. They warned, however, against assuming a constant response to ADS and suggested that consumer demand might have been greater in the early days after restrictions on international travel were lifted.

Tour Operator Relations

Tour operators are important intermediaries between the travel trade in source markets and destinations, yet comparatively little research has been published on their operations and their interactions with other tourism sector players. In their study of German travel companies operating in Turkey, Batman and Hüseyin Soybali (1999) focused mainly on management and organizational structure rather than the interaction between tour operators from very different parts of the world and the challenges that this may offer. In a later study of the business relationship between tourism intermediaries, Medina-Muñoz and Medina-Muñoz (2004) explored the interorganizational relationship between tour operators from both Germany and the United Kingdom and their accommodation providers. Here again, although tour operators from two different countries were investigated, it was their relationship with hotels rather than each other that was the focus. More relevant to this study is the research of Lumsdon and Swift (1999), who examined the relationship between tour operators in four South American countries and their UK counterparts. However, here the tour operators were located in developing country destinations and consequently many of the key issues encountered, such as the lack of infrastructure in the destination, are not relevant to this research.

Also of interest here are studies by March (2008) and King, Dwyer, and Prideaux (2006), who, with a focus on Chinese inbound tourism to Australia, considered unethical practices in international tourism and the damage to tour operator relations. The authors suggested that visitors' expectations, for example, might not be consistent with the services promised and/or provided by tour operators and travel agents. Furthermore, quality issues appear to be primarily associated with excessive shopping and the inclusion of hotels of a lower standard than originally advertised, which consequently leads to diminished tourist satisfaction, reduced repeat visitation, and negative word of mouth.

Cross-Cultural Business Practice

The potential of the Chinese market for all destinations with ADS is considerable, and competition between destinations for Chinese tourists is now intense. The importance of establishing effective relationships between the destination tour operators and their Chinese counterparts was stressed by Pan and Laws (2001) in order for the destination to expand its share of the Chinese tourism market and justify its status as an approved destination. Different business practices can inhibit the development of strong relationships between tourism industry players, which in turn has the potential to impact negatively on the business outcomes (Pan, 2003; Pan & Laws).

Herbig and Martin (1998) suggested that China is one of the most difficult countries for Westerners to understand and adapt to, with cultural misunderstandings being the main reason for failure of business between Western countries and China. The cultural traits prevalent in Chinese negotiation were identified by Woo and Prud'homme (1999) as status, face, trust, friendship, ambiguity, patience, Chinese protocol, and *guanxi* (the basic dynamics in the complexity of interpersonal influence and social relationships, which is a central concept in Chinese society and was discussed in some detail by Leung, Heung, & Wong, 2008). Understanding the Chinese business style is critical for Western businesses; O'Keefe and O'Keefe (1997) compared Chinese and Westerners' behaviors in business and how those behaviors were perceived by each nationality. Although not writing in the context of tourism, their research has significance for international tourism businesses, particularly those in the supply chain, now that China is becoming such an important generating market and destination.

Research Design

In order to explore the changes in the relationship during the first 5 years after ADS was granted, empirical research was carried out in both China and the United Kingdom between 2006 and 2011. Data were collected from tour operators by means of 24 in-depth, semistructured telephone interviews and five e-mailed questionnaires that consisted mainly of open-ended questions. The topics addressed included the finding of business partners; product development; the working relationship with tour operators of the other nationality; the expectations of Chinese tour operators and the traveling public; and how the future might unfold. The respondents were both male and female but no attempt was made to stratify them because the samples were small and the respondents were speaking on behalf of the company rather than providing their own views. The data were analyzed manually; because the interviews were carried out by different people and in different languages, it was not felt appropriate to use a qualitative data analysis software package.

All of the Chinese travel companies that were approached were accredited to organize overseas trips and were located in Beijing and Shanghai. Most of the companies were large with about 100–200 employees and branches in several of the main cities. The respondents all worked in departments specializing in the development and sales of UK and European tours. Twelve companies agreed to participate in the telephone interviews, representing a response rate of 24%, and these were carried out either in Mandarin or in Shanghai dialect by one of the authors who is a native speaker. It was felt that telephone surveys were a more appropriate means of collecting data rather than e-mail questionnaires, because respect is a major feature of interpersonal communication in China (Milliman & Von Glinow, 1998).

The British tour operators were selected from a list of 122 UK suppliers authorized by the Chinese government to deal with incoming package holiday groups from China (CNTA, 2008). Only the companies that offered general package tours were selected for the sample; those specializing in, for example, purely transport, the theater, or travel for students at language schools were not approached. Because the purpose of this research is to explore the relations between British inbound and Chinese outbound tour operators, Chinese companies based in the United Kingdom were also excluded from the sample. Seventeen companies participated in the research, for a response rate of 26%. Twelve interviews were carried out by telephone and in five cases where the respondents had no time to talk, the questions were e-mailed to them for completion at a less busy time.

A limitation of the research is that comparatively few tour operators were interviewed. The reluctance of many of the companies approached to participate in the research, ostensibly due to time constraints, supports Paxson's (1995) observation that response rates may be below 20% when surveying organizations. However, because the intention was to explore the situation rather than to carry out a qualitative analysis, the data were still considered to be of value.

Research Findings

Establishing a Working Partnership

Most commonly, UK and Chinese tour operators make contact at trade fairs or through introductions; in some cases, British tour operators use agents to find them compatible partners. In addition, foreign embassies may supply a list of travel companies to Chinese tour operators or organize free exploration trips, such as the visit to Britain by a delegation of Chinese tourists and VIPs that was arranged post-ADS in July 2005 (British Broadcasting Corporation [BBC], 2005). Language differences were not considered a problem by any of the respondents because many Chinese now speak English and British tour operators often employ Mandarin- or Cantonese-speaking staff. Financial strength and reputation are seen by the Chinese as essential qualities, and prior experience working with the Chinese is desirable due to familiarity with Chinese business practices. Surprisingly, offering a portfolio of low-cost products is not usually considered important because, as one Chinese respondent observed, customers do not mind paying an additional 10–15% of the total price for a holiday package as long as they get a good quality holiday.

Issues Associated With Product Development

Perspective of Chinese Tour Operators. Currently the market is very young, and although Chinese visitor numbers are increasing, demand for a greater range of packages is not. The classic UK tour, which visits some or all of London, York, Edinburgh, Cambridge, Oxford, and the Lake District, is still the most popular, although it may be customized for a group to some extent depending on the length of their visit. The Chinese have voiced some frustration over the lack of new itineraries being developed. Although now that many tour operators have been on familiarization trips to the UK, they sometimes design their own itineraries and then contact British tour operators to quote for them. The trend over the last five years has been toward a reduction in group size and tours with greater depth, which cover less ground but in more detail.

At present there is limited potential for niche or special interest products, although there are already tours designed for football supporters or golf enthusiasts. These groups are considered by some Chinese tour operators to be too expensive and high risk, but for others they are an attractive option as this market segment is not price sensitive:

> Those who can play golf in China are very rich. They gather together in a golf club and then the travel company promotes the golf trip to the UK among them and ask for their feedback, such as the time of the holiday, which is the main issue to those people. They do not care about the price at all. Showing off is one of the motivations. (Chinese respondent 1, 2006)

Also becoming much more popular are tours for groups of prospective students who want to study abroad, so that they can get an idea of the country—the culture, the food, and so on—and its educational environment through visits to selected university campuses.

The Chinese groups travel with a tour manager and on arrival in Britain they are provided with a Mandarin-speaking local guide registered with the British Tourism Authority. All respondents felt that the guides were very experienced and were very well received by the visitors, despite the fact that most were not professionally trained, although some respondents felt that the guides would still benefit from more language training and professional knowledge.

The Perspective of British Tour Operators. According to the British respondents, Chinese tourists' expectations are very high.

> They want what they booked and nothing else will do. (British respondent 6, 2008)

They expect to travel comfortably and to have the opportunity to visit and have their photo taken in front of the monuments or scenery that they have seen in the media. They do not look for immersion into British culture so, for instance, they are happy to eat most of their meals in Chinese restaurants. The British countryside never fails to please them when they compare it to back home. They always want to be doing or seeing something in order to fit as much into the shortest time possible, with very few days free. The most popular attractions are the main London heritage attractions, such as Big Ben and the Houses of Parliament. The tourists like to have some information about what they are visiting but prefer curiosities and stories that they can remember easily rather than a history class from a verbose guide. They consider the entrance costs to be very high and reported that not enough information is provided in Mandarin.

There is, however, a considerable discrepancy between their expectations and reality, especially with regard to transport, service quality, and hotel facilities, none of which is as good as they expect. They find the minibuses cramped, the hotels old, and the rooms very small. Although the Chinese are familiar with multinational hotel chains such as Holiday Inn and Hilton, local guesthouses, bed and breakfast providers, and hostels are new to them. They like American-style hotels with as many comforts as possible, but when visiting Britain they seldom have a large enough budget to stay in them and so are often disappointed because the hotels, especially those in London, are of a lower standard than their equivalent in China. They prefer modern to traditional hotels, with spacious lobby areas with a lot of chrome and glass, plentiful staff, and bedrooms with large bathrooms and Internet access. They complained of the lack of Chinese food in hotel restaurants and reported that there are few choices for breakfast. For Chinese tourists, high-quality accommodation is a requirement when on holiday, unlike many Europeans, who consider their hotel primarily a place to sleep. One company provides photos of the accommodation to business groups because they pay more, but this is rarely done in the case of leisure tourists because it would cost too much, given the number of customers.

Chinese tour operators contract Chinese meals where possible because most older and middle-aged travelers are not used to the food in Europe and prefer to eat their own dishes in UK hotels or eat out in a Chinese restaurant, although visitor feedback suggests that they do not find Chinese food in Britain particularly appetizing. A Western dinner may be offered as a highlight and is well received. In contrast, most young travelers want to try local foods and business groups can opt to try other restaurants as long as there is demand from participants.

Working Relationships and Cultural Issues

In all of the interviews, the Chinese tour operators were warm in their praise of UK tour operators, describing them as helpful and eager to do business with the Chinese and cooperative in providing information when asked. As the British become more familiar with the needs and characteristics of the Chinese market, they are responding more quickly and more appropriately to new requests. Overall, it was felt that there were few, if any, serious cultural issues affecting the working relationship. Understandably, the Chinese consider there to be advantages in working with British tour operators who have Chinese employees in Britain or representatives in China or with those who already have experience of working with the Chinese and are consequently familiar with the Chinese market and business culture, because this minimizes cultural differences. UK companies were seen as open to feedback and suggestions, making changes to their products or prices where possible:

> Very happy cooperation. UK tour operators are trying their best to meet our requirements. They know that Chinese market demand is changing slowly. (Chinese respondent 7, 2011)

It was recognized, however, that different ways of thinking and different business practices could give rise to misunderstandings or create problems in the initial period of working together.

In contrast, the British respondents generally felt that the Chinese tour operators were not easy to work with and that it takes a huge effort to build relationships:

> Chinese requests are very demanding in the first stages—they want everything priced up a year in advance and all the information. I think they then tend to shop around. (British respondent 2, 2011)

Because Chinese tour operators lack understanding of British hotel and meal standards, their expectations are unrealistic and greatly exceed what their budget can provide. Other problems identified were the propensity of the Chinese tour operators to change their minds, their lack of flexibility, and difficulties with regard to obtaining payment. In the early interviews, all of the British respondents complained that the Chinese tour operators frequently request last-minute alterations to the itinerary before their arrival in Britain and then additional changes as the tour proceeds, creating logistical complications and making additional demands on the UK staff involved. It was felt that many Chinese tour operators were inflexible and reluctant to reach a compromise where there was a discrepancy between what was requested and what was supplied, often due to unforeseen circumstances beyond the control of the British supplier. After several years of working together, many conceded that the Chinese have become more familiar with British tourism products; they are consequently better placed to make decisions early and stick to them. This makes working together now much more harmonious.

More serious were the comments about payment. One tour operator observed that the Chinese were quick to demand a refund if things did not go strictly according to plan; others advised that it was necessary to monitor payment transactions once a group had left the United Kingdom. However, in contrast, it was felt that as long as the service agreed on was provided, things ran smoothly and the groups themselves caused very few problems and were always very enthusiastic about the holidays. It is difficult to ascertain exactly how serious these claims are and they need contextualization; one British tour operator did in fact observe that the Chinese were much better about payment than many other nationalities.

Barriers to Market Development

The Visa Application Process. The greatest barrier to market development was identified by over half of the Chinese respondents as the visa application process. A tourist visiting Europe and wishing to include Britain on the itinerary must have both Schengen and UK visas. A Schengen visa is considered much easier to obtain and is much cheaper than a UK visa and it is valid for longer. To save time, tour operators often send their customers' visa applications to an agency that handles the transactions, but this incurs an additional charge.

It was thought that the reason the British government is cautious about issuing visas to Chinese tourists is that they fear that the better standard of living will attract some to remain in the country illegally. One respondent observed that 90% of travel companies have a record of having tourist visa applications rejected, despite trying their utmost to prevent this happening:

> There are not many companies empowered to organize trips to the UK, so all those companies treat it very seriously. The travel agents check the documents for visa application very carefully. They make follow-up calls and ask all the applicants some sensitive questions. They will reject a customer in a polite way (e.g., this holiday has been cancelled, but in fact, it's not) if they think there is any opportunity for the British embassy to reject the application. The Chinese tour operator will be punished by not allowing any group holiday to the UK for three months if just one tourist has left the group in the UK by any means. (Chinese respondent 2, 2011)

Tourists with a new passport and therefore no visa history usually have more difficulty obtaining a UK visa. Original documents may be requested at very short notice before the trip and sometimes there is not enough time to process the visa. If applicants want or need their documents back quickly, they will not risk a delay but decide against going to Britain and apply only for a Schengen visa to visit Europe.

It was suggested the main reason that tourist visa applications are rejected by the UK government is that the tourists offer fake documents or that they have a criminal record, which was recognized as being largely the fault of the travel company, who is careless when checking the documents. Evidence of a substantial bank account is also required, and visas may be refused if the applicant has not had adequate savings in a bank account for a long enough period. It was explained that the Chinese traditionally tend not to put money in the bank but save or invest it in other ways. Should one person in the party have his or her visa application rejected, the final number in the group may be reduced, which makes the cost of the holiday greater for all participants.

The Value of the Chinese Business. Some smaller UK tour operators did not feel that the Chinese business was worth the effort it required. Half of the respondents saw little or no change in demand since Britain acquired ADS and any increase was not worth pursuing. The difficulties in communication, low budget, and "whistle stop" approach to touring, where tourists arrive at an attraction and get off the coach to take a quick photo before continuing on to the next stop, were not in accord with the UK tour operators' business ethos and the standards of care for their customers. In view of the low profit margins, they preferred dealing with the European market. However, they admitted to watching how the Chinese market would develop so that they could enter it if they felt it would be worth their while.

The Future

The Chinese respondents considered that the UK as a destination is developing slowly and it needs more time to mature. The Chinese have increasing disposable income and they want to travel and get to know about other countries in the world; the number of younger outbound travelers is increasing, with many travelers in their 20s and 30s. The United Kingdom is currently not as popular a destination as France or Italy. To assist market development, it was suggested that the primary goal should be to improve the current situation with regard to obtaining visas and for Britain to join the Schengen agreement; in the meantime, training from the UK government for visa applications would be very welcome. It was also suggested that information should be provided in Mandarin not only at tourist attractions and shops but also in public places, such as railway and underground stations, places of interest, and airports:

> There should be more Chinese brochures available at attractions and hotels, especially at the attractions. And stations and the airport. It would be good if there are more Chinese people working in tourism, especially in hotels and shops, those places having direct contact with Chinese tourists. (Chinese respondent 9, 2011)

The British respondents suggested that Chinese agents who sell the holidays to Britain should be better trained so that they more accurately represent the situation in Britain and that VisitBritain should distribute more information about Britain as a destination when promoting the country. They thought that some form of mutual cultural awareness sessions might be helpful and that workshops on British/Chinese business practice and expectations would improve planning and operational performance, reduce stress on both sides, and resolve payment issues. In addition, it was suggested that the Chinese should be warned against Chinese operators based in London, who offer an inferior (and cheaper) product using illegal vehicles and guides; these should be brought within the regulations.

Both sets of respondents stressed the need to minimize costs and work toward cheaper air fares. The cost of a visit is a major factor for Chinese, given the lower salaries in China. The provision of higher quality, lower priced two- to three-star hotels would help in this regard.

Discussion

There can be no doubt that the issue of visas—the cost, the difficulty in obtaining a UK visa, complicated by the fact that the UK is not a signatory to the Schengen agreement—is the greatest hindrance to Chinese tourism to Britain, as observed by Haden (2011).

To address this, in June 2009, it was announced that the British government was looking into the possibility of some sort of harmonization of the UK visa with the Schengen visa to facilitate the process for the Chinese (Tyler, 2009), but no progress appears to have been made. In addition to the cost, the level of inconvenience associated with UK visa application is such that many Chinese feel that is not worth visiting the UK and instead opt for one or more Schengen destinations. This may be one reason why so many more Chinese visit France than visit the UK.

Another issue appears to be the dissatisfaction of the tourists with the quality of the accommodation and food they receive. There appears to be a significant discrepancy between the expectations of the Chinese visitors and the reality of the accommodation booked for them. There is clearly a case here for improving the information provided to the agents who sell the trips, and there is perhaps a role here for VisitBritain when promoting the United Kingdom in China. In addition, better education of the traveling Chinese in this regard is required, although it is difficult to see how this might be accomplished. It would be interesting to know where they acquire their image of Britain from in the first place, and further research in this area might indicate the most cost-effective means of modifying this image to make it more realistic. The Chinese respondents reported that increasingly Chinese tourists are obtaining travel information from the Internet and are becoming more seasoned travelers and know better what they like or want from their trip.

There is obviously a mismatch between what the Chinese like in terms of hotels and what the British have to offer. The predilection of the Chinese for spacious, modern hotels with a lot of glass and chrome is unlikely ever to be satisfied by the available two to three-star accommodations that are within their budget. The tour operators suggest that it is too expensive to provide photos of the hotels for their prospective clients to view when booking a holiday, but it may also be that they do not want the appearance of the hotels to put them off booking the trip. The danger of tourists perceiving (rightly or wrongly) that their hotels are of a lower standard than advertised was stressed by King et al. (2006). The Chinese who are able to afford a holiday in Britain are a wealthy segment of society, so it is not surprising that they are unhappy with British two- to three-star accommodations. It is questionable how many wealthy British travelers would be satisfied with two- to three-star accommodations at their holiday or business destination.

Very little has changed over the past 5 years in terms of the feedback on accommodations. Because Britain cannot offer glamorous hotels to please the Chinese customers, maybe the sales strategy should be changed. Britain could perhaps be sold as a quaint and old-fashioned destination where the visitor "lives the experience" rather than observes it from the comfortable sidelines. Theme parks are very popular in East Asia, and the idea of living the fantasy might appeal to the Chinese. Alternatively, there should be investment in a number of higher quality, lower priced two- to three-star hotels, designed exclusively to please the Chinese, as is done in other destinations to suit particular markets.

With regard to the food, it appears that younger visitors are more adventurous and prepared to try a wider range of dishes, whereas older travelers stick to what is familiar. Because currently older travelers are in the majority, there is a possible scope for arranging exchange visits for Chinese chefs for refresher courses or for courses delivered in digital media format for distance learning. However, if the trend toward younger Chinese travelers continues, it will become less of a challenge to provide good quality Chinese food, because they will be happy to sample more international cuisine.

The fact that language is not a major issue for tour operators working together is not grounds for complacency. Though the number of Chinese arrivals remains comparatively small, the groups can be handled by relatively few tour operators and it may be worthwhile employing Mandarin-speaking staff. Nevertheless, as the number of visitors increases, potential entrants into the market may be discouraged by the additional cost that employing a Mandarin-speaking guide would incur, especially if they are small enterprises. Such companies need support because they offer the kind of tailor-made service that is most appropriate for this market and is hard for larger businesses to emulate. It is unclear whether many UK tour operators are in fact fully committed to dealing with the Chinese market. Feedback suggests that the Chinese inbound market is viewed as low volume, low profit, and a lot of work has to be done, which is not worth the effort. Of the approved UK suppliers approached for an interview, 19 companies (29%) admitted to not handling Chinese groups despite being authorized to do so.

Interestingly, the Chinese tour operators raised no concerns about working with the British, no doubt for cultural reasons, despite being interviewed by a compatriot. In contrast, the British were much more forthcoming when voicing opinions about the Chinese. There does appear to be a case here for some cross-cultural education programs. Reports that the Chinese are unreliable regarding payment raise issues of trust; poor planning or frequent alteration of components of the program may be the result of different working practices. Some sort of cross-cultural seminar program in both the UK and China might fall within the remit of VisitBritain or an institution such as the British Council.

With regard to the product, the Chinese are definite that the UK will mature as a destination, although much more slowly than the British would expect or indeed wish. With regard to the itineraries, some new areas/cities could be included, not only to attract repeat visitors but also to begin familiarizing those destinations with Chinese practices, because this is potentially a large and lucrative future market. Scotland already markets itself as a separate destination, so it might be possible to develop tours that focus mostly on England and Wales and offer Scotland as an "add-on" for those wishing to stay longer in the UK. This would require only small changes in marketing and would allow time for visiting areas like the Cotswolds, with its rich royal history, usually missed by the majority of tour itineraries.

There is a general feeling that for the Chinese market to be expanded faster, things need to change. As Mok and DeFranco (2000) and Jang, Yu, and Pearson (2003) observed, the Chinese are seriously interested in brands and shopping, so extending retail opening hours would be beneficial. In addition, much more tourist literature and support services need to be translated into Mandarin. Again, with reference to France, the Louvre publishes pamphlets in Mandarin and has a Chinese Web page; shop assistants in the big department stores speak Mandarin; and hotels offer their Chinese guests TV channels in their native language (Wang, 2011). It would not require major investment and would remove another disincentive to visiting the UK.

Conclusions

The purpose of this research was to explore the developing relationship between British and Chinese tour operators as Chinese tourism to the United Kingdom increases. Overall, there appear to be very few problems of any magnitude that cannot be resolved over time. The British recognize that the Chinese market is of enormous importance to them, especially in the short term when many of their traditional generating markets are suffering a major economic slowdown. With intense global competition between desti-nations for Chinese tourists, there needs to be swift action taken by the British govern-ment to improve UK visa regulations, which was identified as a major obstacle to the growth in Chinese arrivals. In the short term, training of Chinese tour operators could facilitate visa application, but there is an increasingly urgent need for greater action, which might take the form of either a major overhaul (and simplification) of the system in tandem with a reduction in the cost of visas or, alternatively, membership of the Schengen group. Failure to address this issue could result in Britain losing market share and being marginalized as a Chinese outbound destination.

It would be foolhardy not to recognize that there are significant cultural differences between the two sets of industry players and that any business interaction will inevitably result in areas of friction, which may need to be confronted and resolved. Some sort of cross-cultural training would be welcomed by tour operators of both nationalities and, given the potential of the Chinese market, even quite a modest investment would reap considerable rewards. Further research in this area is needed to evaluate the extent of the demand and to identify the most cost-effective format for such a training program. There is also work to be done in product development to reduce the disparity between the supply of tourism and visitor expectations and to enhance their understanding and experience through the provision of information in a more accessible form. It is expected that the situation will improve as the market becomes more sophisticated. Over the last 5 years positive changes have already been seen not only in tourists' perceptions of aspects of the destination and a readiness to accept the differences but also in the understanding between tour operators. With support and monitoring, the development of an excellent working relationship should be achievable, to the benefit of both British and Chinese.

References

Arita, S., Edmonds, C., La Croix, S., & Mak, J. (2011). Impact of approved destination status on Chinese travel abroad: An econometric analysis. *Tourism Economics, 17*(5), 983–996.
Batman, O., & Hüseyin Soybali, H. (1999). An examination of the organisational characteristics of selected German travel companies in Turkey. *International Journal of Contemporary Hospitality Management, 11*(1), 43–50.
British Broadcasting Corporation. (2005, July 24). *First China tourists arrive in UK*. Retrieved from http://news.bbc.co.uk/1/hi/uk/4711755.stm
China National Tourism Administration. (2008). *UK approved supplier list*. Retrieved from http://zhuanti.cnta.gov.cn/ziliao/other/UK%20Approved%20Supplier%20List%2020080609.xls
China National Tourism Administration. (2011a). *China tourism statistics bulletin 2007*. Retrieved from http://en.cnta.gov.cn/html/2008-11/2008-11-9-21-35-50326.html
China National Tourism Administration. (2011b). *CNTA releases tourism-related economic operation data for February 2009*. Retrieved from http://en.cnta.gov.cn/html/2009-3/2009-3-25-14-48-14525.html
China National Tourism Administration. (2011c). 我国公民自费旅游目的地国家和地区达 140 个 [Over 140 countries and regions now tourist destinations for our citizens]. Retrieved from http://www.cnta.gov.cn/html/2011-4/2011-4-13-8-48-80796.html
China Outbound Tourism Research Institute. (2011). *Current situation of the Chinese outbound tourism*. Retrieved from http://www.china-outbound.com/index.php?option=com_content&view=article&id=110&Itemid=103
Haden, L. (2011). *China outbound—April 2011*. London, England: Mintel Group Ltd.

Herbig, P., & Martin, D. (1998). Negotiating with Chinese: A cultural perspective. *Cross Cultural Management: An International Journal*, *5*(3), 42–56.

Jang, S. C., Yu, L., & Pearson, T. (2003). Chinese travellers to the United States: A comparison of business travel and visiting friends and relatives. *Tourism Geographies*, *5*(1), 87–108.

Jinman, R., & Pai, H-H. (2005, June 27). Chinese tourists flock to UK in search of Clarks, fog and the "big stupid clock." Retrieved from http://www.guardian.co.uk/uk/2005/jun/27/china.world?INTCMP=SRCH

King, B., Dwyer, L., & Prideaux, B. (2006). An evaluation of unethical business practices in Australia's China inbound tourism market. *International Journal of Tourism Research*, *8*(2), 127–142.

Lehman, Lee, & Xu Law Firm. (2011). *How shall employees take their paid annual leave?* Retrieved from http://www.lehmanlaw.com/resource-centre/faqs/human-resources/how-shall-employees-take-their-paid-annual-leave.html

Leung, T. K. P., Heung, V. C. S., & Wong, Y. H. (2008). Cronyism: One possible consequence of guanxi for an insider: How to obtain and maintain it? *European Journal of Marketing*, *42*(1/2), 23–34.

Lim, C., & Wang, Y. (2005). *A time series analysis of Chinese outbound tourism to Australia.* Retrieved from http://www.mssanz.org.au/modsim05/papers/lim_c.pdf

Lumsdon, L. M., & Swift, J. S. (1999). The role of the tour operator in South America: Argentina, Chile, Paraguay and Uruguay. *International Journal of Tourism Research*, *1*(6), 429–439.

March, R. (2008). Towards a conceptualization of unethical marketing practices in tourism: A case-study of Australia's inbound Chinese travel market. *Journal of Travel & Tourism Marketing*, *24*(4), 285–296.

Medina-Muñoz, R. D., & Medina-Muñoz, D. R. (2004). Control and success in collaborative strategies. *The Service Industries Journal*, *24*(2), 81–101.

Milliman, J., & Von Glinow, M. A. (1998). Research and publishing issues in large scale cross-national studies. *Journal of Managerial Psychology*, *13*(3/4), 137–142.

Mok, C., & DeFranco, A. L. (2000). Chinese cultural values: Their implications for travel and tourism marketing. *Journal of Travel & Tourism Marketing*, *8*(2), 99–114.

O'Keefe, H., & O'Keefe, W. M. (1997). Chinese and Western behavioural differences: Understanding the gaps. *International Journal of Social Economics*, *24*(1–3), 190–196.

Pan, G. W. (2003). A theoretical framework of business network relationships associated with the Chinese outbound tourism market to Australia. *Journal of Travel & Tourism Marketing*, *14*(2), 87–104.

Pan, G. W., & Laws, E. (2001). Attracting Chinese outbound tourists: Guanxi and the Australian preferred destination perspective. In D. Buhalis & E. Laws (Eds.), *Tourism distribution channels: Practices, issues and transformations* (pp. 282–297). London, England: Thomson Learning.

Pan, G. W., Scott, N., & Laws, E. (2006). Understanding and sharing knowledge of new tourism markets. *Journal of Quality Assurance in Hospitality & Tourism*, *7*(1–2), 99–116.

Paxson, M. C. (1995). Increasing survey response rates: Practical instructions from the total-design method. *The Cornell HRA Quarterly*, *36*(4), 66–73.

Qu, H., & Lam, S. (1997). A travel demand model for Mainland Chinese tourists to Hong Kong. *Tourism Management*, *18*(8), 593–597.

Ryan, C., & Mo, X. (2002). Chinese visitors to New Zealand—Demographics and perceptions. *Journal of Vacation Marketing*, *8*(1), 13–27.

Tourism Australia. (2011). *Visitors by country of residence.* Retrieved from http://www.tourism.australia.com/en-au/documents/Corporate%20-%20Research/ABS_Sep_2011.pdf

Tretheway, M., & Mak, D. (2006). Emerging tourism markets: Ageing and developing economies. *Journal of Air Transport Management*, *12*(1), 21–27.

Tyler, R. (2009, June 8). *UK may reform visa system to entice Chinese.* Retrieved from http://www.telegraph.co.uk/finance/yourbusiness/5475469/UK-may-reform-visa-system-to-entice-chinese.html

UK Border Agency. (2011a). *UK Border Agency in China: Applying for a UK visa in China— Approved Destination Status*. Retrieved from http://www.ukba.homeoffice.gov.uk/countries/ china/applying/?langname=UK%20English

UK Border Agency. (2011b). *Visiting the UK: General visitors*. Retrieved from http://www.ukba. homeoffice.gov.uk/visas-immigration/visiting/general/documents/

United Nations Statistics Division. (2011). *National accounts main aggregates database: Growth rate of GDP: People's Republic of China*. Retrieved from http://unstats.un.org/unsd/snaama/ dnllist.asp

United Nations World Tourism Organization. (2003). *Chinese outbound tourism*. Retrieved from http://www.etc-corporate.org/resources/uploads/chinastudy.pdf

United Nations World Tourism Organization. (2011a). *The Chinese outbound travel market with special insight into the image of Europe as a destination*. Retrieved from http://www.e-unwto. org/content/m006q3/?sortorder=asc&p=ca554307c2794c7a8b0a18c36dc15268&o=0

United Nations World Tourism Organization. (2011b). *Outbound tourism, international tourism expenditure*. Retrieved from http://unwto.org/facts/eng/pdf/indicators/ITE.pdf

United Nations World Tourism Organization. (2011c). *UNWTO tourism highlights: 2011 edition*. Retrieved from http://mkt.unwto.org/sites/all/files/docpdf/unwtohighlights11enhr_1.pdf

Uren, J. (2009). *The Chinese outbound travel market: Part 1*. Retrieved from http://www. insights.org.uk/articleitem.aspx?title=The%20Chinese%20Outbound%20Travel%20Market:% 20Part%201

VisitBritain. (2011). *Market and trade profile: China*. Retrieved from http://www.visitbritain.org/ Images/China_tcm29-14678.pdf

Wang, G. (2011). *Booming Chinese outbound travel changes world tourism landscape*. Retrieved from http://news.xinhuanet.com/english2010/indepth/2011-06/01/c_13905680.htm

Woo, H. S., & Prud'homme, C. (1999). Cultural characteristics prevalent in the Chinese negotiation process. *European Business Review*, *99*(5), 313–322.

World Travel and Tourism Council. (2011). *Travel and tourism economic impact: China 2011*. Retrieved from http://www.wttc.org/site_media/uploads/downloads/china_.pdf

The Chinese Gaze: Imaging Europe in Travel Magazines

旅游凝视—中国旅游杂志中的欧洲意象

JULIO ARAMBERRI
CHUNMEI LIANG

Growing attention has been paid in the general tourism literature to destination imaging and branding. Usually the literature refers to images of developing destinations among international travelers from developed countries and ignores the increasing number of tourists from developing countries and their images of destinations abroad. This article takes a different tack in analyzing how three Chinese travel magazines present Europe to their audiences. Reverse analysis suggests that these consumer media pattern Europe in a way similar to that in which most Western media portray exotic destinations. Additionally it examines how such a benchmark is adapted to the idiosyncratic expectations of the local audience.

Introduction

Modern mass tourism is a recent occurrence in China. After the initiation of the Open Door policy in 1978, tourism grew exponentially (Sofield & Li, 1998; H. Zhang, Chong, & Ap, 1999). Inbound tourism, by both Chinese living outside the Mainland and foreigners, replaced the formerly tiny groups of politically motivated travelers (Richter, 1983; W. Zhang, 1997). Simultaneously, domestic and outbound tourism grew by leaps and bounds in lockstep with economic growth.

In 2010, China's estimated gross domestic product (GDP) at purchasing power parity reached US$10.1 trillion and its GDP per capita went up to US$7,600 (Central

Intelligence Agency [CIA], 2011). Between 1979 and 2010 the GDP increased approximately 20 times (CIA, 2011).

Economic growth has induced deep and rapid social changes. Above all, a tidal wave of migration from the countryside has flooded the cities. Consumption standards have risen, whereas not so long ago basic subsistence was a major concern for many citizens. Urbanization and new consumption patterns usually go hand in hand with an expansion of the middle classes. A local study (Chinese Academy of Social Sciences [CASS], 2003) defined them in terms of resources, including all people that in 2001 had assets ranging between CNY150,000 (US$18,137) and CNY300,000 (US$36,275). They were estimated at 19% of the population—around 250 million people. The study also forecast that in 2020 the middle classes would comprise 40% of the Chinese population; that is, somewhere around 400 million people (CASS). Other sources cited by Hsiao (2010) reached different conclusions: In 2004, the French bank Paribas reported that about 50 million households belonged to this group. In 2006, Merrill Lynch estimated that this number would reach about 350 million by 2016, and McKinsey estimated this number as 100 million households by 2009 and over 520 million individuals by 2025. According to such estimates, which were obtained through different methods and open to discussion, the country would have the largest middle class in the world by 2025 (Li, 2010)

Even though much travel is subsidized as incentive travel, increasing numbers of Chinese have sufficient disposable income to pay for travel expenses out of their own pockets. This is especially true for urbanites, whose disposable income has increased 7.4% annually (He, 2003). According to official statistics, in 2010 it reached 18% of total income for urban households (National Statistics Bureau of China [NSBC], 2011). In 2003 household tourism expenditures had risen to 14% of disposable income in urban areas (Gu & Liu, 2004).

As a consequence, large numbers of Chinese can engage in tourist activities. Most travel occurs within the Mainland. In 2006, domestic tourism reached around 1.4 billion travelers (NSBC, 2008). In 2010, it increased to 2.1 billion residents (NSBC, 2011). Revenue generated by domestic tourism shot up 23.5% to CNY1.26 trillion.

The number of outbound Chinese travelers has also risen quickly—they nearly trebled between 2001 and 2006 (from 12.1 to 34.5 million), due in part to a growing liberalization of travel abroad by the Chinese government (G. Zhang, 2006). The number of China's outbound visitors in 2010 totaled 57.39 million, up 20.4%. Of this total, 51 million were on private visits, a year-on-year increase of 22.0%, or 89.8% of all outgoing visitors (NSBC, 2011).

The United Nations World Tourism Organization (UNWTO, 2009) forecast that outgoing Chinese market will reach 100 million in 2020, thus becoming the main generating market in the world. Other sources estimate that the target will be reached earlier. For CLSA Asia-Pacific Markets (2005), in 2020 there will be 115 million outgoing Chinese travelers. The German weekly *Der Spiegel*, possibly due to a typo, announced that the 100-million threshold would be reached by 2010 (Wagner, 2007). The basic figures of this development can be seen in Table 1.

Outgoing tourism expenditures have also increased at a quick pace (Table 2) although their index lags considerably behind that of departures abroad.

One should stress that this centrifugal movement does not travel equally far and in all directions. In 2007, 85% of outgoing Chinese tourism traveled to nearby destinations (the top five, Hong Kong, Macau, Vietnam, South Korea, and Japan), leaving around 8 million trips for the rest of the world (CLSA Asia-Pacific Markets, 2005). However, this may change, because China's outgoing tourism is still in a bourgeoning stage. The

Table 1. Outbound Chinese Tourism Departures.

Year	# (000)	Index
2000	10,472	100
2001	12,000	115
2002	16,600	159
2003	20,220	193
2004	28,850	275
2005	31,000	296
2006	34,523	330

Note. Data from "China's Outbound Tourism: An Overview," by G. Zhang, 2006, retrieved from http://www.som.surrey.ac.uk/WTM/GuangruiWTMChinaOutboundTourism2006text.pdf

Table 2. Outbound Chinese Tourism Expenditure.

Year	US$ (billion)	Index
2000	13,114	100
2001	13,909	106
2002	15,398	117
2003	15,187	116
2004	19,149	146
2005	21,795	166

Note. Data from "China's Outbound Tourism: An Overview," by G. Zhang, 2006, retrieved from http://www.som.surrey.ac.uk/WTM/GuangruiWTMChinaOutboundTourism2006text.pdf

number of all outbound tourists remains below 3% of the total population. The equivalent figure is 15% for Japan, 35% for Taiwan, and 25% for the United States (CLSA Asia-Pacific Markets). Therefore, it has ample room to grow. Indeed, the top five destinations will still have the largest share for the next few years. Quite possibly, though, Chinese tourists will also start to spill over to other Asian destinations. Thailand expected that China would be its main market by 2011 (Tourist Authority of Thailand [TAT], 2008), which was close to the mark; in 2011 Chinese tourists to Thailand were the second market after Malaysia. If, despite the uncertainties derived from the financial crisis of 2008, China's economy keeps growing, there will be plenty of opportunities for other destinations.

In addition to the general economic background, other favorable factors for outgoing tourism have to be reckoned. By 2011, those in the 20–34 age group were expected to have the highest average income in the country, for a total of 30% of all revenue (Euromonitor, 2007). Members of this age group are young and therefore more adventurous; they have more formal education than their parents; and their heavy use of the Internet will make them more conversant with international problems, current affairs, culture and history; and they will want to expand their horizons (Euromonitor). This market will require special attention and new tools will have to be sharpened to reach it. However, only recently have institutions such as China's Outbound Tourism Research Institute (COTRI) started to fill the gap (Arlt, 2010).

Academic attention to the trend is growing, though at a slow pace. In addition to case studies (Wen & Carr, 2004), Arlt (2006) published an interesting general study of Chinese outbound tourism in which he reasonably acknowledged that "[w]ith a quarter of all international travelers already originating from cultures not based on occidental values, the simple picture of 'white' guests or 'brown' or indeed 'yellow' hosts is becoming blurred" (p. 8). Others have started to research the behavior of Chinese tourists on package tours (Wong & Lau, 2001) or the thorny relations between some Chinese tourists and the locals at their destination (Chan, 2006). With a scope limited to Germany, the issue of how to relate to the incoming Chinese guests has led to a reevaluation of the importance of Chinese culture and a quest to understand Chinese tourist behavior (Ehrhardt & Klossek, 2003; Wohlfahrt, 2007). This bourgeoning interest shows the urgent need for the tourism industry to gain a better knowledge of this market. One of the first introductions to the values and expectations of Chinese tourists was sponsored by the German Chambers of Commerce (Lott, 2007).

Still, much about how the Chinese perceive their European destinations remains unknown. It is known that when they travel to Europe they usually do it in a way that recalls Japanese behavior 20 years ago. Chinese tourists arrive in groups at an airport in central Europe and begin a bus tour that takes them to 10 countries in 14 days. *If it is Tuesday, this is Belgium*. There is not much time for reflection or deep knowledge of local cultures; just quick visits to well-known landmarks and back to the bus for the next one. Some think that this rush has its roots in the travel behavior of the premodern Chinese gentry and their canon of must-see attractions (Nyíri, 2005), but this seems far-fetched. In fact, being so hard pressed for time and with so many pictures of themselves in front of well-known Western spots to be taken, it is a wonder that they may still have time for their other main pastime—shopping around for the best European brands, definitely something without precedent in premodern Chinese gentry mores.

How and where does the rookie Chinese tourist obtain relevant information for a trip? One can point to many sources, including word of mouth (today in great measure WOW or Word of Web), literature from destination management organizations, and tips from their guides. This article, however, stresses the role of what might be called *educational media*; that is, those that contribute to creating the images of destinations conveyed by parts of the media industry, such as guidebooks or travel magazines.

The Chinese Gaze

Methodology and Goals

Consumer education as well as tourism education is the outcome of interactions between audiences and message senders. Their interaction is furthermore colored by the social context in which communication takes place. Audiences react to similar economic and cultural factors in different ways. In what follows, tourism education in China will be followed through the study of a group of travel communicators (three glossy travel magazines published in China) and their audiences, mostly made of groups of affluent Chinese consumers.

When it comes to travel, above all, Chinese consumers want reliable information on where and how to spend their disposable income (World Travel & Tourism Council [WTTC], 2006); that is where travel magazines come into the picture. Although not the sole source of information, they play a role among those consumers who are ready to engage in tourist activities. They offer information on a wide range of destinations, both domestic and international, and in so doing they contribute to the travel education of increasing numbers of Chinese.

This article analyzes the images of some of the main European destinations that appeared in the issues of three travel magazines between 2003 and 2005—a total of 1,835 icons and 219 articles. The time span corresponds to a still bourgeoning period of outgoing Chinese tourism, but it is also the point at which images of foreign countries began to crystallize. Once they do, changes in the stereotypes will not appear quickly. The European destinations selected were the 13 that appeared among the top 25 destinations in the world by number of arrivals according to the UNWTO (2005), in alphabetical order: Austria, Croatia, France, Germany, Greece, Hungary, Italy, The Netherlands, Poland, Portugal, Spain, the United Kingdom, and the Ukraine.

The three Chinese publications used to create this universe (*National Geographic Traveler* [*NGT*], *Traveler*, and *National Parks* [*NP*]) were selected due to their perceived leading position in upscale markets, which are the most likely to engage in European visits.

What are the main features of their audiences? Information is limited. The most extensive comes from *Traveler*, which boasted a monthly circulation of 338,000 copies and a total audience of over three million—nine readers per copy—in 2007 (*Traveler Magazine*, 2007). It was also *Traveler* that offered the most complete picture of its followers. Its median reader was either a man (52%) or a woman (48%) living in Beijing, Shanghai, or Guangzhou; between 25 and 44 years old; well educated (98% had a college degree or higher); high-level managers and officials; making between CNY40,000 (US$5,000) and CNY120,000 (US$15,000) per year at median 2007 exchange rates. Within the expanding base of the Chinese middle classes, *Traveler* aimed for the top. Not many other people could afford its cover price of CNY18. Given their contents and their cover price (CNY15 and CNY20 respectively for *NP* and *NGT*), one could say that the readers of the other two magazines are not too different. After target selection, Dann's method of iconic analysis (Dann, 1996a, 1996b, 1996c, 2005) was used. It progresses in two stages. The first consists of a quantitative appraisal of the pictures in the brochures examined and their classification into categories according to whether images include people or not. Where people are represented, pictures are subsequently categorized into tourists only, locals only, and locals and tourists together. Based on a combination of those factors and the accompanying literature, qualitative analysis is the following step.

Scenes with large numbers of people—for instance at festivals—were labeled as a mix of locals and tourists in the understanding that at least some of the attendees might come from beyond the boundaries of the locality portrayed. Others with fewer people wearing ethnic attire and/or working in pre-industrial settings were classified as locals. Finally, we counted persons or groups of people in urban clothing and/or engaged in what are usually seen as tourist activities—visiting heritage sites, enjoying treatment at spas, trekking and mountaineering, sightseeing tourist attractions, etc.—as tourists.

Europe

The 13 European destinations resulted in 1,835 icons. *NP* had the lowest number of European pictures of all three magazines (226 or 12% of the total), whereas *NGT* (782 pictures and 43%) and *Traveler* (827 and 45%) had a similarly balanced offer. This was not surprising, because although all three magazines are interested in travel, *NP* predominantly devotes its attention to Chinese themes, above all the many national

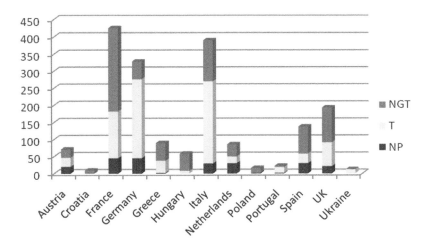

Figure 1. Distribution of icons: Countries (color figure available online).

parks to be found in the country. Despite its many natural attractions, Europe is no rival to China for *NP*'s attention on this level. On their side, *NGT* and *Traveler* cast a much wider net.

Although 13 European countries were initially selected, clearly the three publications did not consider them equally important. Figure 1 shows that there is a chasm between the three top destinations highlighted (France, Germany, and Italy) and the remaining destinations, with Spain and the UK in intermediate positions.

Among the three top destinations, the iconic total reached 1,143 pictures; that is, 62% of the total. With the addition of Spain and the United Kingdom, all five top 80% of the icons. Some countries do not register, such as Croatia, Poland, Portugal, and Ukraine. Croatia only gets 9 pictures in one *NGT* issue and none in the other two magazines; Poland does not show in *Traveler*; Ukraine only registers there.

Far from representing idiosyncratic Chinese tastes stemming from old gentry mores, this ranking coincides with the choices of people traveling from the United States (Office of Travel and Tourism Industries [OTTI], 2008), Canada (German National Tourism Board [GNTB], 2008), and Japan (GNTB) to Europe. With little variation, Brazilians, South Koreans, and Australians share in the same distribution (GNTB). These five countries have played central roles in the modern history of Europe and include some of its best-known cultural attractions. Therefore, one might expect that the Chinese travel magazines analyzed would reinforce the widely shared image of Europe as a continent of culture and heritage.

This would be a mistake. In fact, Chinese travel magazines have their own peculiar focus. What is there to see in Europe? One main point was offered by the interest in the two main categories: no people/people icons. Let us start with the first. For the Chinese travel magazines, Europe is interesting above all because of its people and their represented behavior. Only 765 icons or 40% of the total archive portray areas with no people. If one takes a sharper view separating icons that only deal with nature (8%) and those devoted to man-made structures, the latter win by far. Despite its usual interest in nature, even *NP* allocates a paltry 10% of its 167 no people pictures to nature. For *Traveler* it is less than 2%.

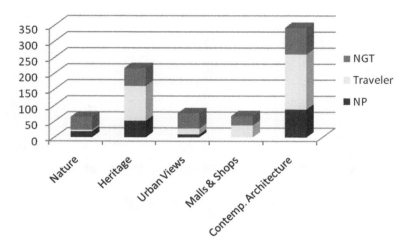

Figure 2. Distribution of icons: No people (color figure available online).

Urban man-made structures are the places where most people spend their lives. They are usually divided between heritage places and everyday life areas. One should expect that, because the European continent has a long history, the Chinese travel magazines would give preferential attention to heritage; however, this is not the case. Heritage comes up to about 30% of all no people icons in *NP* and *Traveler* and only 20% in *NGT*. So, if Europe as seen through Chinese eyes (that is, the way Chinese readers are invited by the travel magazines to see Europe) is not configured by nature and monuments, how do they help construct the collective gaze? Attention is overwhelmingly focused on daily life as represented by cityscapes; that is, areas such as neighborhoods, contemporary buildings, or shops and malls where urban Europeans spend most of their daily lives (Figure 2). In total, nearly two thirds of the visual space offered by the three magazines in the no people category represents such venues.

Even *NP* focuses on contemporary architecture more than in heritage, although it does not inform its audience that one can find things such as malls in Europe. The other two magazines also direct their readers to contemporary architecture, but they are well aware that shopping is a favorite travel activity of their readers and they pay close attention to it. *NGT* and *Traveler* devote over 10% of their no people icons to malls and other shopping venues. The no people category, accordingly, presents Europe as a place of contemporary culture and urban life, treating nature and heritage as two residual categories.

What about people? Sixty percent of the visual space is devoted to them. The focus of attention is the local population, which occupies two thirds of it in the people category. Tourists follow with an additional quarter, and icons depicting common activities between locals and tourists reach less than a tenth. It is the locals, therefore, that provide the main show for the Chinese reader. A show indeed it is, because locals provide visual information on what Chinese tourists may expect when they reach the destination and offer them an anticipation of the activities in which they may share. Their travel magazines aim at providing general information and mutual identification above and beyond reciprocal understanding between tourists and locals (see Figure 3).

How are the locals represented? What do they do? Above all, the Chinese magazines have very little interest in anything premodern (used here in the sense of

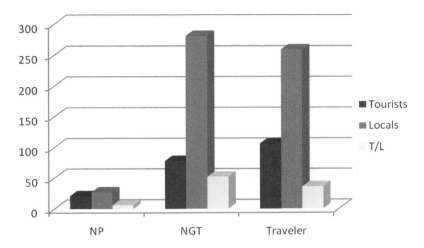

Figure 3. Distribution of icons: People (color figure available online).

pre-industrial, agrarian, or rural). Even though at times they depict people in premodern types of jobs or involved in handicraft making, they do not highlight them. Altogether only 38 pictures out of 566 in the locals' category depict people using premodern tools or techniques. The rest are devoted to different aspects of modern life. When they are seen working, locals mostly act as vendors, servants, or entertainers (VSE). In discharging those roles, some may don old-time or traditional clothing (as in Bavarian beer gardens with servers wearing *lederhosen* and waitresses clad in *dirndln*), but it is clear that they do so tongue-in-cheek, playing on a themed or typical subtext. The rest of the people at work are bank tellers, shop attendants, clerks, and occasionally fashion models. In a nutshell, nostalgia for the past does not seem to be a popular commodity for Chinese tourists. The overwhelming majority of Europeans appear while at leisure in their daily lives—walking, taking care of pets, having dinner or drinks, and shopping. This aspect will be examined in more detail in the next section.

At any rate, Europe as a place of history and heritage does not register high in the image offered to Chinese readers of the selected magazines (Figure 4).

The Big Three: Setting the Score

This is a broad conclusion that refers to the continent as a whole. There are, however, important differences in the way particular European destinations are presented, especially the three countries that are the main magnets for Chinese tourists (France, Italy, and Germany; the Big Three). As stated, they occupy nearly two thirds of all the visual space devoted to our 13 European destinations.

All three magazines share a common interest in the Big Three, but it is up to *NGT* and *Traveler* to provide the main aspects of their images. *NP*'s total contribution to this feature is quite limited given the small size of its related iconic archive. In total, it carries 119 pictures of all three, less than 10% of the total icons. With such a limited interest, it is difficult to draw conclusions about its views on the destinations.

NGT and *Traveler* show an interesting slant. *NGT* devotes more than half of its total Big Three icons to France, leaving Germany (slightly over 10%) out of the frame.

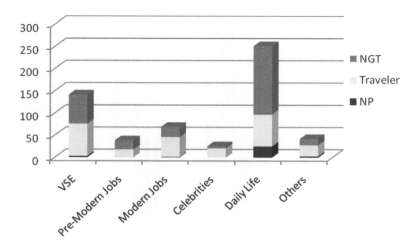

Figure 4. Distribution of icons: People activities (color figure available online).

Even though it shows more balance, *Traveler* downgrades France in comparison to the other two destinations. This may be due to the limited timespan considered (years 2003–2005) and may have not been the case in previous or later years. At any rate, it is worth noting.

What is the comparative image of the three countries that *NGT* and *Traveler* offer to their readers? A portrait may be obtained by measuring visual intensity along six main parameters: heritage, contemporary architecture and arts, urban views, shops and malls, the presence of vendors/servants/entertainers, and daily life depictions (mostly of local people at leisure). Nature as a subject was not included because all three magazines do not include nature in their depictions of Europe.

NGT has a rather well-rounded view of France (see Figure 5). Most of its dimensions seem to have a similar value. Only urban views had a slightly higher ranking than others, but this was compensated for by the relatively lower ranking of daily life scenes. Heritage is also well represented in relation to other dimensions. This is not the case for *Traveler*. Shops (with a prominent presence of wine and food) and malls are well balanced with the rest.

All of this contrasts with the images of Italy and Germany, which are less balanced. This should not lead to quick conclusions in the case of Germany, which receives only fleeting attention in *NGT* (52 icons in total). In both Germany and Italy the image is clearly anchored by the attractions of daily life. Portrayals of a laidback urban life dominate the panorama for Italy, passing over contemporary arts, food and wine, and even heritage as the main attraction. The least intensively communicated value is the presence of VSE, even though the latter include participants and revelers in local parades and events.

Traveler conveys a markedly different view (Figure 6). First, the number of icons for Italy (241) and Germany (231) compensates for their relative inattention in *NGT*. Additionally, despite its lesser intensity, France still receives considerable notice (137 icons). This allows for somewhat more solid conclusions in all three cases.

Traveler's readers receive a similar view of France and Germany. Both countries practically overlap in the shape of their attractions, adopting a butterfly-like contour where those dimensions with medium to lower importance are heritage and malls and

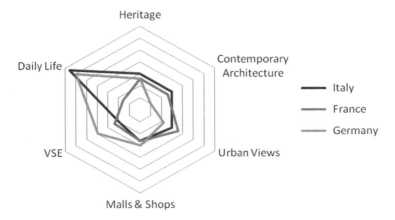

Figure 5. Comparative images of the Big Three in *NGT* (color figure available online).

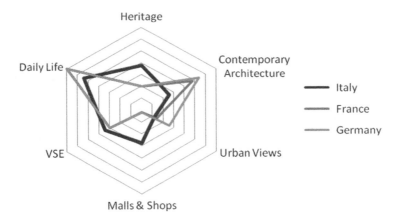

Figure 6. Comparative images of the Big Three in *Traveler* (color figure available online).

shops. This does not mean that these attractions are considered unimportant but that they are usually portrayed more as part of daily life than as still-life icons. For *NGT* French wines or Napoleonic shrines are products to be highly revered; *Traveler* presents them as objects of desire—to be experienced rather than worshipped. For instance, in Germany, beer cannot stray from the leisure patterns of real human beings; it is not the final product of a complex alchemy that is alien to the reader. It is difficult to escape here Barthes' (1972) reflection on the ornamental cookery of French magazines. Though *Elle* portrayed its dishes as a symbol of reverence that should somehow be left untouched, *L'Express* showed its well-heeled readership dishes similar to those they experienced in the restaurants they frequented in their daily lives. Daily life at leisure, together with the neighborhoods where it is conducted, similarly tops *Traveler*'s list of European attractions that its readers can afford.

Italy is only a slightly different story. All of its dimensions pivot around the center and have similar importance. In this way, the views of the country run closer to the mainstream notion of a living museum where even the expensive shops that are portrayed (all of the well-known global Italian brands) become unique pieces for the connoisseur.

However, in what seems to be *Traveler*'s trademark, it is finally the *dolce vita* that comes upmost in its image of the country. Art and the good life graciously stem from people who know how to enjoy the pleasures of life. Therefore, in all three countries, the axis that runs between a pleasant daily life including well-built surroundings and the work of VSEs (who usually are the most frequently depicted category of the three in each country) practically overlap.

The Big Three: Getting to Know You

Crunching numbers is half of the story. It helps to figure that the Chinese gaze on Europe has its own features. For the Chinese, Europe is an old continent full of historical places and both ancient and modern art. However, this does not seem to have much traction with present-day Chinese consumers. Their own culture antedates that of medieval and modern Europe. Their knowledge of European history may also be quite limited. Perhaps the still limited social groups that can engage in long-haul travel see it more as a status symbol to be confirmed by the acquisition of costly European goods rather than an occasion for cross-cultural exchanges.

Regardless, Europe is epitomized in the Big Three destinations singled out by the Chinese travel magazines as a topmost space for consumption and leisure that contrasts with life at home. This narrative is mainly conveyed to the Chinese through three main conduits—the contrast between Chinese modernity and European life, the role of successful events and personalities in Chinese mass culture, and the formation of a number of local stereotypes to pin down the expected basic features of the European identities as seen through Chinese eyes. To some extent, this concurs with Craik's (1997) hypothesis that expectations, fantasies, and mythologies about destinations that are generated in the visitors' culture have a greater weight on their experiences than local attractions.

New China takes great pride in its own modernity and shuns the postmodern mindset of Europe. Long deprived of the comfortable Western way of life portrayed in print media, on television, and on the Internet, Chinese consumers revel in their own view of modernity's accouterments. In their newly attained prosperity and self-assurance, they also want to show that they are even more modern than their Western peers and as skilled at modern technology as anybody else. They especially pride themselves in their urban planning skills. They feel that their cities can rival and even surpass any other Asian and U.S. cities (Tokyo, Singapore, Taipei, Hong Kong, Los Angeles, Chicago, New York) in the creation of successful (whatever this may mean) urban structures. Modern architecture and its technological exploits has thus become their measuring rod for modernity.

Nyíri (2002, 2007) has stressed its importance in the expectations of Chinese tourists visiting European destinations. Although he did not offer much substantive evidence for his views, he surmised that Europe does not stand up to their challenge on this score. One of his informers, a Chinese guide in Berlin, noted that many of her customers criticized the lack of high-rises and broad avenues in the town. They compared them unfavorably with urban landscapes in Shanghai and Hangzhou, implying that Berlin looked backward by comparison (Nyíri, 2005). The way in which Chinese travel magazines cover contemporary architecture with preference to heritage sites treads on the same footsteps.

The new cohorts of Chinese tourists on long-haul travel to Europe have interests other than history. Where do they originate? One possible answer is mass culture. Chinese consumers want to identify with the personalities and follow the trends that, in their view, have shaped or are shaping our world as conveyed in print media, on television, and on the Internet.

The special issues devoted by *Traveler* to the Top Three destinations (Issue No. 110 for France, No. 114 for Germany, and No. 120 for Italy) require some attention at this juncture. The ways in which France and Italy are depicted have many similarities. In a nutshell, one can say that they are great shopping malls for conspicuous consumption over a background of art and history made by grand personalities or associated with mass culture. How to get to know Paris best? Follow the *Da Vinci Code* steps. It will take you to the Tuileries gardens, to the new glass pyramid in the Louvre, and to Saint Sulpice. The 2003 bestseller is presented as a better approach to the city than any guidebook. Before being banned by the government in June 2006, the movie version had drawn millions of moviegoers (British Broadcasting Corporation [BBC], 2006). What about Montmartre? That's where Amélie Poulain of the eponymous movie (*The Fabulous Destiny of Amelie Poulain* in English) lived. The film made a great impression in China. If you follow the places seen there, it is surmised, you may see the hill under a better light than the Impressionists could ever capture. Is there anything other than Paris to be seen in France? Yes, it is. However, travel routes may be better organized by following the places where Napoleon (another mass culture figure in China) spent his life: From Corsica to Toulon to Paris (see the Louvre whose collections he enriched), from La Malmaison in Rueil (where he lived with Josephine Beauharnais) to Grasse, one of the places where some of the best French perfumes originate from. The reader is reminded that Napoleon himself was one of their greatest promoters.

Then forget about the rest and go shopping. With a nod to rural tourism through the eyes of a Chinese student engaged in the grape harvest, readers are informed that wine making and wine drinking are two of the grand pleasures the French enjoy. But wine is only one—and not the most important—of the many items that tempt the Chinese consumers. A series of articles in the special issue show them the best places to spend their money, a lesson apparently quickly learned by its readers. According to *Traveler*, the expenditure of Chinese tourists in France ranked second only to that of the Japanese and was double the daily expenditure of U.S. tourists. A study by ACNielsen (cited in Xie & Li, 2008) reported that the mean expenditure of Chinese travelers in Europe in 2007 was US$1,408, making them the top spenders on the continent.

The mix was similar for Italy. A long section in the special issue was devoted to Italian art, but the whole revolved around the contribution of Leonardo—of *Da Vinci Code* fame. This was followed by the great Italian cities of Rome, Florence, and Venice, where Marco Polo lived. Once again, there was a nod to food and wines and, indeed, to Chinese culture. Italians love pasta, pizza, and other specialties similar to others found in Chinese cuisine. Once again, though, food is in the background. The real action is in the great shopping streets in Rome and Milan, which are amply portrayed by the magazine with detailed explanations of where to find the best apparel, cosmetics, and fashion brands. Original Italian items can be found in Beijing, Shanghai, and Guangzhou as well, but they do not have the same glitter as those bought in Europe when shown to friends and relatives. They are also cheaper there than at home, because the Chinese fiscal authorities charge considerable duty on luxury imports.

Germany is no exception to the rule, but leisure and consumption are shown in a different light. The special issue starts with a glimpse at recent German history and Nazi rule, one of the few periods of foreign history that impacts Chinese mass culture. After reporting some of the atrocities of the period, the article notes that Germans have shown great courage in facing their terrible history and have completely disowned it, thus regaining the respect of the world. This view might make some people frown, but the magazine offers it as a definite moral to the story. Then the reader is propelled to the great personalities in German history, including Konrad Adenauer, Martin Luther, Karl Marx, Albert Einstein, Johann W. Goethe, and Sophie Scholl, with a recommendation to visit the places where they lived.

Shopping for high fashion and top-quality nondurables is accompanied by another object of desire in mass culture, especially in modern Chinese mass culture—the car. There, one is told, cars are one of the main components of collective identity. The descriptions of the machines (Mercedes and BMW topmost) are quite detailed and the tourist routes recommended are those that have found favor with the car crowd: the *Romantische Strasse* (Würzburg-Rothenburg-Dinkelsbühl-Augsburg-Freiburg-Füssen), the *Märchenstrasse* (Hanau-Kassel-Hameln-Bremen), and the German *Alpenstrasse* (Berchtesgaden-Prien-Kirchen-Lindau). Note that most other German attractions (with the exception of some passing mention of the Rhine cruises) are not mentioned.

The third element in imaging Europe through Chinese eyes is exoticism; that is, the way in which Chinese magazines represent their view of European identities. Exoticism has had a consistently bad press among mainstream academic thought. Following Said (1979, 1993), it is usually seen as the way in which Western culture portrays different ethnic groups (the Other) as subject to infantile beliefs, awkward mores, or inferior lifestyles. This notion has been criticized (Aramberri, 2010) as circular, scarcely attentive to facts, and reifying so-called Western culture—a discussion, however, that will not be dealt with within the mainly descriptive framework of this article.

Exoticism, as surmised by the Said school of thought, usually finds expression in the use of a number of stereotypes that justify in shorthand the alleged superiority of Western moral and intellectual standards and traditions. This notion, however, ignores at its own risk the fact that stereotypes are also a basic tool of communication. The world has an infinite diversity. We never find "trees" or "animals" or "doctors" but individual members of the *Quercus* or *Salix* or other specific genera, likewise for the *Panthera leo* or the *Drosophila melanogaster*, or for this obstetrician or this dentist. Motley individuals make each one of those species and we could not grasp them without concepts or stereotypes that allow communicating meaning with great economy of means. Concepts or stereotypes can indeed be wrong, but trying to exorcize them from language is futile. Additionally, the Saidian notion cannot bloom without a normative prejudice about which are good stereotypes and which are not. Because there is nothing in their own nature to justify one single type of selection, accepting or objecting to them rather seems to be in the eye of the beholder.

Nevertheless, the Chinese gaze seems to hold its own. It has already been noted that, through Chinese eyes, Europe does not measure up to modernity in a full way and is above all a space for consumption and leisure. Europeans are usually portrayed having a good time in parks, cafes, restaurants, or festivals. Hard work and scientific and technological advances do not register in this view of Europe. For example, Munich is depicted as a huge open-air restaurant where people happily enjoy beer and diverse pork products; this stereotype, however, may help place Munich in the set of eventual destinations evoked by potential Chinese consumers.

More specific features follow this general characterization. The copy in the analyzed travel magazines uses a number of qualifiers to define some regularities that in the copy of their writers characterize social life in those European countries. France is gorgeous, Italy delicate, Germany efficient, Spain a dreamland, Greece extremely colorful. In Britain, aristocracy is the defining quality. Even people not born to privilege, the reader is told, behave in a noble way. Accordingly, one should not be surprised that the most recommended British attractions for Chinese tourists are the castles and the churches that epitomize its aristocratic traditions, the educational institutions (Eton, Oxbridge) that contributed to forming the ruling class, and gentlemen's sports (polo, cricket, golf, horse riding). In a notable departure from their relative lack of interest in the main cities of Europe, the Chinese magazines describe London in more detail, reminding readers of the many places where the British aristocratic identity has forged a unique atmosphere.

Exoticism does not end after showing the optimal features of the Other; it also highlights those that are extremely different from our own and may surprise, shock, or titillate the reader. Germany scores highest in this respect. *Traveler*'s special issue discusses at length what their authors consider a highly sexualized social environment. The publication informs its readership that, together with The Netherlands, Germany has no legal ban on the sex industry; that many people prefer to live together instead of getting married; that sexual freedom in the country is higher than anywhere else; and that the sex industry is quite prosperous. Berlin takes the title of Europe's Sex Capital on behalf of its Love Parades and its openness toward homosexuality. Germany is also presented as the birthplace of the *Freikörperkultur* (FKK) or Free Body Culture; therefore, it is not uncommon to see nude sunbathing in many public areas like the *Englischer Garten* in Munich. Not a small distance from the usual restraint shown by Chinese denizens in their public behavior, it may confirm the exoticism of the place to the Chinese reader planning to visit Germany.

Conclusion

As increasing numbers of Chinese have paid vacations and higher disposable income, they have begun to travel in great numbers. The overwhelming majority of trips are taken within the country, but many travel abroad as well—a pattern that will grow considerably in the near future. Both categories of tourists look for information about eventual destinations, and this information is provided by many sources, including independent travel magazines. Their impact has not been widely studied, even though they seem to be a key factor in building destination images, which will require detailed attention from European marketers and destination management agencies.

This article analyzed the contribution of three travel magazines published in Chinese to the image of Europe. To this effect, it selected a number of icons and articles referring to some of the main European destinations that appeared between 2003 and 2005—a total of 1,835 icons and 219 articles. In agreement with Dann's methodology (1996a, 1996b, 1996c), the first part of the study provides a quantitative analysis of the ways in which the visual icons were used. In the second part, a more qualitative approach is described to define the main aspects of Europe's image as a tourist destination. The overall analysis offers a picture of the main features of the continent when seen through Chinese eyes.

The quantitative analysis revealed a number of thought structures. Above all, an image of Europe as such does not exist for the travel magazines analyzed. Although 13 European destinations were selected, just three (France, Italy, and Germany) attracted more than 60% of the material. If one adds icons depicting Spain and the United Kingdom, the total reaches over 80%. These five countries have played central roles in the modern history of Europe and include some of its best known cultural attractions. One might think that the Chinese travel magazines reinforce the widely shared image of Europe as a continent of culture, but this is not so. In fact, the Chinese travel magazines have their own peculiar line of attack. A majority of icons depict human subjects rather than areas with no people. The first conclusion is that Chinese magazines think that their readers are mostly attracted by European life in general. This first conclusion is reinforced when one bears in mind that the majority of pictures with no human component portray man-made structures over nature's views. Additionally, despite the expected image of Europe as a historical and heritage destination, the man-made structures depicted are overwhelmingly of contemporary architecture and urban landscapes; that is, the places where most Europeans go about their daily business.

Local people appear foremost in the iconic representation of Europe. What do they do? The Chinese magazines show very little interest in any type of premodern or nonurban life. Except for a few icons, the majority are devoted to different aspects of modern life. When they are seen working, locals mostly act as VSEs; the remainder are bank tellers, shop attendants, clerks, and occasionally fashion models. The overwhelming majority of Europeans, however, appear while at leisure in their daily lives, above all wining, dining, and shopping. In a nutshell, nostalgia for the past does not seem to be a popular commodity among present Chinese tourists, and Europe as a place of history and heritage does not register high. This broad conclusion refers to the continent as a whole. There are, however, important differences in the way particular European destinations are presented, especially the three countries that are the main magnets for Chinese tourists (France, Italy, and Germany).

What is the comparative image of the three countries that Chinese travel magazines offer to their readers? France and Germany practically overlap in the shape of their attractions, adopting a butterfly-like contour where the dimensions with medium to lower importance are heritage and malls and shops (Figure 6). Italy tells a slightly different story. All of its dimensions pivot around the center and have similar importance, so one could say that the views of the country run closer to the mainstream notion of a living museum. However, it is finally the *dolce vita* that comes upmost in the image of the country. People who know how to enjoy the pleasures of life graciously combine art and the good life. Therefore, in all three countries, the axes mainly run around a pleasant daily life including well-built surroundings.

Qualitative analysis of the texts adds to the idea that through Chinese eyes Europe is above all a space for consumption and leisure that contrasts with life at home. This descriptive approach runs along three main dimensions—the contrast between Chinese modernity and European life, the role of successful European events and personalities recognized by Chinese mass culture, and the formation of a number of local stereotypes to pin down the basic features of the European identities as seen through Chinese eyes. The first deals with the definition of *modernity*. For present-day Chinese, modernity means above all the capacity to master the challenges of social life by means of modern technology. In this way, China, especially when it comes to urban planning and architecture, is seen as superior to old Europe in building modern environments. This may be one of the reasons why Chinese magazines do not pay much attention to heritage.

The second thread is mass culture. Chinese tourists want to identify with the personalities and to follow the trends that, in their view, have shaped or are shaping our world as conveyed in print media, on television, or on the Internet. The best way to capture Europe is by consuming European products, whether high-quality nondurables in France or Italy or technological marvels such as German cars.

The third thread in imaging Europe through Chinese eyes is exoticism; that is, the way in which Chinese magazines construct European identities. Exoticism, however, does not end after showing the surprising or distinct features of the Other; it also highlights those that are extremely different from our own and may surprise, shock, or titillate the reader. German attitudes toward sex offer a way for Chinese magazines to compare them with their own behavior.

Such a mind-set or gaze has long been lamented by a well-established academic tradition (Dann, 1996b; MacCannell, 1999; Wang, 2000). The issue, however, lies elsewhere—how to explain that Chinese tourists, at least those who have the money to visit Europe, for all their differences, gaze at the continent through mechanisms that closely resemble those of Western mass tourists in faraway destinations. After all, that well-meaning academic tradition imagined that it should be the exclusive purview of the new Golden Hordes coming from the West or the North. It still remains to be explained why the experience remains so similar when the world (Europe in this case) is looked at through Chinese eyes. This is, however, a discussion that would go beyond the mostly descriptive analysis this article has adopted.

References

Aramberri, J. (2010). *Modern mass tourism.* London, England: Emerald.

Arlt, W. (2006). *China's outbound tourism.* London, England: Routledge.

Artl, W. (Ed.). (2010). *China's Outbound Tourism Research Institute (COTRI) yearbook 2010. China's outbound tourism development.* Munich, Germany: Martin Meidener Verlag.

Barthes, R. (1972). *Mythologies.* New York, NY: Hill and Wang.

British Broadcasting Corporation. (2006). *Chinese ban Da Vinci Code movie.* Retrieved from http://news.bbc.co.uk/2/hi/entertainment/5059658.stm

Brown, D. (2003). *The Da Vinci code.* New York, NY: Doubleday.

Central Intelligence Agency. (2011). *The world factbook: China.* Retrieved from https://www.cia.gov/library/publications/the-world-factbook/geos/ch.html

Chan, Y. W. (2006). Coming of age of the Chinese tourists: The emergence of non-Western tourism and host–guest interactions in Vietnam's border tourism. *Tourist Studies, 6*(3), 187–213.

Chinese Academy of Social Sciences. (2003). 当代中国社会阶层研究报告 [A report on the study of contemporary China's social strata]. Beijing, China: Social Sciences Literature Press.

CLSA Asia-Pacific Markets. (2005). *Dreaming with the BRICs.* Retrieved from https://www.clsa.com/public/login.asp?secure=1&

Craik, J. (1997). The culture of tourism. In C. Rojek & J. Urry (Eds.), *Touring cultures: Transformations of travel and theory* (pp. 113–136). London, England, and New York, NY: Routledge.

Dann, G. (1996a). *The language of tourism: A sociolinguistic perspective.* Wallingford, UK: CAB International.

Dann, G. (1996b). The people of tourist brochures. In T. Selwyn (Ed.), *The tourist image: Myth and myth making in tourism* (pp. 61–81). New York, NY: John Wiley & Sons.

Dann, G. (1996c). Tourists' images of a destination: An alternative analysis. *Journal of Travel and Tourism Marketing, 5*(1/2), 41–55.

Dann, G. (2005). Content/semiotics analysis: Applications for tourism research. In J. Aramberri & R. Butler (Eds.), *Tourism development: Issues for a vulnerable industry* (pp. 27–42). Clevedon, England: Channel View.

Ehrhardt, A., & Klossek, A. (2003). Die relevanz kultureller unterschiede in der deutsch-chinesischen zusammenarbeit. In M. Nippa (Ed.), *Marrkterfolg in China: Erfahrungsberichte und Rahmanbedingungen* (pp. 58–69). Berlin, Germany: Physica Verlag.

Euromonitor. (2007). *Asia winning the battle for Chinese tourists.* Retrieved from http://www.euromonitor.com/Asia_winning_the_battle_for_Chinese_tourists

German National Tourism Board. (2008). *GNTB market research.* Retrieved from http://www.germany-tourism.de/ENG/about_us/market_research.htm

Gu, H., & Liu, D. (2004). The relationship between resident income and domestic tourism in China. *Tourism Recreation Research, 29*(2), 25–35.

He, G. (2003). China's economic restructuring and banking reform. In Yomiuri International Economic Society (Ed.), *Emerging China and the Asian economy in the coming decade.* Retrieved from http://www.iima.or.jp/pdf/paper12e.pdf

Howard, R. (2006). *The Da Vinci code* (film). Hollywood CA: J. Calley and B. Glazer (producers).

Hsiao, H. H. M. (2010). Placing China's middle class in the Asia-Pacific context. In C. Li (Ed.), *China's emerging middle class* (pp. 3–31). Washington, DC: The Brookings Institution.

Jodidio, Ph. (2007). *Architecture in China.* Köln, Germany: Taschen.

Li, C. (2010). The middle class in the middle kingdom. In C. Li (Ed.), *China's emerging middle class* (pp. 245–263). Washington, DC: The Brookings Institution.

Lott, S. (2007). *Was Sie schon immer über Chinesische Touristen wissen wollten.* Berlin, Germany: DIHK Verlag.

MacCannell, D. (1999). *The tourist: A new theory of the leisure class.* Berkeley, CA: University of California Press.

National Statistics Bureau of China. (2008). *Statistical yearbook 2007.* Retrieved from http://www.stats.gov.cn/tjsj/ndsj/2007/indexeh.htm

National Statistics Bureau of China. (2011). *Statistical yearbook 2010.* Retrieved from http://www.stats.gov.cn/was40/gjtjj_en_detail.jsp?searchword=domestic+tourism&channelid=9528&record=1

Nyíri, P. (2002). From class enemies to patriots: Overseas Chinese and emigration policy and discourse in the People's Republic of China. In P. Nyíri & I. Saveliev (Eds.), *Globalizing Chinese migration: Trends in Europe and Asia* (pp. 208–241). Aldershot, England: Ashgate.

Nyíri, P. (2005). *Scenic spot Europe: Chinese travelers on the Western periphery.* Retrieved from http://www.espacestemps.net/document1224.html

Nyíri, P. (2007). *Scenic spots: Chinese tourism, the state and cultural authority.* Seattle, WA: University of Washington Press.

Office of Travel and Tourism Industries. (2008). *Profile of U.S. residents travelers visiting overseas destinations: 2007 outbound.* Retrieved from http://tinet.ita.doc.gov/

Ren, X. (2011). *Building globalization: Transnational architecture production in urban China.* Chicago, IL: The University of Chicago Press.

Richter, L. K. (1983). Tourism politics and political science: A case of not so benign neglect. *Annals of Tourism Research, 10*(3), 313–335.

Said, E. (1979). *Orientalism.* New York, NY: Viking.

Said, E. (1993). *Culture and imperialism.* New York, NY: Knopf.

Sofield, T., & Li, F. (1998). Tourism development and cultural policies in China. *Annals of Tourism Research, 25*(2), 362–392.

Tourist Authority of Thailand. (2008). Chinese travelers expected to become Thailand's number 1 market in three years. Retrieved from http://www.tourismthailand.org/news/release-content-943.html

Traveler Magazine. (2007). Introduction for our readers. Retrieved from http://www.traveler.com.cn

United Nations World Tourism Organization. (2005). *World top tourism destinations*. Retrieved from http://unwto.org/facts/eng/pdf/indicators/ITA_top25.pdf

United Nations World Tourism Organization. (2009). *Long-term trends: 2020 vision update*. Retrieved from http://www.mots.go.th/ewtadmin/ewt/mots_km/download/article/Knowledge_Base/Tourism/long_term_thai.pdf

Wagner, W. (2007). *Journey to the West: Chinese tourists do Europe—In 14 days*. Retrieved from http://www.spiegel.de/international/europe/0,1518,druck-500550,00.html

Wang, N. (2000). *Tourism and modernity: A sociological analysis*. New York, NY: Pergamon Press.

Wen, J, & Carr, N. (2004). Visitor satisfaction: An analysis of mainland Chinese tourists on the Australian Gold Coast. *International Journal of Hospitality & Tourism Administration*, *5*(3), 31–48.

Wohlfahrt, F. (2007). *Chinesische Touristen in Deutschland—Schwerpunkt Köln. Eine Empirische Untersuchung*. Hamburg, Germany: Diplomica Verlag.

Wong, S., & Lau, E. (2001). Understanding the behavior of Hong Kong Chinese tourists on group tour packages. *Journal of Travel Research*, *40*(1), 57–67.

World Travel & Tourism Council. (2006). *China, China Hong Kong SAR and China Macao SAR: The impact of travel & tourism on jobs and the economy*. Retrieved from http://www.wttc.org/bin/pdf/temp/chksar2006cn.html

Xie, Y., & Li, M. (2008). An analysis of the tourist flow in China's outbound tourism. In K. Ferfet (Ed.), *Proceedings of Tourism in the new Eastern Europe: Global Challenges–Regional Answers, 29–30 November 2008* (pp. 35–44). Warsaw, Poland: Warsaw College of Tourism and Hospitality Management.

Zhang, G. (2006). China's outbound tourism: An overview. Retrieved from http://www.som.surrey.ac.uk/WTM/GuangruiWTMChinaOutboundTourism2006text.pdf

Zhang, H., Chong, K., & Ap, J. (1999). An analysis of tourism policy development in modern China. *Tourism Management*, *20*(4), 471–485.

Zhang, W. (1997). China's domestic tourism: Impetus, development and trends. *Tourism Management*, *18*(8), 565–571.

When the Global Meets the Local in Tourism—Cultural Performances in Lijiang as Case Studies

旅游中的全球化与地方化—以丽江文化表演为例

YUJIE ZHU

As one of the most popular tourism destinations of China, the World Heritage Site Old Town of Lijiang has attracted millions of tourists from around the world. The commoditization of local culture and its manifestation in the indigenous religion have emerged to satisfy the demand of its booming mass tourism. Taking three cultural performances as case studies—namely, Naxi Ancient Music, Lijiang Impression, and Naxi Marriage Courtyard—this article aims to explore the influence of globalization and localization on the development of tourism in Lijiang. It examines how these performances are interpreted and transformed into cultural productions by the local tourism market. During this endless flow between the global and the local, cultural performances show the dynamic forms of encounter, combining the homogenization of global capital and the heterogenization of local ethnicity.

Introduction

International tourism has become one of the most significant beneficiaries and vehicles of globalization in the last few decades, constituting both the site and the source of direct cultural contacts in large-scale flows between Western and non-Western cultures. Cultural performance, which is the presentation, perception, and interpretation of local cultures, is an intrinsic part of international tourism and helps (re)build the place-bound identity in mediating the influence of global forces. Both local people and local cultures are not merely recipients of global forces; however, they actively mediate these forces by comprehending, containing, and controlling tourism development within a host community. In this sense, the mediation between the global and the local strengthens a continuity of cultural forms of the past and synthesizes transnational cultures in different places through reinvention and innovation.

In the late 1980s and early 1990s, Lijiang began to market itself as an international tourist destination. Since then, it has attracted millions of tourists from around the world. In particular, Westerners are fascinated by this remote town, which has been described as "a magic Kingdom of wealth, scenic beauty, marvelous forests, flowers and friendly tribes"[1] (Rock, 1947, viii). After being included in the World Heritage List by the United Nations Educational, Scientific and Cultural Organization (UNESCO) in 1997, Lijiang became one of the most popular destinations in China for both inbound and domestic tourists. The commoditization of local culture and its manifestation in the indigenous religion and folk festivals have emerged as a reinvention of tradition (Hobsbawm & Ranger, 1983) to satisfy the demand of its booming tourism.

Cultural performances are central to the development of the town's tourist industry. Three of the most important forms of performances, *Naxi Ancient Music* (*naxi guyue* 纳西古乐), *Lijiang Impression* (*yinxiang lijiang*印象丽江) and *Naxi Marriage Courtyard* (*naxi xiyuan* 纳西喜院), have been staged in the tourism market of Lijiang. These performances produce and represent various images of Naxi culture and ethnicity and have become the most popular tourist attractions of the site. Taking these three cultural performances as case studies, this article explores the influence of globalization and localization on the development of tourism in Lijiang. It examines both Western and domestic tourists' interpretations and imaginaries of these performances and how the local cultural capital is transformed into cultural productions by the local tourism market. It addresses the consciousness of cultural flows made by the mutual communication between local culture and tourism as one part of the global dynamics.

In this study, tourism is conceptualized as a transnational and contradictory process that embodies a mix of both homogenizing and diversifying forces. The complex process of globalization and localization needs to be understood through the cultural flows and internal shifts of power, which move from a binary opposition to an intertwined reality. This research also attempts to stimulate the discussion on the nature and scope of possible alternatives to the identity and cultural representation of tourism studies in China.

This article is structured into three major sections. The first section conceptualizes globalization and localization and illustrates the framework in relation to cultural performance in the context of tourism. The second section delineates the study's methodology and contextualizes Lijiang's response to tourism development and its status as a World Heritage Site. The third section examines three cultural performances to reveal how they have evolved in terms of Lijiang's tourism market as a global–local nexus. This article concludes by emphasizing that cultural performances both produce and are conditioned by the dynamic cultural flow between global capital and local culture.

Globalization, Localization, and Cultural Performance

Tourism has changed dramatically in the last decade in response to transitions in the global economy and political sphere (Butler, 1992). In the globalized world, tourism has become a process of interconnectedness and interdependency, expanding the cross-cultural production of local meanings, self-images, representations, and modes of life (Appadurai, 1996), thus complicating culturally static representations of tourism that have been and continue to be created and circulated (Salazar, 2006).

Tourism is complex. It transforms local culture into cultural capital, making it diversifiable and consumable. Cultural capital (Bourdieu, 1986) acts as a social relation within a system of exchange that includes the accumulated cultural knowledge that confers power and status. It can be further distinguished into three states: the embodied state (knowledge and skills that individuals possess), the objectified state (expressed in a form of cultural goods), and the institutionalized state (represented by actual documents and other proof of cultural status, Bourdieu).

Cultural performance, as one form of cultural capital, attaches to both the objectified and institutionalized states. It is objectified, thus formulating consumption as the interpretation of cultural and social values of material goods (Sherlock, 2001). It is institutionalized to develop and express collective belongings, social capital, and identity (Giddens, 1991; Jackson, 1996). In this approach, cultural performance is seen as the locus of an ongoing dialogue between tourists and locals, between the universalistic requirements of tourism and the particularities of a given tourist destination. Tourism generates a demand for cultural performance by promoting the whole society to stage their culture for its global audience. In reply to this demand, local people construct alternative cultural performances based on their indigenous system of reference and their understanding of the tourists' expectations and imagination. Through the representation that is implicated, embedded, and intertwined with the local culture, cultural performance helps to construct, folklorize, and ethnicize the local authenticity and distinctiveness (Salazar, 2005). The production, distribution, and consumption of performances create imaginaries about the shared lifestyle and values of locals (O'Connor & Wynne, 1996; Warde, 1994).

The emergence of cultural performance and its transition into local cultural capital is the result of globalization in the context of tourism development. Globalization is a powerful force that increases the mobility of capital, people, ideas, and information on a universal scale (Harvey, 1989; Ohmae, 1990). Processes of globalization continue to homogenize and standardize societies (Rosenberg & White, 1957). This is commonly regarded as a threat to local cultures. However, globalization should not be seen as overbearing; it is always mediated by local factors, producing unique outcomes in different locations (Mak, Lumbers, & Eves, 2012). Appadurai (1996) contended that though globalization homogenizes the world to some extent, the disjuncture in globalization also produces heterogeneity. Both sides of the globalization coin can produce infinite contestations of sameness and difference on a stage characterized by the radical disjuncture between global flows and uncertain landscapes (Appadurai). This exemplifies how globalization produces homogenization and concomitantly provides an impetus for transforming the nature and meaning of the local, which engenders heterogenization (Appadurai).

Correspondingly, Urry (1990) referred to the influence of globalization on cultural performance in tourism as the *tourist gaze*. By using the term he viewed tourism as a function of social structural differentiations with a collection of signs. This term, originally from Foucault (1973), presupposes a narcissistic subject within which there is a deterministic fit between self and society. Urry brought the tourist gaze to tourism studies with a philosophical concern for the human subject and subjectivity. In his second edition of *The Tourist Gaze*, Urry (2002) linked the tourist gaze to globalization by tourism reflexivity, a set of procedures and criteria that enable each place to evaluate and develop a potential for tourism with material and semiotic resources. He argued that there has been a massive shift from a single tourist gaze to a proliferation of tourist gazes, embodied in a variety of discursive forms. Through the complex and interconnected process of a multiple tourist gaze, the flow of images, local people, and the emerging practices of tourist reflexivity are conceptualized as global hybrids that influence the local culture. In the third edition, *The Tourist Gaze 3.0*, Urry and Larsen (2011) clarified the relationship between the sense and the gaze and developed an embodied and multisensuous approach to gazing, which they call *embodied gazing*. They further argued that tourism itself is an embodied practice that accomplishes something as a contingent process (Schieffelin, 1998). From this approach, cultural performance highlights tourists' experiences of places in multisensuous ways that involve both bodily sensation and affect (Urry & Larsen). It reveals a heterogeneous interpretation of the community and the place and brings to light the dynamic interplay of individual and collective meanings of the tourist gaze, enabling tourists (guests) and people from the local community (hosts) to interpret, impart, and share their own cultural codes.

Nevertheless, in this process of communication between hosts and guests (Smith, 1977), the hosts, rather than being passive objects of the gaze, are in fact active agents gazing on the tourists as well. Both hosts and tourists are simultaneously performers and audience, combining to form a space of tourism in "the mutual gaze" (Maoz, 2006, p. 211). In other words, the top-down global perspective on tourism and the one-dimensional influence of globalization on cultural capital in the form of cultural performance should also include considerations of bottom-up local forces (Chang, Milne, Fallon, & Pohlmann, 1996). The local does not exist as an oppositional reality to the global but rather constitutes a dynamic cultural negotiation between the changing structures of a political economy, a negotiation in which dominant structures are mediated by individual agencies (Oakes, 1993).

The local is defined as being part of the nation state, though not necessarily corresponding to any territorial configuration. Rather, it should be seen as a fluid and relational space, constituted in and through its relation to the global (Hall, 1998). Generally, the local connotes a small space characterized by close-knit social relationships, place-based identities, and the realities of everyday life that turn a location from a physical space into a place (Teo & Li, 2003). But the local is best understood as a realm established at the junction of the global and the local and between tourists and tourism workers, who form a relational identity marker of connection with the locality. Local people have an emotional investment in the host community and often provide both labor and financial support for community services with their connotation of belonging and commitment to the place (Sherlock, 2001). Local particularities, cultures, and identities are juxtaposed with global influences (Massey & Allen, 1984) and are mobilizing and projecting the interests of their members beyond their political, economic, and social arena. Hence, localities are not merely recipients of global forces but are actively involved in their own transformation (Teo & Li).

In the course of transformation, localization has received considerable attention as a method of involving intrasocietal or intranational cultural processes that define and strengthen local cultural practices. Through local organizations and networking, localization is proposed as one way of folkorizing, ethnicizing, and exoticizing the cultural, economic, social, and physical resources of the local place. These are not a homogeneous block but a fragmented and continually changing network of social ties (Sherlock, 2001). Rather than being a passive host community, the empowerment of local tourism development requires localized horizontal networking among producers and vertical networking by external intermediaries, consumers and partnership with the state, agencies, and large operators (Buhailis & Cooper, 1998). As a result, localization does not reflect the shift of hegemonic power from global to local but instead it relates the intersection of heterogeneous discourses.

Notwithstanding this, there is an asymmetrical power relationship between the global and the local in creating and shaping tourism products (Chang et al., 1996). Hannerz (1992) illustrated the relationship by formulating a modular structure of periphery and the core, where the periphery is at the fore of cultural generation and diffusion; in the core, the power of identity is constructed and contested. Cultural performance follows this structure and acts as a certain contact zone (Clifford, 1997) between the commoditized and mystified version of the global (the periphery) and the reflected and legitimatized mirror of local truth and reality (the core). The core and the periphery are interwoven by the socioeconomic power relation that constructs the global and local communication (Hughes, 1992). This relation, therefore, structurally illuminates the dynamic nature of cultural performance in the process of transition from globalization to localization in tourism.

To conclude, globalization can be seen as a threat but also as an impetus that opens up new opportunities through localization for the reinvention of local cultural products and identities (Mak et al., 2012). The dialogues between the local and the global are not fixed monolithic discourses; rather, they achieve real values through their mutual interaction, proximity, and differences. Global values and ideas are negotiated and adapted to suit local needs, thereby leading to the reconstruction of local traditions or forms of particularity with other cultural entities (Robertson, 1992). The existing literature has recognized cultural performance through the representation of local cultures in tourism as one of the major consequences of globalization and localization. In this article, cultural performances in Lijiang will be discussed to broaden the current theoretical approaches to tourism studies.

Methodology

Denzin (1997) stated that interpretations of human activities are always shaped by the cultural values and life practices of the day and culture in which they are formed. Based on this philosophical stance, this study builds from ontological assumptions of interpretive and reflexive ethnography research (Okely, 1996), which refers to the multiple constructed realities of the social world, the dynamic interactions between researchers and the research objects, and the value-laden nature of the research.

In this study's attempt to understand the discursive meanings surrounding cultural performances in Lijiang and their relation to sociospatial contexts, a qualitative textual analysis of both primary and secondary source materials has been deployed. Firstly, a textual analysis of literature related to theories on globalization, localization, and cultural performances, as well as statistics of the site, government documents on planning and development, and tourism promotional materials was conducted. By analyzing these materials, the author has learned how the process of local tourism development matches national and global patterns of socioeconomic development. Secondly, a fieldwork study in Lijiang that lasted 8 months (July–December 2010 and July–August 2011) was carried out. Qualitative methods, particularly methods of interpretive ethnography such as situ observation, participation, and interviews, were used to assess the significance, experiences, and processes that emerge in social interactions. Through ethnographic research on local experiences and attitudes toward the development of tourism in Lijiang, the author was able to interpret the data from the perspectives of the host and global tourists by attending various cultural performances in Lijiang during the period of fieldwork study. Focusing on a single tourist site has provided the author great ethnographic details and a deep engagement with each performance of the site. Studying Lijiang ethnographically has also offered primary data that is essential in untangling the complexities of the ongoing development of cultural performances in Lijiang and its impact on local tourism in general.

To obtain more detailed and accurate information about the local perspectives of cultural performances and their interaction with globalization, interviews were conducted with cultural performers, tourism and heritage officials, and some local scholars in the studies of tourism and culture. Interview questions include the historical development of cultural performances, their understanding of tourism and cultural heritage, conflicts between local and global encounters, and future visions.

Lijiang—A Local Setting for Global Flows

Located in Yunnan Province in southwest China, the Old Town of Lijiang lies in the center of the Lijiang basin. Lijiang was listed as a World Heritage Site because of its unique urban fabric and residential buildings and its vernacular landscape of custom, religion, music, and pictographic written language. It is an ancient town set in a dramatic landscape and has retained its coherence and sense of history, making it different from many other Chinese cities.

Lijiang is dominated by the *Naxi* community, which has retained a number of its traditional everyday cultural activities. As the old indigenous religion of the *Naxi*, the *Dongba* religion incorporates Lamaism, Buddhism, and Daoism and bonds *Naxi* people closely with important life events such as birth, marriage, and death. *Dongba* rituals, centering on maintaining harmony between human and nature, consist of offerings and dances to worship ancestors and nature and to expel evil spirits (McKhann, 1992). As an extraordinary system of hieroglyphics formed in the 13th century, the ancient *Naxi* language aids in the recitation of ritual texts during rituals. In 2003, UNESCO formally included the ancient *Dongba* manuscripts in the Memory of the World Register. This title, together with the Old Town as a World Heritage Site, distinguishes Lijiang further from other destinations.

China's modernization process has allowed some amount of soft power to integrate the peripheral regions into the mainstream of the Chinese society (Su & Teo, 2009), where tourism is a central component of globalization and domestication. The Chinese government has made a point of promoting ethnic equality and advertising the contributions of minority nationalities to Chinese culture. Tourism development in China in the post-Mao era has fulfilled China's desire to be globally recognized with an open-door policy. Consequently, the politicization and commoditization of ethnic tourism encapsulates the whole country to serve the national goals of modernization on the one hand and remains loyal to socialism on the other in the transitional period (Su & Teo).

Lijiang is a "hot spot" tourism heritage site in China, with frequent population migration and cultural flows. In 2009, Lijiang attracted 7.6 million visitors with 8.8 billion yuan (ca. US$1.3 billion) in revenue drawn from tourism (Lijiang Bureau of Statistics, 2010). The influx of modern tourists has accelerated the production of new cultural and social capital, bringing dramatic change to the place and its culture. By linking capital and politics, the process of heritage production has converted *Naxi* ethnic culture and the town into "a predominantly capitalistically organized place driven by the inherent and defining social dynamics of the system" (Britton, 1991, p. 475). The image of *Naxi* culture, including its *Dongba* religion, has been interpreted as a new form of tradition and vividly represented in cultural performances, folk festivals, music, and dance. Among these new inventions, three performances—*Naxi Ancient Music*, *Impression Lijiang*, and *Naxi Marriage Courtyard*, which are revitalized and staged as cultural products in front of the floods of mass tourists—attract the most global flows of tourism to Lijiang. As a result, tourism integrates the town into a web of global capital relations in which local cultural capital becomes produced, consumed, and commoditized.

Searching Authenticity in *Naxi Ancient Music*

Lijiang's experience with globalization began at the turn of the 20th century with the entrance of Western scholars and global media. The first image of Lijiang was invented by James Hilton's (1933) novel *Lost Horizon* as a paradise of Shangri-la, where the town was viewed as a romantic forgotten place, frozen in time (Su & Teo, 2009). Later, Joseph Rock (1947) and Peter Goullart (1957), who had both stayed in Lijiang, published descriptive texts of the town, reinforcing the image of China's peripheral area as an oriental paradise with the symbols of ancientness, tradition, and nature. The landscape was further depicted as ideal for trekking and a possible backdoor to Tibet. These media-constructed imaginaries about the picturesque landscape attracted Western and Japanese tourists to the town en masse for the first time in the mid-1980s. To concretize the picture of *Naxi* culture and ethnicity, the local population opened cultural performances to the increasing numbers of tourists. The music concert *Naxi Ancient Music* was staged as the first performance for the tourism industry in Lijiang in the late 1980s.

Naxi Ancient Music, initially called *Lijiang Ancient Music*, is organized by the Dayan Ancient Music Association (*Dayan Guyuehui* 大研古乐会), which formerly operated as a folk art association and later became a privately owned company. *Naxi Ancient Music* is a musical genre with varied ethnic affiliations, adapted from its original traditional and religious purposes to fit the needs of secular entertainment in the booming tourism industry of Lijiang. The first concert of *Naxi Ancient Music* was held on July 22, 1988. With English-language commentary from the leader Xuan Ke, the performance mainly targeted foreign visitors, especially English-speaking tourists and tourists from Hong Kong and Taiwan. From 1998 to 2007, the price of tickets steadily rose from 35 yuan (ca. US$5.5) to 180 yuan (ca. US$28). In 2007, people from over 30 countries saw the concert, bringing more than 5 million yuan (ca. US$0.7 million) to Lijiang (Yang, 2009). The concert has since become world famous. It is performed daily in the Old Town and is regularly shown in countries around the globe, including the United Kingdom, Germany, Denmark, and the United States. Since 2000, it has appeared frequently on local, provincial, national, and overseas television channels and has been mentioned in various travel guides and newspapers and on the Internet.

Why has the performance of *Naxi Ancient Music* become so successful? And why has this commercial performance attracted so many foreigners? In addition to the growth of Western backpackers in Lijiang and the fame of *Naxi Ancient Music* in the world, the successful marketing by Xuan Ke, the leader of the Dayan Ancient Music Association, is the main reason. Benefiting from his educational background and personal experience,[2] Xuan markets his cultural products specifically to Western tourists. In late 1980s, most Western tourists traveling to Lijiang had become tired of the elaborately staged performances of other tourist venues, but they were fascinated by the ethnic culture of this remote area that seemed to present the backyard of China. Responding to this thought, Xuan changed the name of his concert from *Lijiang Ancient Music* to *Naxi Ancient Music* to emphasize ethnicity.

Furthermore, Western tourists search for what they believe to be authentic culture in China. From their perspectives, the performance of *Naxi Ancient Music* has an aura of unspoiled authenticity, even though it is actually *Han* Chinese, not *Naxi* in origin. There are three "olds," as Xuan Ke propagates, to create this image of authenticity in his concert. The first old concerns the musicians themselves. Most performers are over 60 with flowing white beards; according to Xuan, this lends a sense of "timeless" dignity to the performance. The other two olds include the old music notation and the old instruments, which came from central China hundreds of years ago and were conserved in this remote area and have been handed down from father to son ever since. After Lijiang successfully became a World Heritage Site, one more old was put forward to increase cultural authenticity: the location of the concert was an 800-year-old town.

In addition to the propaganda of these olds, the ramshackle setting of the stage and the visual impression of the performance with the romantic atmosphere also attract foreign audiences (Rees, 2000). The concert is held in a slightly dilapidated and old mansion in a winding alley. The electric lighting is dim, darker and noisier than other performances in the town. Black-and-white photos of former members of the association are suspended on the roof beam, and classical Chinese paintings decorate the background. Furthermore, Xuan Ke acts as a charismatic speaker who reads his foreign audience's mind very well. He skillfully creates an atmosphere of romantic timelessness by his presentation in the concert. He introduces the history of the music, emphasizing the ancient historical continuity of the musical tradition, instruments, and musicians, which was lost from their origins in central China but well preserved in Lijiang. He talks about the remoteness of Lijiang and its *Naxi* locals and emphasizes the unbroken transmission of the music, even during tumultuous periods in Chinese history. He also identifies the ethnic minorities of the players and specifically the "*Naxi* spirits" elements in the music, capitalizing on foreign interests in minority culture as well as in history (Rees).

Xuan Ke successfully inserts Goullart's (1957) romantic description of *Naxi* music in the 1940s into the picture he designs for his foreign audience. The picture contributes to the commercial viability of the genre, which in turn helps push its candidacy as a cultural ambassador of Lijiang (Rees, 2000).

> The old musicians, all formally dressed in long gowns and . . . [jackets], took their seats unhurriedly, caressing their long white beards. . . . [The music] was majestic and inspiring and proceeded in rising and falling cadences. Then, as a climax, the great gong was struck. I have never heard in China such a deep and sonorous gong: the whole house seemed to vibrate with its velvety waves. Then, rising from their chairs, the elders sang a sacred ode in a natural voice and with great reverence and feeling. . . . It was a recital of the cosmic life as it was unfolding in its grandeur, unmarred by the discordant wails and crashes of petty human existence. It was classical, and timeless. It was the music of the gods and of a place where there is serenity, eternal peace and harmony. . . . Let us hope that this treasure of music in Lijiang may be secure from the ravages of the modern age. (Goullart, 1957, pp. 216–217)

Through Xuan's interpretation and commentary, the description from Goullart (1957) matches the imaginaries of the tourists with their global gaze of *Naxi* and its ethnic culture. Western tourists, mainly backpackers conceptualized by scholars as existential tourists, tend to come to the remote Lijiang—600 kilometers and 20 hours by bumpy long-distance bus from Kunming, the capital of the province—to search for spirituality outside modernity by approximating themselves to China's native people and culture (Cohen, 1988). They are greatly impressed by the dignified and elderly musicians and their continuation of a long-standing artistic tradition in the face of a modernizing world (Rees, 2000). Different from most staged shows elsewhere, the performance seems to be authentic.[3] The history of the music and musicians and the ethnic perception of *Naxi* attach the performance to the nature of tradition, credibility, and authenticity.

National and local governmental policies also play a central role in promoting *Naxi Ancient Music*. Because the performance has generated international acclaim and high revenues, the government politically and economically supports it. It does so to attract more tourists to the town and to preserve its heritage. The government positively encourages local minorities to develop and claim their own distinct and differentiated art forms and traditions, raising local presentations of a self-conscious identity. By using internal and external forces to add the notion of ethnic identity, official policies have contributed to the molding of certain habitués (Bourdieu, 1977) among minorities and *Han* Chinese. This partly explains why the Lijiang ancient music has recently acquired the name *Naxi Ancient Music*. Xuan Ke did not create it alone; rather it is a product of a conscious collective effort by both the *Naxi* inhabitants and the Chinese government.

As the main actor of the performance, Xuan and his associates label themselves as the ambassadors of *Naxi* ancient music. They claim social and political responsibility to the inheritance of cultural heritage. However, due to the huge economic gain that is generated from the cultural capital, his work has been criticized as a cultural commercialization by selling "ancientness" to tourists. It has been argued that *Naxi Ancient Music* cannot be regarded as the representation of *Naxi* classical music; instead, it is simply the name of a performance and a brand for commercialization (Wu, 2003). Nonetheless, the emergence of *Naxi Ancient Music* has influenced the influx of foreign tourists since the beginning of tourism development in Lijiang in the 1980s. Since 2007, the transformation of the tourism market from international tourism to domestic mass tourism has made ancientness and authenticity difficult selling points. The market for *Naxi Ancient Music* is gradually losing its popularity.

Daydreaming in *Impression Lijiang*

With the open-door policy in the 1990s, China has begun a variety of discursive campaigns to bolster its socioeconomic transitions. Such campaigns include "getting on track with the world" (*yu shijie jiegui* 与世界接轨) and "creating a global brand name" (*maixiang guojihua* 迈向国际化) (Noble, 2003, p. 6) for accelerating globalization and raising mass consumption. New cultural performances act as reflexive representations of Chinese culture to the world and resistance to dominant global media. China's desire to build its own cultural capital, or soft power, highlights its need and motivation to connect with the global market.

Impression Lijiang is an outdoor tourism spectacle directed by the famous Chinese film director Zhang Yimou, based on his *Impression Liusanjie* set in Yangshuo of

Guangxi Province. He has established the "Impression Series" as a benchmark for the cultural tourism market, targeting both international and domestic tourists. Zhang applies the term *impression* with his signature cinematic and storytelling style to simplify complex cultural resources, expressing visual sensations and repackaging them to a larger audience. The show is grandiose. It incorporates the performances of singers, dancers, and acrobats and is illuminated by pyrotechnic and special effects. Like other shows in the same series, *Impression Lijiang* is directly financed by a private company and preferential policies granted by the Lijiang government. In 2005, the Impression Lijiang Tourism Company was founded and invested 250 million yuan (ca. US$30 million) in building an outdoor theater at the base of the Jade Dragon Snow Mountain, sacred to the *Naxi* (Gao & Zhou, 2010). Since 2007, the theater has launched the show two or three times a day depending on the weather. As a result of the support of the company, the show has become exceedingly successful—600,000 tourists viewed the performance in 2008, which generated approximately 6.7 million yuan (ca. USD$1 million; Gao & Zhou).

The outdoor theater is located 3,100 meters above sea level affixed to the splendid scenery of the Jade Dragon Snow Mountain, which is symbolically important to the *Naxi* religion and culture. The setting of the stage is decorated in natural tones; it is open to the elements and the seats are disordered. Wild stones are the only ornaments to be found. This design shortens the distance between humans and nature. Because of this setting, the audience can witness the seasonal changes of nature. Just like the lines of the performance read: "This is a magic place. Call the heaven and the heaven will answer. Call the earth and the earth will answer."[4]

The success of *Impression Lijiang* derives from the development of the domestic tourism industry in recent years. Nowadays, tourism in China is no longer a luxury for the rich but a broadly accepted leisure and relaxation method for the mass. Different from the main selling points of *Naxi Ancient Music* of ancientness and ethnicity, *Impression Lijiang* aims to encapsulate a representational narrative of *Naxi* identity and religion that is natural, mysterious, and sacred. A particular atmosphere is created by the stage and the imaginaries of tourists, both international and domestic, from the remotest parts of China to its major metropolitan centers (Gao & Zhou, 2010). It renders a liminal space, inviting tourists to escape their ordinary stressful urban lives and participate in various forms of transgressions, and it enables their secret selves to be displayed while pursuing an unrestrained hedonic experience (Redmon, 2003).

Impression Lijiang is more than a mere liminal spectacle. It is a site of ethnic performance and production. For example, the first session represents *Naxi* horse cavalcades and drunken happy men. Five hundred local farmers from *Naxi*, *Bai*, *Yi*, *Lisu*, and other ethnic groups are the main performers. They shout to heaven: "We are farmers. We cannot sing. When friends come, we sing. We are farmers. We cannot dance. When friends come, we dance. When friends leave, we drink. When friends leave, we drink!" (recorded and translated by author).

This enactment of peasant life is exactly what the Western tourists yearn for. They fly several thousand miles from their homes to this remote area of China not to find a Broadway show but a representation of what they believe to be the nonmodern ethnicity of China and to authenticate their biased imaginaries. In Wang's (2011) article, she stated that in the continuous drinking and celebrating, *Impression Lijiang* tries to create a carnival image of the ethnic Chinese. Using Bakhtin's (1984) notion of carnivalesque, Wang argued that the carnival theme creates a unique sense of time and space that shortens the distance between the performers and the audience.

The middle session of the performance, named "Heaven on Earth," tells a touching love story in which a couple dies in love at the edge of the sacred Jade Dragon Snow Mountain. Committing suicide in the name of love (*xunqing* 殉情) is a longtime tradition in *Naxi* culture and has been described in the *Naxi* ancient narrative poem *rubanrurao* (鲁般鲁饶). Quoting from the poem, the couple in the performance says, "We have kin but we do not want to know them. All we need is love" (recorded and translated by author). This suggests that young people lack interest in their own kin as prospective marriage partners and would pursue partners on their own. Lovers believe that they share the same notion of paradise and eternal reunion through *xunqing*. The idea of rebirth in paradise makes them bind their bodies together to ensure a collective transmission to heaven. Currently, this image has been propagated by the mass media in the context of Lijiang's tourism promotion (Zhu, 2012a). The theme has been used in the performance of *Impression Lijiang* to engage the audience in relating with the sad and romantic story and to evoke nostalgia for a real and pure love.

After the theme of "Heaven on Earth," the performance enters into the phase of the sacred *Dongba* ritual. This is the last session and presents the creation of new life and hope. The audience is asked to raise their hands to heaven with the *dongba*[5] and bow down to pray in front of the Jade Dragon Snow Mountain. The ritual commences with drums thundering and *Dongba* chanting, and the snow mountain becomes a performative operation that is embedded in the space created by the stage. Although the visitors recognize that they are watching a theatrical performance, the status of the participants and the interaction between self and place still create an embodied experience for the in-betweenness of the sacred and the profane, belief and disbelief, and sensibility and rationality.

To conclude, if we consider *Ancient Naxi Music* as a cultural performance promoted by the local cultural broker Xuan Ke, who mainly targets international tourists, the main reasons for the success of *Impression Lijiang* are its specific operation model (cooperation between a private company and the local government), the presentation of Chinese ethnic culture, and the fame of Zhang Yimou and his associated production team. Zhang Yimou's "Impression Series" derives from the rising importance of Chinese culture as a new soft power and the country's economic creativity in the global entertainment and tourism market. The "Impression Series" appeals to international consumers by incorporating essential images that not only link the product with stereotypical images of Chinese culture but simultaneously offer the appeal of the exotic locale (Keane, 2011). Compared to the use of authenticity as a soft power in *Naxi Ancient Music* and its connection to the global tourism market, *Impression Lijiang* highlights ethnicity, naturalness, and sacredness as the cultural capital. This relates to Zhang Yimou's show in the Opening Ceremony of the Beijing Olympics in 2008. This also becomes a model for franchising contemporary artistic events in other parts of China. For instance, a similar attempt is being made by the Chinese film director Chen Kaige to launch another outdoor tourism spectacle show in Dali, Yunnan Province.

Impression Lijiang does not solely target international tourists. It also aims at fostering domestic appeal. Since 2007, China has been searching for original culture (*yuanshengtai* 原生态). *Yuanshengtai* indicates the original and natural state of culture, which has captivated urban populations. From *yuanshengtai* dances and songs to *yuanshengtai* literature, the *yuanshengtai* culture boom indicates a demand or nostalgia for originality, which has arisen in conjunction with the influx of modernity and industrialization. This *yuanshengtai* approach closely resembles modern tourists who are looking for authenticity on stage (MacCannell, 1973).

Through the multi-sensuous tourist gaze (Urry, 2011), both Chinese and Western tourists have their collective interpretation of the local community. As Wang Chaoge and Fan Yue, the other two deputy directors of the show, said, "It is not a show with professional performances, but a daydream for all the people under the sunshine and snow mountain (Wang, 2011, p. 69)." With the gaze of otherness, both Western and Chinese tourists undergo a romantic and nostalgic experience that is located in a simple and happy daydream.

Experiencing Romance in *Naxi Marriage Courtyard*

The rapid tourism development in Lijiang since the new millennium has accelerated population migration and culture flows. With about 7 million domestic visitors in 2009 (compared to 0.35 million international tourists), the local community has been influenced by the incoming flood of Chinese tourists and the intensified culture exchanges (Lijiang Bureau of Statistics, 2010). As a result, mass tourism development has brought dramatic change to the peace and tranquil daily life of the *Naxi* community. Global demands of consumption have led the cultural flow from urban cities into Lijiang, putting new romance and exotic flavor into it. For example, the mysteries of walking-marriage customs and indigenous love traditions have been interpreted by urban tourists as a modern image of romance (Zhu, 2012a). The theme of love has been broadly used in the tourism market by different media, including books, magazines, newspapers, and the Internet, turning the town from the "Lost Kingdom," an icon of oriental paradise for the Westerners, to the "Town of Romance," an exoticized holiday destination for modern Chinese. The commercially constructed cooperation between the media and businesses has brought new ways of consumption and creativity. However, in the process of commercialization, Western tourists have lost their interest in the town due to the fading of its original aroma.

In 2005, the Lijiang Heritage Conservation and Management Bureau and a local private enterprise[6] colaunched a heritage tourism project called "Walking Into *Naxi* Family" (*zoujin Naxi renjia* 走进纳西人家) to diversify Lijiang's heritage tourism products and enhance Lijiang's tourism image and brand. Ten traditional courtyards in the Old Town of Lijiang were selected as platforms for cultural presentation and exhibition with different themes of *Naxi* culture, such as handicrafts, clothing, music, religion, food, and weddings. Most of the courtyards are open to the public for free; some profits are made from services such as handicraft production and the wedding ceremony.

As one of the theme courtyards, *Naxi Marriage Courtyard* presents the *Naxi* traditional wedding celebration and arranges *Dongba* marriage as paid services to tourists and locals. *Naxi*, the ethnic group of Lijiang, has its own marriage tradition, which is under the auspices of *dongba*. After the long process of Hanization, the form of *Naxi* traditional wedding ceremony acculturated *Han* culture as well as the Confucian practice. In modern times, local residents in the Lijiang basin are still familiar with the *Dongba* rituals in the wedding ceremony, although most of the locals are married in their houses and arrange a big party with dinner for the creation of social prestige associated with hierarchy and material displays. In mountain areas, the wedding rituals conducted by *dongbas* for the marriage ceremony still exist.

The wedding ceremony and marriage performance in *Naxi Marriage Courtyard* is viewed as a form of reinvention of tradition (Hobsbawm & Ranger, 1983). Building on the ethnic culture and religion, this cultural tourism project tries to attract tourists and local residents to get married in the courtyard by presenting a complete traditional *Naxi* marriage package, including *Dongba* wedding rituals, performance, dinner, and shows. It starts with a welcome ceremony at the entrance of the Old Town. A group of grandmas dressed in traditional *Naxi* clothes guide the couple and the visitors to the *Naxi Marriage Courtyard*. After entering into the courtyard, the couple is asked to dress in *Naxi* ethnic clothes; meanwhile, all the guests start their wedding dinner and watch the marriage ceremony, which includes singing, dancing, and the wedding ritual.

   Naxi Marriage Courtyard hires a *dongba* to conduct the *Dongba* wedding ritual: *Siku*.[7] This *dongba* came from a village in the mountain area of the Lijiang Basin and was trained in the *Dongba* Research Academy of Lijiang. He works in *Naxi Marriage Courtyard* and sometimes goes back to his home village to conduct rituals for villagers (Zhu, 2012b). Unlike other parts of the ceremony, which emphasize the tie between the households of the bride and the groom in the form of show and dinner, the *Siku* ritual is primarily concerned with establishing the new household—consisting of the bride and the groom—as a separate entity and drawing boundaries between the new household and the bride's old household (Chao, 1995). *Siku* involves Gods that are associated with the health and wealth of the household (McKhann, 1992). By offerings, *Dongba* script readings, incense and lights burning, and blessings with yak butter, the entire ritual places importance of the marriage on inviting the bride's *Si* to join the groom's family and on inviting the house God and making an offering to him to secure a blessing for the couple and their household. Though *Siku* is concerned with integrating the new bride into her husband's household, the ritual also aims to establish the couple as a new productive and reproductive entity in the household (Chao).

   Due to the limitation of time and space, the text of the *Siku* ritual has been shortened and simplified by the *dongba*. The original 3-day ritual is reduced to a 5-minute performance. Compared with the original scriptures the *dongba* uses for the marriage ritual in his village, the scriptures are much simpler but all the important proceedings as formerly mentioned still exist, such as offerings, readings, God invitation, and blessings. However, the *dongba* as the ritual performer and most of the tourists who get married there consider the wedding ritual an impressive and authentic experience.

   After the sacred ritual, the ceremony enters into a more profane session. When celebratory bonfires are made at the center of the courtyard, the staff of *Naxi Marriage Courtyard* invites the couple, their friends, and guests to dance and sing around the fire pit with happy *Naxi* songs. The show ends with a lantern ceremony[8] outside the courtyard along the canal. The couple puts a lighted lantern in the canal and makes a wish for everlasting happiness and a brand new life after the marriage with the guests as witnesses.

   The *Naxi Marriage Courtyard* has conducted over 70 wedding rituals with marriage ceremonies. Most couples come from cities outside of Lijiang. They are cosmopolitan travelers or new inhabitants working in bars and hostels of the Old Town. In addition to offering real marriage ceremonies, *Naxi Marriage Courtyard* also arranges performances and dinner for group tourists. In the past, the staff acted as the bride and bridegroom, but currently, two tourists in the group are invited to participate to experience the ethnic marriage. This has made the performance an entertainment-oriented game. Although the wedding ceremony in *Naxi Marriage Courtyard* is a paid service, it still, aims to protect and inherit local culture for education and heritage conservation.

The emergence of *Naxi Marriage Courtyard* in Lijiang as an ethnic tourism activity reflects the transition of contemporary Chinese society. The social, political, and cultural conversion in modern China have sped up the rhythm of urbanization, modernization, and industrialization in the context of globalization. Chinese people, especially the younger generation, are fed up with modern urban life with conventional social norms and regulations. It is their demands to get into the liminal space of tourism, which provides them opportunities to participate in temporary forms of transgressions and rites of consumption. After Chinese tourists dominate the tourism market of Lijiang, the picture created by the Western imaginaries of Lijiang as a remote Shangri-la has been transfigured into a popular honeymoon or holiday destination for leisure and mass consumption. For Chinese tourists, Lijiang as a World Heritage is no longer the main motivation to visit the site. Instead, they are attracted by the place of Lijiang because it is continuously romanticized with the theme of love, which is lost in modern capital cities. In other words, the cultural heritage site has been transformed into a town of romance, in which the appearance of *Naxi Marriage Courtyard* increases the flavor and highlights the theme of romance of the remote ancient town. The ethnic marriage ceremony thus becomes a flow from urban space to peripheral space, demonstrating a persistent exchange between global forces and local specificity and diversity through the social, cultural, and economic development.

When the Global Meets the Local: Cultural Performance in Tourism

From the authenticity of *Naxi Ancient Music* to the daydreaming images of *Impression Lijiang* and the romance of *Naxi Marriage Courtyard*, cultural performances in Lijiang have constructed a contact zone (Clifford, 1997) of visual contestations, which in turn has converted the site from a "Lost Kingdom" to the current "Town of Romance." These cultural performances indicate that the role of tourism in the social construction of Lijiang is interwoven with socioeconomic power relations between the global and the local and between the core and the periphery (Fees, 1996; Hughes, 1992). The relationship involves diffusion and differentiation. It also consists of a kind of creolization of global culture, which emerges alongside the creative uses of imported and local resources (Hannerz, 1992).

Western backpackers are fascinated by the mystery of *Naxi* ethnicity and the fantasy of the *Naxi Ancient Music*. Modern tourists bow to the sacred Jade Dragon Snow Mountain before sounds of religious drumming and ritual chanting; and urban couples ride horses into the town to marry. Chinese also travel to the site, bringing new capital and urban consumption patterns to the town. Such experiences between international and national foreigners and the town highlight the impact of globalization on Lijiang, an impact that is, as has been shown, influenced heavily by Lijiang's cultural performances. These performances have constructed an attractive image for the town of an authentic historicity that is both marketable and consumable. Tourism, in turn, has influenced the nature and meaning of Lijiang, creating new or reinventing local varieties of culture. As emphasized by tourism, communication between the global and the local is a continuous dialectical process that calls to mind the tourism system's capability to respond to the multiple inputs that comprise its constitution.

The initial encounter between Lijiang and global forces began as a manifestation of Western tourists searching for cultural authenticity. Later, this shifted to indirect Chinese contact in their yearning for modernity. The transition involved exploring how global markets interact with political rule, social forms, and the production of cultural values. During this endless flow between the global and the local, cultural performances, as the exterior representation of culture, show the dynamic forms of encounter, combining the homogenization of global capital and the heterogenization of local ethnicity. In the process of globalization, local cultural performances will continue onstage in front of the global world.

Notes

1. A description written by Joseph Rock in his book *The Ancient Na Khi Kingdom of Southwest China* published in 1947. This book is the very first work introducing Lijiang to Western readers.
2. Because family members used to serve for the missionaries in Lijiang, Xuan Ke received a Western education but had a dramatic life trajectory. Xuan was in jail for more than 20 years during the Cultural Revolution. This experience has become a myth, and he often uses it as a strategy to attract his Western audience.
3. Though there is no one single word in Chinese that carries all of the ramifications of the English word *authentic*, a term often employed in the musical context is *traditional* (*chuantong* 传统).
4. These lines of the performance *Impression Lijiang* are recorded and translated by the author during the several times he attended the show.
5. As ritual practitioners of *Dongba* religion in Lijiang, *dongbas* traditionally perform divinations and a variety of rituals either in home settings for individuals or families or in public spaces for lineages or the entire village population, including exorcisms, healing, funerals, and annual sacrifices to heaven (Chao, 1995).
6. The enterprise called *Naxi* Cultural Industry Company mainly contributed to cultural education, presentation, and cultural tourism development in Lijiang. The Lijiang Heritage Conservation and Management Bureau is an administrative bureau, which is mainly responsible for the implementation of urban planning, drafting policies on heritage preservation, collecting maintenance fees, and supervising construction projects. In recent years, the agency gradually extended its functions to regulating the tourism business, providing daily security to tourists, and leasing public houses to private investors. These two institutions have worked together on many projects since 2000, including heritage tour guide training, cultural tourism activities, etc.
7. *Siku* is the ritual of family God worship in a traditional *Naxi* wedding. According to the *Naxi* traditional belief, *Si* is the life God of the whole family.
8. The lantern ceremony is another reinvention of tradition. *Naxi* has its tradition of memorizing their ancestor by putting a lantern in the canal on July 15 of the Lunar Calendar—the Chinese Ghost Festival. The company creates this romanticized image for its own use. Nowadays, the lantern ceremony is very popular with tourists in Lijiang.

Acknowledgments

This article is based on field research supported by the Cluster of Excellence "Asia and Europe in a Global Context" at Heidelberg University. My gratitude goes to Nelson Graburn, William Nitzky, and two anonymous reviewers for their valuable comments. I thank Paul Fletcher for his generous help and constructive suggestions. I am especially grateful to Anna Li for her continuous and insightful support.

References

Appadurai, A. (1996). *Modernity at large: Cultural dimensions of globalization.* Minneapolis, MN: University of Minnesota Press.

Bakhtin, M. M. (1984). *Rabelais and his world.* Bloomington, IN: Indiana University Press.

Bourdieu, P. (1977). *Outline of a theory of practice.* Cambridge, England: Cambridge University Press.

Bourdieu, P. (1986). The forms of capital. In J. Richardson (Ed.), *Handbook for theory and research for the sociology of education* (pp. 241–258). Westport, CT: Greenwood Press.

Britton, S. (1991). Tourism, capital, and place: Towards a critical geography of tourism. *Environment and Planning D: Society and Space, 9*(4), 451–478.

Buhalis, D., & Cooper, C. (1998). Competition or cooperation? Small and medium sized tourism enterprises at the destination. In E. Laws, B. Faulkner, & G. Moscardo (Eds.), *Embracing and managing change in tourism: International case studies* (pp. 324–346). London, England: Routledge.

Butler, R. (1992). Tourism landscapes: For the tourist or of the tourist. *Tourism Recreation Research, 17*(1), 3–9.

Chang, T., Milne, S., Fallon, D., & Pohlmann, C. (1996). Urban heritage tourism: The global–local nexus. *Annals of Tourism Research, 23*(2), 284–305.

Chao, E. (1995). *Depictions of difference: History, gender, ritual and state discourse among the Naxi of Southwest China* (Doctoral dissertation, University of Michigan). Retrieved from ProQuest Dissertations and Theses. (Accession No. AAT 9542805).

Clifford, J. (1997). *Routes: Travel and translation in the late twentieth century.* Cambridge, MA: Harvard University Press.

Cohen, E. (1988). Authenticity and commoditization in tourism. *Annals of Tourism Research, 15*(3), 371–386.

Denzin, N. K. (1997). *Interpretive ethnography: Ethnographic practices for the 21st century.* Thousand Oaks, CA: Sage Publications.

Fees, C. (1996). Tourism and the politics of authenticity in a north Cotswold town. In T. Selwyn (Ed.), *The tourist image: Myths and myth making in tourism* (pp. 121–146). Chichester, England: John Wiley.

Foucault, M. (1973). *The birth of the clinic: An archaeology of medical perception* (A. Sheridan, Trans.). London, England: Tavistock.

Gao, Y., & Zhou, F. (2010). STP战略在印象西湖和印象丽江中的应用 [The application of STP strategy in Impression Xihu and Impression Lijiang]. 云南科技管理 [Yunnan Science and Technology Management], *3*, 85–86.

Giddens, A. (1991). *Modernity and self-identity: Self and society in the late modern age.* Stanford, CA: Stanford University Press.

Goullart, P. (1957). *The forgotten kingdom.* London, England: Reader's Union.

Hall, C. (1998). The institutional setting—Tourism and the state. In D. Ionndies & K. G. Debbage (Eds.), *The economic geography of the tourist industry: A supply-side analysis* (pp. 199–219). London, England: Routledge.

Hannerz, U. (1992). *Cultural complexity: Studies in the social organization of meaning.* New York, NY: Columbia University Press.

Harvey, D. (1989). *The condition of postmodernity: An enquiry into the origins of cultural change.* Oxford, England: Blackwell.

Hilton, J. (1933). *Lost horizon.* London, England: Macmillan.

Hobsbawm, E., & Ranger, T. (1983). *The Invention of tradition.* Cambridge, MA: Cambridge University Press.

Hughes, G. (1992). Tourism and the geographical imagination. *Leisure Studies, 11*(1), 31–42.

Jackson, P. (1996). Towards a cultural politics of consumption. In J. Bird, B. Curtis, T. Putnam, & L. Tickner (Eds.), *Mapping the futures: Local cultures, global change* (pp. 207–228). London, England: Routledge.

Keane, M. (2011). *Zhang Yimou's impressions: Adaptation, innovation and creativity in China.* Retrieved from http://creativeasia.squarespace.com/storage/Zhang%20Yimous%20Impressions_adaptation%20innovation%20and%20creativity%20in%20China.pdf

Lijiang Bureau of Statistics. (2010). *Lijiang statistical yearbook 2010.* Lijiang, China: Author.

MacCannell, D. (1973). Staged authenticity: Arrangements of social space in tourist settings. *American Journal of Sociology, 79*(3), 589–603.

Mak, A., Lumbers, M., & Eves, A. (2012). Globalisation and food consumption in tourism. *Annals of Tourism Research, 39*(1), 171–196.

Maoz, D. (2006). The mutual gaze. *Annals of Tourism Research, 33*(1), 221–239.

Massey, D., & Allen, J. (1984). *Geography matters!: A reader.* Cambridge, MA: Cambridge University Press in association with the Open University.

McKhann, C. F. (1992). *Fleshing out the bones: Kinship and cosmology in Naqxi religion* (Doctoral dissertation, University of Chicago). ProQuest Dissertations and Theses. (Accession No. AAT T-31812).

Noble, J. S. (2003). *Cultural performance in China: Beyond resistance in the 1990s.* (Doctoral dissertation, The Ohio State University). ProQuest Dissertations and Theses. (Accession No. AAT 3088877).

Oakes, T. (1993). The cultural space of modernity: Ethnic tourism and place identity in China. *Environment and Planning C: Society and Space, 11*(1), 47–66.

O'Connor, J., & Wynne, D. (1996). Introduction. In J. O'Connor & D.Wynne (Eds.), *From the margins to the centre: Cultural production and consumption in the post-industrial city* (pp. 1–14). Brookfield, VT: Arena.

Ohmae, K. (1990). *The borderless world: Power and strategy in the interlinked economy.* New York, NY: HarperBusiness.

Okely, J. (1996). *Own or other culture.* London, England: Routledge.

Redmon, D. (2003). Playful deviance as an urban leisure activity: Secret selves, self-validation, and entertaining performances. *Deviant Behavior, 24*(1), 27–51.

Rees, H. (2000). *Echoes of history: Naxi music in modern China.* Oxford, England: Oxford University Press.

Robertson, R. (1992). *Globalization as a problem.* London, England: Sage.

Rock, J. (1947). *The ancient Na-Khi kingdom of Southwest China.* Cambridge, MA: Harvard University Press.

Rosenberg, B., & White, D. M. (Eds.). (1957). *Mass culture: The popular arts in America.* Glencoe, IL: The Free Press.

Salazar, N. B. (2005). Tourism and glocalization: "Local" tour guiding. *Annals of Tourism Research, 32*(3), 628–646.

Salazar, N. B. (2006). Touristifying Tanzania: Global discourse, local guides. *Annals of Tourism Research, 33*(3), 833–852.

Schieffelin, E. (1998). Problematizing performance. In F. Hughes-Freeland (Ed.), *Ritual, performance, media* (ASA Monographs 35, pp. 194–208). London, England: Routledge.

Sherlock, K. (2001). Revisiting the concept of hosts and guests. *Tourist Studies, 1*(3), 271–295.

Smith, V. (1977). *Hosts and guests: The anthropology of tourism.* Philadelphia, PA: University of Pennsylvania Press.

Su, X., & Teo, P. (2009). *The politics of heritage tourism in China: A view from Lijiang.* London, England: Routledge.

Teo, P., & Li, L. (2003). Global and local interactions in tourism. *Annals of Tourism Research, 30*(2), 287–306.

Urry, J. (1990). *The tourist gaze: Leisure and travel in contemporary societies* (1st ed.). London, England: Sage.

Urry, J. (2002). *The tourist gaze* (2nd ed.). Thousand Oaks, CA: Sage.

Urry, J., & Larsen, J. (2011). *The tourist gaze 3.0.* London, England: Sage.

Wang, Y. (2011). 文本 现象 文化 媒介批评视野中的印象丽江 [Text, phenomenon, culture, on Impression Lijiang in the view of media criticism]. 四川教育学院学报 [Journal of Sichuan College of Education], *27*(4), 68–70.

Warde, A. (1994). Consumption, identity formation and uncertainty. *Sociology*, *28*(4), 877–899.

Wu, X. (2003). 纳西古乐是什么东西? [What is Naxi Ancient Music?]. 艺术评论 [Arts Criticism], *1*, 21–26.

Yang, H. (2009). 丽江本土文化产业的调查与总结—以纳西古乐、东巴宫为例 [Research and summary on local cultural industry of Lijiang: Case study of Naxi Ancient Music and Dongba Palace]. 民族艺术研究 [Ethnic Art Study], *4*, 37–45.

Zhu, Y. (2012a). Shifting tourism images: The world heritage site Lijiang, China. *Heidelberg Papers in South Asian and Comparative Politics*, *67*, 58–68.

Zhu, Y. (2012b). Performing heritage: Rethinking authenticity in global tourism. *Annals of Tourism Research*, *39*(3), 1495–1513.

Culture-Based Interpretation of Vacation Consumption
度假旅游消费的文化释义

XIAOXIAO FU
XINRAN Y. LEHTO
LIPING A. CAI

Drawing on typologies of consumption values, this study identifies and interprets the cultural divergence reflected in vacation experience. Through analysis of reviews by tourists from China and the United States, three salient themes of vacation experience emerged: scenery, food, and social interaction. Although all three aspects were addressed by both Chinese and American tourists, a closer look revealed that they had been assessed from quite different perspectives. The divergence in values is found to be instigated by unique cultural dispositions, which in turn links to tourist behavioral characteristics. Findings from the current research would help destinations in providing services to Chinese tourists.

Both societies (the United States and China) believe they represent unique values. . . . China's exceptionalism is cultural. It is the heir of the Middle Kingdom tradition.

Henry Kissinger in *On China* (2011, xvi)

Introduction

Since its inception, the notion of consumption values has drawn significant interest in the field of consumer choice behavior. The theoretical framework, along with many subsequent typologies of value perceptions (Holbrook, 1999; Sweeney & Soutar, 2001), have been validated across a variety of consumption settings, including consumer goods (Kim, Forsythe, Gu, & Moon, 2002; Tse, Wong, & Tan, 1988) and service businesses (Long & Schiffman, 2000). Though attempts have been made to explore cross-cultural differences in the context of retailing (Gnepta & Petrosky, 2001), empirical evidence of cultural divergence in the tourism setting has been rare. Vacation, as a tourism product, is an experience. The intangible, experiential nature of a vacation experience suggests that the appreciation of a destination is likely to stem from subjective interpretations. This subjectivity, in turn, can be influenced by an individual's cultural background; culture and values are critical in shaping consumers' lifestyles, motivations, and preferences (Tse, Francis, & Walls, 1994). Understanding cultural differences that account for unique consumption values is important for delivering quality experience to consumers in the travel marketplace.

The rise of emerging markets, such as Brazil, Russia, India, and China (BRIC), has been shown by the significantly growing roles that these countries play in the globalized market (Enderwick, 2007). Marketing theories and practices developed in conventional contexts are being challenged, as acknowledged by Sheth (2011) two decades after he proposed the consumption values framework. Sheth noted that these economies, along with their aspirations, will move from the periphery to the core of the global market and thereby change the landscape of many industries. As one of the BRIC countries, China has experienced phenomenal growth in outbound tourism. The World Tourism Organization (WTO, 2001) has forecast that by 2020 China will produce 100 million outbound tourists, ranking fourth with respect to market size. A recent *Wall Street Journal* article (LaVallee, 2011) noted that Chinese consumers are pushing the country to top Japan and become the largest market for luxury goods in 2011. Therefore, the booming influx of Chinese tourists in the global marketplace is expected to bring economic benefits to destination countries in a number of ways. Though outstanding opportunities have been acknowledged, challenges arise, because the majority of studies about this market are limited due to their descriptive nature (Hsu, Cai, & Li, 2010). In particular, knowledge on what constitutes a valuable consumption experience for the Chinese is mostly lacking. Chinese values have been recognized as different from those of Westerners (Doctoroff, 2005). Some studies have argued that Chinese values have been transformed by the rise of consumerism (Gerth, 2010), whereas others have maintained that the millennia-old cultural heritage is still entrenched in many spheres of Chinese life and its deep influence cannot be easily eradicated (Lin & Wang, 2010). As a result, the value frameworks developed in the Western context may not account for the uniqueness of consumption values of Chinese consumers. In addition, different interpretations may arise based on the same framework. With such a backdrop, this research intends to analyze tourists' valuations of a vacation experience. This assessment was conducted by contrasting Chinese tourists with American tourists. Similarities and differences in consumption values were examined through analysis of textual data of customer reviews of their experiences in two comparable destinations. The underlying cultural influences of such phenomenon were identified and examined.

Literature Review

Consumption Values

Consumption values are defined as perceived utilities delivered by a choice alternative (Tse et al., 1988) and serve as justification for the actual purchase of products and services (Xiao & Kim, 2009). Sheth, Newman, and Gross (1991) identified five different dimensions of consumption values that affect consumer choices and eventual satisfaction. Revolving around a choice's utility, the five domains of value are functional value, social value, emotional value, epistemic value, and conditional value. *Functional value* refers to a product's practical attributes. *Social value* is the value associated with a certain status or perception that helps the consumer fit into a social group. *Emotional value* compels the consumer to make a purchase when certain feelings are evoked by an alternative. *Epistemic value* drives market choices by motivating the pursuit of novelty, new knowledge, and new experience. *Conditional value* relates to the situational capacity that certain products satisfy, such as seasonal or a special occasion. The framework of consumption values has been tested and evidenced across various settings. Most recently, Hallem and Barth (2011) assessed the multidimensional values in a medical tourism context. Based on a thematic analysis that consisted of 208 postings on a health forum, functional value was identified as the major contributor to the overall perception of the medical tourism experience. However, the researchers argued that the importance of other values, such as social dimensions, to the overall experience should not be neglected.

The dimensions of consumption values also laid the groundwork for many subsequent studies that aimed to develop value measures (Boksberger & Melsen, 2011). Furthering Sheth and his colleagues' (1991) conceptualization, researchers have proposed a number of typologies of values perceived in consumptive situations, such as functional value, social value, and emotional value (Sanchez, Callarisa, Rodriguez, & Moliner, 2006; Sweeney & Soutar, 2001) and utilitarian, social, and hedonic value (Rintamaki, Kanto, Kuusela, & Spence, 2006). As one of the most cited conceptualizations, Sweeney and Soutar developed a 19-term measure to assess the perceived value of consumer goods. As a result, four distinct dimensions were identified: functional value (price), functional value (quality), emotional value, and social value. Similarly, Sanchez et al. proposed a scale of measurement for post-purchase perceived values. Based on evaluations of a tourism package, the measure consisted of six dimensions: functional value of the travel agency, functional value of professionalism, functional value of quality, functional value of price, emotional value, and social value. Assessing the perceived value of department store shopping, Rintamaki et al. developed a three-dimensional measure for shoppers. The dimensions are utilitarian value regarding monetary savings and convenience, social value concerning status and self-esteem, and hedonic value relating to entertainment and exploration. P. T. Chen and Hu (2010) reviewed many typologies of values identified by previous research and determined functional value and symbolic values as two major dimensions among existing classifications. Apparently, consumers perceive value in terms of both functional aspects and symbolic aspects when assessing the quality of goods and services consumed. In terms of functional values, previous studies have used labels including *utilitarian, monetary, price, quality, convenience,* and *efficiency.* Symbolic dimensions, on the other hand, emphasize nonfunctional aspects of values including hedonic, aesthetic, social, emotional, and reputational features. Based on a sample of 949 coffee shoppers, P. T. Chen and Hu found that both functional and symbolic values influenced postconsumption satisfaction and served as strong predictors of customer loyalty.

Research on value has established value's linkage with satisfaction and loyalty (P. T. Chen & Hu, 2010; Hu, Kandampully, & Juwaheer, 2009) and seems to support the proposition that positive post-purchase evaluation of a product is reflective of a product experience where consumption values are fulfilled. Yet, if values differ cross-culturally, one may assume that similar products may not necessarily yield the same level of satisfaction. This assumption has been assessed in a consumer product context in which Chinese and Korean female shoppers were compared concerning their value perception of apparel (Kim et al., 2002). However, there is a lack of literature on utilizing value typologies to understand the consumption experience in a vacation context.

Culture and Consumption Values

Culture, defined as "socially acquired behavior patterns common to the members of a society" (Sheth et al., 1991, p. 45), has been seen to have a strong influence on consumption values. As a product of subjective interpretation, value is a culturally driven phenomenon and needs to be understood in a broad cultural context. A certain value that is interpreted as prominent in one culture may not be the same in another. For instance, in an empirical study conducted among 356 participants from three countries (154 from the United States, 109 from France, and 93 from the Ivory Coast), social value was relatively more salient for Ivorian youth when buying jeans. In the same consumptive situation, their French and American counterparts were driven by the emotional dimension (Gnepta & Petrosky, 2001). The authors pointed out that the Ivory Coast was more socially conservative than France and the United States and that there may be limits on when Ivorian consumers could wear jeans. As such, their consumption values were largely affected by cultural norms.

Although it is difficult to describe a national culture for the United States due to its size and diversity (Mill & Morrison, 2009), Americans generally focus on individual values, including life, liberty, and the pursuit of happiness as stated in the Declaration of Independence. As a result, American tourists have demonstrated travel behaviors such as love of originality, desire to be near culture, freedom to move, and individual-ism (Pizam & Mansfeld, 1999). Chinese culture, on the other hand, emphasizes the importance of hierarchy, relationships, and social harmony as conveyed by Confucianism (Markus & Kitayama, 1994). In a society that gives prominence to social order, customers may hold different consumption values as opposed to their American counterparts. Previous studies that attempted to explain Chinese culture are largely based on the framework of individualism and collectivism (Hofstede, 1980; Triandis, 1995). However, the framework may not comprehensively explain Chinese behavioral characteristics because it focuses on addressing China as a collectivist society and fails to take into account other dimensions in Chinese value systems. Dating back in history, Chinese culture has been a fusion of cross-flowing ideas and beliefs. Much philosophical thinking has emerged since the Zhou dynasty (1045–256 BC) and has had profound influences on social and political changes in China. Pan (1990) proposed a dual structure for Chinese culture in which "humanism and monarchy, rationalism and ritualism, individualism and collectivism restrained and interpenetrated each other to form a special stability" (p. 75). Lin and Wang (2010) further claimed that Chinese culture is heterogeneous in nature, with contradictory and conflicting values often coexisting. To illustrate, the authors noted that the values of thriftiness and extravagance, self-constraint and self-expression, and asceticism and political engagement are shared by both elite and grassroots groups. Hence, Chinese consumption values may have unique aspects that demand further scrutiny.

Objectives of the Study

Within the context of vacation experience, no study has investigated the consumption values of Chinese and American tourists, especially the potential commonalities and divergences demonstrated among island vacationers from the two cultures. Consequently, the objectives of the study are to examine the interpretation of consumption values by comparing and contrasting tourists' reviews of their island experiences and to explore whether any differing interpretations were related to underlying cultural influences. The specific goals are (a) understand Chinese tourists' consumption values of their vacation experience in Hainan, as reflected in online reviews; (b) understand American tourists' consumption values of their vacation experience in Puerto Rico, as demonstrated in online reviews; (c) compare and contrast the differences in the interpretation of an island experience; and (d) understand the differences in interpretation from a cultural perspective.

Methodology

The current study utilized inductive thematic analysis to analyze vacation experiences evaluated by Chinese and American tourists, with the aim of uncovering major vacation experience themes with consumption value differences and cultural differences. Inductive thematic analysis was defined by Braun and Clarke (2006) as a bottom-up way of coding data without attempting to fit data into a preexisting framework or researchers' analytic preconceptions. The technique starts with line-by-line coding to identify emerging patterns and then to organize patterns into descriptive categories or themes. The outcome of inductive thematic analysis is to propose a series of analytical themes that represent reviewers' interpretation of the data (Thomas & Harden, 2008). In other words, the data analysis leads to the generation of themes that are abstract and analytical enough to explain all of the initial descriptive categories or themes.

Data Collection

Two destinations, Hainan, China, and Puerto Rico, United States, were chosen for the analysis because they are comparable in many aspects. Geographically, they are both tropical islands. Additionally, both are popular vacation destinations within their respective regions. Puerto Rico and Hainan are versatile destinations that are categorically similar, embracing both natural and cultural/historical resources. Puerto Rico possesses natural and cultural resources (Puerto Rico Convention Bureau, 2012). Similarly, the official Web site of the Hainan government promotes a variety of popular nature- and culture-oriented theme travels (People's Government of Hainan Province, 2012).

The data were gathered from five customer review Web sites, including tripadvisor. com, virtualtourist.com, lonelyplanet.com, elong.com (Chinese), and ctrip.com (Chinese), as well as 10 travel blogs maintained by individual tourists. The data collection phase was conducted during a 3-month period from September to

November 2010. A Google search was conducted to identify the commonly used tourist review Web sites according to Google-based ranking and popular travel blogs depending on both ranking and visitor numbers. Virtually any review that was posted on the listed sources during the period of time was eligible to be chosen. The sampling process, following the chronological order of the publishing date, started with the first eligible entry. Guided by the research aim, keywords related to the evaluation of the island experience were recorded. The step was repeated on the subsequent entries. When similar keywords reoccurred, they were tentatively grouped into subthemes. As the analysis proceeded, the subthemes were continuously refined and keywords regrouped to allow new themes to emerge. For instance, the most frequently utilized keywords or phrases were captured, such as "pure," "friendly," and "drinks are the highlight of the trip." Keywords or phrases related to similar content were grouped into subthemes— for instance, "pure nature," "pristine," and "untouched beauty"—were grouped under "scene." Six subthemes were categorized further into main themes. To illustrate with an example, "scene," mentioned by American tourists, and "spots," mentioned by Chinese tourists, were integrated into the broader theme of "scenery." This process continued until the data became saturated and further data did not lead to the discovery of additional themes. This resulted in 100 entries created by tourists from each country and the average length of the reviews was 100 words.

The primary investigator, who is fluent in both Chinese and English, systematically conducted line-by-line analysis of textual data following an open-coding process. A recruited team including one Chinese graduate student and one American graduate student assisted in the first-order analysis to verify the baseline keywords. In the second- and third-order analyses, all of the researchers of the present study participated in discussion to reach consensus on theme generation and to avoid imposing preconceptions on the data. Both English and Chinese were used to conduct data analysis. Reviews contributed by Chinese tourists were initially analyzed in Chinese and the findings including keywords and themes were later translated into English by the primary investigator for the purpose of reporting. To validate, all of the researchers of the current study translated the results back into Chinese to compare the two versions. This back-translation procedure helps ensure an accurate prose translation rather than a literal English language translation (Brislin, 1983; Werner & Campbell, 1970).

Results and Discussion

Three major domains of themes emerged from the data. They are scenery, food, and social interaction. For each theme, data were further examined contextually with regard to their unique value representations for the two cultures. Figure 1 illustrates these themes and divergent points noted by Chinese tourists and American tourists.

Scenery

Scenery is a prominent theme that was noted by both American and Chinese tourists. Both groups value scenery with a vacation experience. This is not surprising given that the importance of scenery in drawing tourists has been attested to repeatedly in previous literature. According to Mill and Morrison (2009), scenery has been a universal attribute that "serves as the primary definition of the attractiveness of a destination" (p. 18). Though emphasis on the functional and practical features of a destination experience is salient and consistent across the two cultures, how and why the scenery pleases tourists

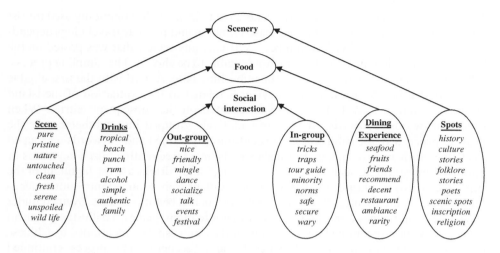

Figure 1. Theme identification of vacation experience.

appear to be somewhat different. American tourists appear to appreciate the pristineness of nature. Their enjoyment encompasses the "pureness" of a place that is in its "organic" state. Following are some of the comments from American tourists:

> It was almost therapeutic if you ask me. The air is cleaner, the water is fresher, and it's just absolutely pure nature.
>
> The rain forest is almost peaceful, serene, and even more beautiful because of its untouched nature.
>
> It is hard to sum up in words the experience . . . magical, euphoric, pure joy, untouched beauty all don't quite suffice. It's one of those places that you feel "in the know" for experiencing; like it is a long kept secret, a hidden door and that you somehow found the key.

Chinese tourists, on the other hand, seem to expect man-made spots at the site of a natural scene. In Hainan, Chinese tourists demonstrate a substantial liking for natural attractions that are stamped with a legend or stories of renowned people in history, such as Nanshan Buddhist Culture Garden and *Tian Ya Hai Jiao* (end of the sky, edge of the sea), which witnessed political exile of many literati in history. Following are some of the comments from Chinese tourists:

> We went to visit two iconic attractions in Hainan, Sanya Nanshan Buddhist Culture Garden and *Tian Ya Hai Jiao* as scenic spots. We heard the two are a must-see for tourists to Hainan. Upon entering the Culture Garden, we felt instantly the splendor and grandeur of Buddhist culture. The quintessence of Nanshan is the statue of the Goddess of Mercy, 108-meter tall and surrounded by the sea in three directions. The Goddess wears a gentle and affable look. It was spectacular indeed.
>
> The spot of *Tian Ya Hai Jiao* has picturesque scenery. Virtually a couple of rocks (with inscription of intellectuals), but the meaning is different. With the combination of beach, palm trees, water, and inscriptions, the scene's worth a visit.

From the perspective of functional value, the pursuit of scenery can be found among both American and Chinese tourists. Nevertheless, the specific attributes that are considered valuable seem to diverge. American tourists appreciate the scene from a more nature-oriented perspective. The pure, untouched, and pristine landscape is of more interest. Chinese tourists appear to find greater interest in the peripheral and contextual elements of natural scenery, specifically the cultural and historical touches on nature. The cultural and historical attachment to the natural scenery is an important part of the expected performance and adds to the value of the site. American tourists are pleased by geological features in their purest form; the fewer human touches, the better. Chinese tourists, however, do not derive the same level of satisfaction if there is no story associated with it, although the human touches can be either tangible, such as a temple in the mountain, or intangible, such as a legendary figure associated with the mountain. The keywords and phrases tourists use to describe their experience are different as well. American tourists tend to use direct descriptors to support their valuations, whereas Chinese tourists rely on peripheral and contextual information to give meaning to the experience.

Such divergence of consumption values can be better understood from a broader cultural perspective. Westerners embrace the idea of nature, untainted and untouched by civilization (Mertens, 2008). In the American mind, as Cronon (1996) indicated, wilderness speaks for "the last remaining place where civilization, that all too human disease, has not fully infected the earth" (p. 67) and is often compared to Eden. Pure and authentic, wild areas are seen as an escape from the perpetual urban chaos brought by industrialization. In fact, the idea of wilderness has been promoted by resorts as a selling point in their marketing scheme, illustrated by "the incomparable Mameyes River, the only river in Puerto Rico untouched by the hands of men" (Rio Mar Beach Resort & Spa, 2010) and "Niihau island, visit this pristine island, untouched by development and crowds" (Niihau Helicopters Inc., 2010).

For Chinese tourists, the interpretation of the natural scenery takes a perspective. They see the human and historical touch as an integral part of the landscape, as evidenced by the Chinese proverb *Shan Bu Zai Gao, You Xian Ze Ming* (The mountain does not have to be magnificent as long as there's a story behind it). Chinese tourists look for a combination of scenery and history. In fact, a Chinese idiom equates attractions with *Ming Sheng Gu Ji* (scenic spots and historical relics), which perceives both scenery and history as a coherent whole. In Chinese travelogues, *Jing Dian* (scenic spot) is a recurring topic. Chinese tourists emphasize the *Dian* (spot) aspect, whereas American tourists focus on the *Jing* (scene). Emphasizing the *Dian* aspect, the story behind the mountain is considered the focal point of the experience. To the Chinese, the scene is expected to be a well-developed and culturally armed area to be appreciated by tourists. Therefore, the vacation experience should include visits to a list of established and administrated entities even if it is a nature-oriented attraction.

Food

Food is another salient and recurring theme addressed by both American and Chinese tourists. To those from the United States, the variety of tropical drinks in Puerto Rico is a "must-have" element to add to the exotic island feel:

> Best thing I did in Puerto Rico . . . all you can drink rum-punch, Medalla beer, and pina coladas, made fresh with Don Q rum (the ONLY rum Puerto Ricans drink).

> One of the things I enjoyed the most about staying in the Condado area was the number of places we could go to in the evening just to grab a drink.

Yet the quest for food is not as important. American tourists are satisfied with simple local food:

> Another great find was the Starbucks in the lobby. They carried all the usual drinks, but what we enjoyed was the homemade local pastries.
> Fantastic experience, great simple food! The food is simple and authentic. Order the bacalito a coco frio and see if you can find a spot on the beach on a downed palm tree to sit and enjoy.

Their Chinese counterparts tend to demand more sophistication regarding food. Chinese tourists appear to place higher importance on the dining experience. The value of a vacation experience seems to be more closely associated with their experience with food. The valuation of food experience is much more integrated with the overall vacation experience. In their trip reflections, Chinese tourists discussed their food experiences more frequently than their American counterparts.

> After I came back, I still miss the seafood I had in Hainan. When I was in Sanya, the most important thing I did was to try the seafood.
> Food isn't much. We were tricked into buying sour fruits after sampling some extremely sweet samples. It was a disastrous trip. I vow not to go back if I could help it.
> The restaurant is famous for its petite bourgeois atmosphere. You can tell this from the luxury cars parked out front. People who dine here must be decent. There are also shows so we were entertained with folk songs and dances while savoring the fine seafood. It is pricy, but in a place like this you don't need to worry about sanitation issues.

In addition, the food experience has much higher social connotations and values for the Chinese tourists than the American tourists. The Chinese tourists' reflections on their food experiences were much more illustrative of the perception that food helps the consumer fit into a social group (Sheth et al., 1991). For instance, Chinese tourists mentioned that they would try exotic dishes so they can boast about the experience to their social circle upon return to their homeland:

> Even before we left home for Hainan, we planned to try some rare, expensive seafood, which in Beijing is sold for over one thousand RMB [US$155] per kilogram. After returning home, we were able to tell our friends about the stuff we tried in Hainan.

Unlike Chinese tourists who dwelled on the food aspect, American tourists place relatively more emphasis on the functional value of drinks. Drinking plays an important role in American vacation culture (Gusfield, 1987; Room, 1984) and it is often associated with the beachfront destination experience. In comparison, the Chinese quest for a quality dining/food experience seems to be driven by social value. Focusing on social and symbolic image rather than utilitarian performance, Chinese tourists seem to link the social value of dining to the enhancement of self-concept (Sheth et al., 1991; Sweeney & Soutar, 2001). In Chinese trip reviews, a close link was shown between the image of social self and food experience because food is symbolic of status in Chinese culture. The rapid growth in the economy today has made the finest food, once only available to the dominant class, attainable to the general public. Therefore, the Chinese are eager to get a taste of the status and prestige once assumed by the hierarchy, as frequently mentioned by Chinese tourists: *Fu He Shen Fen* (Fit into my social status). Therefore, food is valued by Chinese tourists beyond its functional value and is more closely associated with the symbolic dimension.

Social Interaction

Both American and Chinese tourists reported certain levels of social interaction that occurred during vacation. Travel literature from the perspective of Americans demonstrates that tourists are motivated to interact with one another as well as with the locals. Such encounters are often found to be pleasant experiences according to many reviews:

> Caribe Playa Beach Resort is a great place to mingle with other guests if you need some social interaction.
> The street festival has many friendly people. When I asked a man if I could take his picture, he was happy to allow me.
> Casa Armstrong is where the locals go. If you want to meet some locals, then this is the definite place for you.

Chinese tourists, however, seem to exercise a higher degree of caution while interacting with locals. Tourists in package tours usually choose to stay close to their group:

> We were told that tourist traps are a common part of tourism here. Also, the local customs are different so we chose to stay in the hotel at night.
> I am very interested in knowing about the authentic culture and customs of the Li ethnic group on Hainan Island. But I was not sure where to go. There are many negative reports about them online.

According to Sheth et al. (1991), novel knowledge or experience provides epistemic value to a consumer. Such value can be persuasive when the consumer is curious about participating in new social activities or desires to experience another culture. It is evident that both American and Chinese tourists have expressed interest in exploring while vacationing at an island destination. For American tourists, voluntary interaction with local people and culture contributed to the overall experience. They looked for a good local crowd to meet with, as stated in a testimonial from a tourist, "The place has a good mixture of locals and tourists. I highly recommend it! I went there almost every night when I was in San Juan." From the Chinese point of view, curiosity about local culture and customs is also notable, but such desire is often accompanied by a feeling of caution and distrust. Some tourists reported negative social experiences, based on which they evaluated the whole vacation as "very bad." X. Chen, Rubin, and Sun (1992) pointed out that certain social behaviors positively valued by Western society may not be as appreciated in Chinese culture. Chinese people, especially grassroots, are encouraged to be cautious and sensitive (X. Chen et al.) toward a foreign social environment but cooperative and friendly within their "in group" (Yum, 1988, p. 81).

Again, this can be better understood from the broader perspectives of historical and cultural influences in Chinese society, one that had been a centralized feudal state for centuries. Unlike Western societies, which implement Montesquieu's theory of separation of powers, for centuries China has honored the ultimate right of the emperor and the subsequent social hierarchy. In such a structure that defines social boundaries, people tend to be more cautious and more in-group oriented as a means of protecting their self-interests.

Conclusion

The present study aimed to identify and interpret the cultural divergence between American and Chinese tourists in consumption of an island vacation experience. Through analysis of travel literature by tourists from both countries, three major themes emerged from an island vacation experience: scenery, food, and social interaction. Although both groups of tourists addressed similar themes, a closer examination showed that the assessment of an island vacation experience is quite culture specific. The current research sought to understand this phenomenon in light of differences in consumption values in a broader context of cultural influences. For instance, though there is a universal appreciation of beautiful scenes, Chinese tourists appear to be more drawn to the human footprints and touches upon nature than their American counterparts. American tourists seem to have a more direct appreciation and interpretation of the natural scenery, whereas Chinese tourists rely more on historical and human validations for valuation. Cultural differences in the valuation of food and drinks in the food experience between the two countries' tourists seem to be quite palpable. American tourists emphasize the functional aspect of food; the Chinese tend to see more social functions for food and dining. Additionally, the food experience appears to be regarded as a more critical component of a satisfactory vacation experience for Chinese tourists compared to American tourists. In the interactional sphere, both American and Chinese tourists are driven by epistemic value, but the latter act with more caution toward locals. Examined cross-culturally, these divergences attest to different cultural contexts. For instance, the functional role of scene and food in providing gratification varies little across cultural groups, but the symbolic aspects of scene and food and the way people interpret their meanings in specific cultural contexts may vary significantly.

Though exploratory in nature, the findings from the present study extend current literature on consumption values by identifying major themes for clearer interpretation of values in a vacation setting. The value assessment reflected in the dimensions corroborate existing studies that nonfunctional values can also be important contributors to overall satisfaction (P. T. Chen & Hu, 2010; Sanchez et al., 2006). Therefore, a more holistic vision on values is needed to analyze functional values as well as experiential or symbolic values. As Gilbert (1991) identified travel as "a special form of consumption behavior involving an intangible, heterogeneous purchase of an experiential product" (p. 98), valuation of vacation consumption would demand scrutiny to account for its intangible and interactive nature. Furthermore, certain values that appear universal to some extent may suggest markedly different connotations across cultures. For instance, though functional values of scenery are commonly acknowledged, American tourists focus on the pleasure obtained from pure nature, but Chinese tourists appreciate the landscape.

In addition to generating a framework for enhanced understanding of consumption values in a vacation setting, the present findings provide managerial implications for industry practitioners. How to accommodate the influx of increasing Chinese tourists has become a task facing destinations vying for this lucrative market. Chinese tourists are becoming more sophisticated and look forward to not only quality service but also cultural understanding (Li, Lai, Harrill, Kline, & Wang, 2011). The present study is expected to help marketers and operators better interpret the cultural preferences and translate them into marketing guidelines that can be applied at a more concrete level, such as how to focus strategic resources in designing programs that correspond to certain values to produce a desired experience economically. For instance, marketing strategies can revolve around the legendary stories of a mountain when targeting the Chinese, thereby attracting interested tourists.

Limitations and Future Research

The present study has certain limitations that need to be taken into account when considering its contributions. First, the two destinations are comparable but not identical. Therefore, the divergent discovery could be due to specific physical features unique to the destinations under examination. Future research may focus on one specific location to compare and contrast tourists' interpretations of the vacation experience. Second, this study identified and interpreted major themes and values about vacation experience based on customer review data collected from several public domains. Very limited demographic information was available through the method used to conduct the research. Undiscovered demographic information such as gender, age, and travel patterns could potentially account for sources of variances in the data.

Marketing practitioners and researchers have demonstrated a growing interest in customer experience management, especially in a globalized market where different values may exercise distinct effects on consumer behavior. The current study constitutes a first step toward understanding tourists' consumption valuation of an island experience from a cultural perspective. Future studies are needed to further the understanding of island experience domains and may also investigate other cultural, social, and/or environmental factors that account for divergence and/or convergence in consumption values. The identified themes, values, and underlying cultural reasons may lay the groundwork for subsequent quantitative approaches that could be used to validate the themes and values revealed by the present study.

References

Boksberger, E. P., & Melsen, L. (2011). Perceived value: A critical examination of definitions, concepts and measures for the service industry. *Journal of Service Marketing, 25*(3), 229–240.

Braun, V., & Clarke, V. (2006). Using thematic analysis in psychology. *Qualitative Research in Psychology, 3*(2), 77–101.

Brislin, R. W. (1983). Cross-cultural research in psychology. *Annual Review of Psychology, 34*, 363–400.

Chen, P. T., & Hu, H. H. (2010). The effect of relational benefits on perceived value in relation to customer loyalty: An empirical study in the Australian coffee outlets industry. *International Journal of Hospitality Management, 29*(3), 405–412.

Chen, X., Rubin, K. H., & Sun, Y. (1992). Social reputation and peer relationships in Chinese and Canadian children: A cross-cultural study. *Child Development, 63*(3), 336–343.

Cronon, W. (1996). The trouble with wilderness: Or, getting back to the wrong nature. *Environmental History*, *1*(1), 7–28.

Doctoroff, T. (2005). *Billions: Selling to the new Chinese consumer*. New York, NY: Palgrave Macmillan.

Enderwick, P. (2007). *Understanding emerging markets: China and India*. New York, NY: Routledge.

Gerth, K. (2010). *As China goes, so goes the world: How Chinese consumers are transforming everything*. New York, NY: Hill and Wang.

Gilbert, D. (1991). An examination of the consumer behaviour process related to tourism. In C. Cooper (Ed.), *Progress in tourism, recreation and hospitality management* (pp. 78–105). London, England: Belhaven Press.

Gnepta, T. J., & Petrosky, A. (2001). Cross-national comparison of consumption values: A center-periphery perspective. *Journal of International Consumer Marketing*, *14*(2/3), 73–99.

Gusfield, J. (1987). Passage to play: Rituals of drinking time in American society. In M. Douglas (Ed.), *Constructive drinking. Perspectives of drink from anthropology* (pp. 73–91). Cambridge, England: Cambridge University Press.

Hallem, Y., & Barth, I. (2011). Customer-perceived value of medical tourism: An exploratory study—The case of cosmetic surgery in Tunisia. *Journal of Hospitality & Tourism Management*, *18*(1), 121–129.

Hofstede, G. (1980). *Culture's consequences: International differences in work-related values*. Beverly Hills, CA: Sage.

Holbrook, M. B. (1999). *Consumer value: A framework of analysis and research*. London, England: Routledge.

Hsu, C., Cai, L. A., & Li, M. (2010). Expectation, motivation, and attitude: A tourist behavioral model. *Journal of Travel Research*, *49*(3), 282–296.

Hu, H., Kandampully, J., & Juwaheer, T. (2009). Relationships and impacts of service quality, perceived value, customer satisfaction, and image: An empirical study. *Service Industries Journal*, *29*(2), 111–125.

Kim, J.-O., Forsythe, S., Gu, Q., & Moon, S. J. (2002). Cross-cultural consumer values, needs and purchase behavior. *The Journal of Consumer Marketing*, *19*(6), 481–502.

Kissinger, H. (2011). *On China*. New York, NY: The Penguin Press.

LaVallee, A. (2011). China to overtake Japan in luxury demand. Retrieved from http://blogs.wsj.com/japanrealtime/2011/09/06/china-to-overtake-japan-in-luxury-demand/

Li, X., Lai, C., Harrill, R., Kline, S., & Wang, L. (2011). When East meets West: An exploratory study on Chinese outbound tourists' travel expectations. *Tourism Management*, *32*(4), 741–749.

Lin, X., & Wang, C. L. (2010). The heterogeneity of Chinese consumer values: A dual structure explanation. *Cross Cultural Management*, *17*(3), 244–256.

Long, M. M., & Schiffman, L. G. (2000). Consumption values and relationships: Segmenting the market for frequency programs. *The Journal of Consumer Marketing*, *17*(3), 214–232.

Markus, H., & Kitayama, S. (1994). A collective fear of the collective: Implications for selves and theories of selves. *Personality and Social Psychology Bulletin*, *20*(5), 568–579.

Mertens, R. (2008, September–October). Can't see the forest for the trees. *The University of Chicago Magazine*. Retrieved from http://magazine.uchicago.edu/0810/features/the_forest.shtml

Mill, R. C., & Morrison, A. M. (2009). *The tourism system*. Dubuque, IA: Kendall/Hunt Publishing Company.

Niihau Helicopters Inc. (2010). Niihau Island, the forbidden island. Retrieved from http://www.niihau.us/heli.html

Pan, J. (1990). The dual structure of Chinese culture and its influence on modern Chinese society. *International Sociology*, *5*(1), 75–88.

People's Government of Hainan Province. (2012). *Theme travel in Hainan*. Retrieved from http://en.hainan.gov.cn/englishgov/Travel/SightSeeing/Theme/index.html

Pizam, A., & Mansfeld, Y. (Eds.). (1999). *Consumer behavior in travel and tourism*. New York, NY: The Haworth Hospitality Press.

Puerto Rico Convention Bureau. (2012). *Puerto Rico at a glance*. Retrieved from http:// meetpuertorico.com/Puertorico/Default.aspx?c=35&m=11&activemenu=0&activesubmenu=1

Rintamaki, T., Kanto, A., Kuusela, H. & Spence, M. T. (2006). Decomposing the value of department store shopping into utilitarian, hedonic and social dimensions. *International Journal of Retail & Distribution Management, 34*(1), 6–24.

Rio Mar Beach Resort & Spa (2010). Tours and sightseeing. Retrieved from http://www. wyndhamriomar.com/recreation/tours.html

Room, R. (1984). A "reverence for strong drink": The lost generation and the elevation of alcohol in American culture. *Journal of Studies on Alcohol, 45*(6), 540–546.

Sanchez, J., Callarisa, L., Rodriguez, R. M., & Moliner, M. A. (2006). Perceived value of the purchase of a tourism product. *Tourism Management, 27*(3), 394–409.

Sheth, J. N. (2011). Impact of emerging markets on marketing: Rethinking existing perspectives and practices. *Journal of Marketing, 75*(4), 166–182.

Sheth, J. N., Newman, B. I., & Gross, B. L. (1991). *Consumption values and market choices*. Cincinnati, OH: South-Western Publishing Co.

Sweeney, J. C., & Soutar, G. N. (2001). Consumer perceived value: The development of a multiple item scale. *Journal of Retailing, 77*(2), 203–220.

Thomas, J., & Harden, A. (2008). Methods for the thematic synthesis of qualitative research in systematic reviews. *BMC Medical Research Methodology, 8*(45), 1–10.

Triandis, H. C. (1995). *Individualism and collectivism*. Boulder, CO: Westview.

Tse, D. K., Francis, J., & Walls, J. (1994). Cultural differences in conducting intra- and inter-cultural negotiations: A Sino-Canadian comparison. *Journal of International Business Studies, 25*(3), 537–555.

Tse, D., Wong, J., & Tan, C. T. (1988). Towards some standardized cross-cultural consumption values. *Advances in Consumer Research, 15*(1), 387–395.

Werner, O., & Campbell, D. T. (1970). Translating, working through interpreters, and the problem of decentering. In R. Naroll & R. Cohen (Eds.), *A handbook of cultural anthropology* (pp. 398–419). New York, NY: American Museum of Natural History.

World Tourism Organization. (2001). *Tourism 2020 vision: Vol. 7. Global forecasts and profiles of market segments*. Madrid, Spain: Author.

Xiao, G., & Kim, J. O. (2009). The investigation of Chinese consumer values, consumption values, life satisfaction and consumption behaviours. *Psychology & Marketing, 26*(7), 610–624.

Yum, J. O. (1988). The impact of Confucianism on interpersonal relationships and communication patterns in East Asia. *Communication Monographs, 55*(4), 374–388.

The Behavior of Citing: A Perspective on Science Communication Across Languages

援引行为: 一种跨语言科学传播的视角

HONGGEN XIAO
QU XIAO
MIMI LI

This article addresses the perceptions and behavior of Chinese tourism researchers citing foreign language sources in (for) their own studies. Theoretically sensitized to notions of dissemination of knowledge and science communication, and departing from the ongoing measurement of citation impacts, the study adopts a qualitative approach to the scrutiny of citer perceptions and behavior in the instances of citing sources from other languages. Observations and narratives from in-depth interviews with 24 active Chinese tourism researchers amply speak of the dynamics, politics, subjectivity, and at times irrationality of citing from foreign languages. In particular, the inductive analysis complements traditional scientometric perspectives on citation impacts and provides insights into the motivation, perceived benefits, facilitation, and constraints, as well as (re)presentations of cited ideas in the observed instances of science communication in tourism.

Why We Cite What We Cite

"If I have seen a little further it is by standing on the shoulders of the giants."
(Sir Isaac Newton, 1676, p. 416)

Though the connotations of this quote are associated with the rationality of citing for scientific discoveries, the denotations along with its quintessence and idiosyncrasy of citations for knowledge development are often equally implied beyond the words. The sociology of knowledge asserts that the practice of citations reflects the norm of a scientific community to acknowledge not only intellectual connections but also community values such as humility, recognition, and rewards of scholarly work (Merton, 1957, 1961; Mulkay, 1977). More explicitly, citations are developed into indices both as a standard measure and as a technology to generate "an ordered list of cited articles accompanied by a list of citing ones" (Garfield, 1964, p. 650) to indicate impacts in the scientific community (Garfield, 1979a, 1979b). In an increasingly pragmatic world driven by publishers and academic journals, and with the commercialization of institution-based research and the call for accountability of investment through ubiquitous research assessment exercises, the counting and measurement of citations as impact factors of research have gradually evolved into a flourishing business for publishers, an indicator of prestige for journal editors and published authors, and, consequently, served as the basis of a variety of ranking and rating systems. Nevertheless, as a norm of the researching and authoring community, little is known of the behaviors of citers, particularly in the postmodern contexts of science communication facilitated by information and communication technologies (e.g., Internet, search engines, open-access journals), the mobility of researchers across cultural/linguistic boundaries, and the ever-increasing popularities of learning foreign languages for academic purposes.

This article focuses on the perceptions and behaviors of citers, their subjectivity and irrationality of citing, and, consequently, the controversies or issues surrounding citations from foreign languages, which have been subjects of interest among academics for many years and from different disciplines. In documentation and science communication literature, a number of irrational factors have been identified of authors citing what they cite for (or in) their research (Martyn, 1975; Weinstock, 1971). Cronin (1981, 1982), in the theorizing of citation as the norm of a scientific community, described it as "a private process with a public face" (1981, p. 16), in which the underlying reason of why an author cites what he does appears to have always remained a matter of conjecture due to subjectivity in the very act of citing. In their scrutiny of the economics literature, Beed and Beed (1996) reported citation instances ranging from the usefulness of comprehensive literature reviews, to critiques of authorities, to the "halo effects" of citing Nobel Prize winners, and to highly personal idiosyncrasies such as "helping the citer get a job where the cited is in a position of authority" (p. 380). These authors further observed that, in economics, different schools of thoughts, opposing paradigms, and even nationalities of journals can influence the citation of a publication. More recently, in feminist geography, Raju (2006) reported on instances of looking for "theory" in "familiar" faces in which non-Anglophone authors publishing in English feminist journals "have been pushed not only for more theory but for more references to particular theories or theorists currently popular in the Anglophone literature" (p. 156). In addition, there are epistemic discussions on citations and impacts of knowledge in pertinence to behaviors such as self-citations (i.e., an author citing his or her own works), negative citations (i.e., citing a source for the purpose of criticism or refutation), and incidences of sheer uncertainty in which a source not cited in one time period may well be cited in another and vice versa (Broadus, 1971; Price, 1965; Xiao & Smith, 2008).

That citer behaviors have defied reason has also been remarked in tourism studies. For example, in their attempt to rank journals on the basis of a citation analysis, Pechlaner, Zehrer, Matzler, and Abfalter (2004) noted that "citation counts are heavily affected by the popularity of specific research topics and areas within an academic community" (p. 329). Dann (2005), in his harsh criticism on the presentation of literature review in tourism research, referred to citations as mindless trawls through recycling, stirring, and pick-and-mix strategies, in which the irrationality of citing is characteristic of a Teutonic treatise syndrome,

> . . . where authors believe that they have to exhaust a topic totally by overloading their texts with *de rigueur* footnotes and references (some to works which they have never read). Then there are less than useful "catch all" citations (e.g., the collected works of Karl Marx) and obscure quotations (from unpublished or out of print materials, non-academic esoteric sources and unverifiable personal communications with the intellectually rich and famous). There is also an (unwitting?) tendency for some scholars to over-quote persons from their own discipline, nationality and tongue. (In the latter regard, tourism research seems to be dominated by monoglot Anglophones who are either unwilling or unable to learn another language, and hence are blissfully unaware of what is taking place elsewhere in the world). Then there are those individuals who over-cite works published in the same journal as their piece appears, or from books which are advertised in that journal and/or have been sent to them as examination copies. However, perhaps the worst trend of all is to refer unduly to their own published and unpublished material (auto-citation), in which no one else may be even remotely interested. (p. 5)

To a large extent, the above observation on irrationality of citing is also true of dissemination or science communication across linguistic communities in tourism (Xiao, Su, & Li, 2010). In a recent small-scale e-mail survey personally addressed to some of the most cited/most downloaded authors listed on the Websites of leading hospitality and tourism journals, we found that though top citation is indicative of quality in terms of originality, contribution to knowledge, practical value, solid designs and rigorous methods, and clarity of presentation, which largely echo the reports of Seaton (1996) and Yuksel (2003), what is perhaps more interesting and pervasive is the participants' narratives on the irrational features of citers. For example, one U.S.-based author, in response to the probe on why his e-word-of-mouth paper is top cited, noted this:

> [T]here is really nothing special about the paper, other than it caught a hot topic early and we were lucky to get it into a top journal. I think I have done lots of far better work, this article, conceived by a marketing professor, introduced a topic into the tourism literature before the wave of popularity began to crest. And then with the I think overdone value we put on literature

reviews, everyone that follows seems inclined to mention that we were among the first to discuss the topic, rarely indicating that the paper offered anything particularly insightful, which, if you go back and read today, you will learn it did not. It just came early. (From the researchers' "top-cited authors" e-mail survey, November 1, 2011 to February 18, 2012)

Furthermore, in a recent trinet (Tourism Research Information Network) posting on citation as science communication, Kozak (2011) initiated a discussion on ethical concerns of journal editors requesting a publishing author to cite their own journals in terms of acknowledging or building on prior research on the same subject published in the same outlets. In response to this discussion, Ryan (2011) further reiterated the situation, which to him is

> . . . all the more dismaying when this practice is sought by what many might regard as the more senior journals, and is a reflection of the wider environment whereby the intangibles of knowledge creation and dissemination are being forcibly measured by research assessment exercises.

Nonetheless, the argument could also be reversed to the favor of journal editors in that a publishing author on a certain topic should fully build his or her work on prior studies published on the same subject and therefore prior sources yet to be cited could be fully recognized or acknowledged in his or her forthcoming research. As Rennie (2011) put it in support of this position,

> . . . it is standard to place your work in the relevant literature and so I think it is automatic if one is aiming a publication for a particular journal to have some reason for doing so—usually to continue a conversation with other authors/readers in/of that journal—therefore one would logically have referred to articles in that journal.

In tourism, though the irrational behaviors of citers have often been—albeit largely in an anecdotal fashion—discussed (e.g., in trinet postings and at seminar or conference discussions), the subject has nevertheless hardly ever been scrutinized on any empirical grounds, especially the instances of researchers in one language community citing authors or sources in (or from) another language community. In the recent small-scale e-mail survey on top citations alluded to above, one participant working in a Greek institution expressed his concerns about publishing research in non-Anglophone outlets and its consequential citation impacts from English readership:

> This is a major issue that we face here in Greece. For example, if somebody publishes an excellent paper in Greek it is highly unlikely that the paper will be ranked high in terms of citation indexes, etc. simply because few researchers speak Greek at an international level. Does this mean that we should publish only in English? Certainly not! (From the researchers' "top-cited authors" e-mail survey, November 1, 2011 to February 18, 2012)

To a large extent, this has remained a concern for tourism researchers writing and publishing in other non-English communities. As reported by Xiao et al. (2010) on the situation in Mainland China, there has been a remarkable increase over the last 10 years of its researchers citing foreign sources in and for their studies published in the top three Chinese tourism journals. Nevertheless, the rationales and motivations underlying these citations of foreign language sources have remained largely unknown. Notably, though citation counts, rankings, and impacts have been widely documented, hardly ever have any enquires been reported on citer behaviors relying on empirical grounds in the context of science communication across languages.

Building on and departing from the above discussions, the purpose of this article is to examine the perceptions and behaviors of Chinese tourism researchers citing foreign language sources in their studies and to report on their motivations, perceived benefits, and the associated (re)presentational concerns underlying their instances of citing from foreign languages. In so doing, we hope to open up an alternative discussion on citations as science communication in pertinence to citers' perspectives and the quintessential yet undisclosed nature of academic authors citing sources of references from foreign languages.

Chinese Researchers Citing Foreign Language Sources

This study adopts a qualitative analysis to examine the perceptions and behaviors of Chinese citers using foreign language sources in (or for) their tourism research. The inductive/interpretive approach is deemed appropriate due to the exploratory and subjective (and at times irrational) nature of citer behavior and their attitudes toward citing what they cite. In-depth interviews with open-ended questions were used as the study's data collection strategy because they allow flexibility of probing for details and extending to related issues contextually emerged along the interviewer–participant interactions. Though the interviews were conducted and transcribed in Chinese, the researchers' bilingual preparation and familiarity with the Chinese tourism research community facilitated the analysis and interpretation of findings in English.

The Interview and Inductive Analysis

An instrument with broad enquiries was used as a guide for in-depth interviews. To serve the purpose of this study, the open-ended questions pertained to (a) citers' perceptions of Chinese tourism researchers using foreign language sources in their studies (e.g., What is your view of Chinese tourism researchers citing foreign language sources?); (b) whether and why a citer uses foreign language sources in his/her research (e.g., In writing and publishing tourism research in Chinese, do you cite foreign language sources in your own work? Why or why not?); (c) the contexts or circumstances of foreign language citations (e.g., Under what circumstances do you cite foreign language sources in your own research? From what languages, which disciplines or specialized fields, and which media or outlets do you cite foreign language sources? Do you regard your instance or frequency of citing as high, moderate or low compared to your peers?); and (d) citers' opinions of using translated instead of original texts in their foreign language citations (e.g., What is your opinion of Chinese tourism researchers citing translated versus original texts in their research writings?). Probes or follow-up questions were prepared to ensure the depth of enquiry and richness of information generated around these broad enquiries.

The interviews, with durations ranging from 30 to 90 minutes, were conducted with 24 tourism researchers in Mainland China around May 2010 to August 2011. All of the informants were active researchers who publish (or are required to publish) on a regular basis either to complete their research degree or to build strong publication records for promotion and academic career development. Among these informants, we selectively contacted 10 of them for their interest in participating in this study and secured their availability before making our research trips to actually conduct the interviews. In addition, 14 interviews were completed prior to, during, or after the investigators' several conference trips to Mainland China in the past year and a half. Though demographics were not taken at their face value in this analysis, Table 1 presents a background of the interview participants in terms of their research training, disciplinary affiliation for teaching and research, as well as their areas of interest and major publication outlets. For the sake of anonymity, the interviewees' institutions are not reported in this analysis. In addition, to facilitate the reading of this article by its intended (English) readership, the interview participants were assigned pseudonyms, in common English first names, in the following analysis.

At the beginning of an interview, the participant was briefed about the purpose of the study and was made aware of ethics-related concerns such as confidentiality, anonymity, voluntary participation, and informed consent; permissions to tape record their talking and interactions were also sought prior to the start of an interview. The conversations were broadly centered around the aforementioned questions on citer behaviors and perceptions of Chinese tourism researchers citing foreign language sources. As the process of talking unfolded itself, theoretical sampling (Glaser & Strauss, 1967) was exercised as much as possible, where the interviewers listened to what was said and then decided on what issues to raise or what questions to probe next. If new ideas were expressed by a participant or responses to a query were inadequate or ambiguous, clarification was sought by inviting the participant to elaborate on his or her answers. In addition, the researchers also watched for "saturation" during the interview. For example, when ideas given by a participant tended to be repetitive or overlapping, the conversation was then shifted to another open-ended question or eventually to the closing of an interview.

All of the interviews were conducted and transcribed in Chinese for subsequent coding and analysis. To enhance trustworthiness of the study and assure accuracy of what was heard or said, all of the interview transcripts were cross-checked among members of the research team. In addition, member checks (Kirby & McKenna, 1989) were undertaken through e-mail attachments of these transcripts to their respective interviewees, which were positively responded by 17 of the 24 participants in terms of confirming, clarifying, and/or amending what was transcribed out of their previous conversations.

Subsequently, an inductive content analysis was conducted on these interview transcripts, through a three-stage systematic procedure of open, axial, and selective coding. According to Strauss (1987), open coding is the initial stage of unrestricted coding of the data to produce conceptual codes that seem to fit the data; axial coding consists of intense analysis and sorting of open codes around an "axis" to result in a hierarchically higher level of conceptual categories to achieve explanatory or theoretical fit; and selective coding pertains to coding toward the core to identify substantive themes emerged through the iterative and inductive process.

To facilitate this inductive analysis, the researchers first went through the interview transcripts several times to become familiar with the content before assigning labels, descriptors, or open codes to a passage in the transcript. Typically in the process of coding, keywords were highlighted, as were "in vivo codes" (Strauss, 1987, p. 33)— terms directly derived from the transcripts—watched for as terms of references. In

Table 1. Backgrounds of Interview Participants.

Participant/Department (Faculty)[a]	Areas of Interest/Publication Outlets
Jenny, aged 29, lecturer, PhD in Geo-mathematics, Faculty of History, Culture and Tourism (Guilin)	Interests in tourism geographies, geographic information systems (GIS), tourism economics, and ecology; mainly published in Chinese tourism and geography journals, occasionally published in English periodicals such as *Tourism Geographies* and *Geoinformatics.*
Stephanie, aged 34, lecturer, PhD in Cultural and Heritage Studies, Faculty of History, Culture and Tourism (Guilin)	Interests in cultural heritage and tourism development, ethnicity, and tourism; mainly published in Chinese tourism and cultural studies journals.
John, aged 37, lecturer, deputy head, Department of Tourist Guiding (Guilin)	Interests in ethnic tourism and tourism economics; mainly published in Chinese tourism journals.
Mark, aged 43, professor, deputy dean, PhD in Resources and Industrial Economics, Faculty of History, Culture and Tourism (Guilin)	Interests in tourist culture, resort development, tourism resources planning and development, tourist souvenirs, and geological parks; mainly published in Chinese tourism, geography, and cultural studies journals.
Peter, aged 30, PhD in Hotel and Tourism Management, Department of Tourism (Shanghai)	Interests in tour operation and management, tourism marketing, and consumer behavior; more often published in Chinese than in English-language tourism journals.
Steve, aged 29, PhD candidate in Tourism E-commerce, School of Management (Harbin)	Interests in e-commerce, e-tourism, information systems, and business intelligence; mainly published in Chinese tourism and tourism-related journals.
Emily, aged 27, PhD candidate in Tourism E-commerce, School of Management (Harbin)	Interests in e-commerce, e-tourism, and information and communication technology; hoping to get published in Chinese tourism and information technology (IT)-related journals.
Tony, aged 27, PhD candidate in Tourism Planning and Development, School of Tourism Management (Guangzhou)	Interests in theories and methodology, tourist behavior and marketing, and regional tourism planning and development; this author currently has articles under review by English-language journals.

Table 1. Continued.

Participant/Department (Faculty)[a]	Areas of Interest/Publication Outlets
Mathew, aged 44, PhD in History, professor, Department of Tourism Studies (Qingdao)	Interests in tourist culture, consumer behavior, cultural/heritage tourism, history, and tourist souvenirs; mainly published in Chinese tourism, history, and cultural studies journals, occasionally published in English-language journals.
Eric, aged 27, PhD candidate in Geography, College of Tourism (Fuzhou)	Interests in tourism geography, economic geography, and regional tourism planning and development.
Chris, aged 32, PhD in Tourism Planning and Development, associate professor, Tourism College (Shenzhen)	Interests in tourism geography, planning and development, tourism marketing, ecotourism, tourism resources, and tourism education; mainly published in Chinese tourism journals, occasionally published in English-language periodicals such as *Tourism Recreation Research* and *Asia Pacific Journal of Tourism Research.*
Angela, aged 36, MSc in Human Geography, lecturer, Department of Tourism (Fuzhou)	Interests in tourism planning and development and heritage tourism; mainly published in Chinese tourism and geography-related journals.
Tim, aged 48, PhD, associate professor, head of department, College of Tourism (Quanzhou)	Interests in resources planning and management, human and economic geography, and ecotourism; mainly published in Chinese tourism and geography-related journals.
Tom, aged 38, PhD in Management, associate professor, College of Tourism (Quanzhou)	Interests in regional tourism planning and development and marketing and management; mainly published in Chinese tourism and business-related journals.
Alice, aged 32, PhD in Tourism Management, associate professor, Department of Tourism (Fuzhou)	Interests in tourism marketing and management, ecotourism, event, sociology of tourism, and hospitality; mainly published in Chinese tourism and business-related journals.
Helen, aged 29, MSc in Tourism Policy and Planning, assistant professor, College of Tourism (Quanzhou)	Interests in leisure, tourism policy and planning, and governance of protected areas; mainly published in Chinese journals, sometimes in English-language periodicals such as *Environmental Management* and *Journal of China Tourism Research.*

(Continued)

Table 1. Continued.

Participant/Department (Faculty)[a]	Areas of Interest/Publication Outlets
Ada, aged 41, professor, PhD in Anthropology, School of Tourism Management (Guangzhou)	Interests in tourism anthropology, community tourism development, community participation, aboriginal community, and cultural identity; mainly published in Chinese journals relating to tourism, geography, and anthropology and sociology.
Leslie, aged 48, professor, head of hotel and tourism management department, College of Economics and Commerce (Guangzhou)	Interests in hotel management, tourism management, and human resources management; mainly published in Chinese tourism and hotel management journals.
Gloria, aged 45, professor, PhD in Management, College of Tourism (Beijing)	Interests in tourism and leisure studies; mainly published in Chinese tourism and leisure-related journals.
Henry, aged 42, PhD, professor and director of a tourism school (Guangzhou)	Interests in tourism resources, planning and development, and tourism in ethnic communities; mainly published in Chinese tourism and related journals.
Jason, aged 32, PhD in Tourism Management, lecturer, School of Tourism Management (Guangzhou)	Interests in hotel management, outbound tourism marketing, and tourism in ethnic communities; mainly published in Chinese tourism and hotel journals.
Murphy, aged 27, PhD candidate in Tourism Management, School of Tourism Management (Guangzhou)	Interests in community development, conventions and events, and tourism in ethnic communities; mainly submitted research to Chinese tourism journals.
Maggie, aged 41, associate professor, PhD candidate, College of Tourism (Guangzhou)	Interests in tourism management, ecotourism, and event management; mainly published in Chinese tourism journals.
Carolyn, aged 36, lecturer, PhD in Tourism Management, Department of Tourism (Wuhan)	Interests in regional tourism planning and development, ecotourism, and cultural tourism; mainly published in Chinese tourism and tourism-related journals.

Note.[a]Demographics of the participants were recorded as of the date of the interviews around May 2010 to August 2011. For anonymity, institutions of the interviewees are omitted in this table.

addition, the grounded theory approach emphasizes the centrality of an analyst being open to his or her data (Strauss & Corbin, 1998), in which the researchers tried to be freed from preconceived terms or notions in order to come up with as many open codes as possible (Saldaña, 2009). Labels with meaning similar to terms in the transcripts were used to allow voices of the participants to be heard. Moreover, intercoder consistency checks were performed to enhance confirmability in the process of assigning codes and developing categories (Lofland & Lofland, 1995).

In total, over 2,000 open codes resulted from these preliminary readings, which allow their grouping into some 40 descriptor headings under four broad perceptual/ behavioral categories (Table 2). Within each category, the descriptors are presented in the order of recurrences of their open codes mentioned or implied in the transcripts. Some nonrecurring labels or open codes were dropped during the grouping because of their irrelevance or vagueness in relation to this study.

Citations as Quality or Perceived Quality of Research

As it has inductively emerged from this analysis, Chinese tourism researchers view citations of foreign language sources as quality or perceived quality of research. Such perceptions hold not only in their behavior of citing a foreign language source when writing up their research but also in their decisions regarding or selections of a publishing outlet for their own work. It is believed that citations from foreign language sources will equip their work with international standards and global outlooks or perspectives and consequently enhance the quality of their articles, which will in turn be better received in the review and publication process. They tend to cite authoritative titles or credible sources from top-ranked journals or do so when targeting their research at top-quality periodicals. To a large extent, such associations with quality or perceived quality are rather widespread in the broader Chinese tourism research community, encompassing not only the publishing faculty themselves but also reviewers, journal editors, research students, and graduate supervisors. As Stephanie observed in her publication experience,

> The editors, particularly those of established tourism journals, would expect to see an article include foreign language citations in its references because they are evidence of a broad perspective on the topic at hand, and hence are signs of quality of research input, regardless of whether it makes a point or what they are really cited for. . . . (Stephanie, PhD in Cultural and Heritage Studies, January 19, 2011)

This observation on perceived quality was echoed by Jenny,

> If your article has too many Chinese references, its readers will think the issues are not addressed in an international context; the perspectives are too domestic or local. I just completed my doctoral research; my advisor suggested that I should have at least about 50% foreign language citations in my references. (Jenny, PhD in Geomathematics, January 19, 2011)

Interestingly the participants' perceptions of quality are often justified through comparisons of the Chinese research literature with foreign language sources for tourism studies. It is a recurring observation that academic literature in foreign languages

Table 2. Chinese Tourism Researchers Citing Foreign Language Sources: Conceptual Categories Derived from Coding.

Perceptual/Behavioral Categories	Descriptors and Open Codes[a]

Citations as Quality or Perceived Quality of Research	• ***Overall quality or perceived quality*** (e.g., better quality of research, perceived quality of a paper, editor's perception of research quality, favorable editor perceptions, Chinese editor's demand, more likely for a paper to be accepted if it cites more English articles).
	• ***Quality or perceived quality of journals*** (e.g., targeting at a top journal, submission to English journals, credible sources, citing well known journals, citing top-ranked journals vs lower ranked journals, the higher the rank of a journal, the more English citations required).
	• ***Quality or perceived quality of titles or articles*** (e.g., authoritative titles, credible sources, English articles following paradigmatic standards, articles following rigorous methodological process, more persuasive/informative/comprehensive titles, of international standards, of global outlook).
	• ***Comparisons of foreign and Chinese literature for tourism research***
	  – *Differences* (Foreign literature is better in theoretical studies, is more often driven by theory and supported by sophisticated methodology, is more mature, is more innovative, and is more difficult to understand because of technical terms, expressions, and ways of thinking. Chinese literature is easier to understand, has no methodology, and is of limited value but entirely necessary for tourism research).
	  – *Similarities in empirical research* (and hence cite less).

Motivation and Perceived Benefits of Citing	• ***An addition or perceived addition to research innovation, cutting edge research, new perspectives, international focus or standards*** (e.g., of a cited title being innovative research, authoritative viewpoints, foreign authority, seminal/influential titles, a must-read, original work/originality, classics, learning/borrowing from foreign countries, as a window to the outside world, keeping abreast of cutting edge research, broadening horizon, new perspectives, more comprehensive).

Table 2. Continued.

Perceptual/Behavioral Categories	Descriptors and Open Codes[a]
	• *Enhancing usefulness and contribution of a citer's research* (e.g., guiding Chinese practice, enhancing usefulness, changing ways of thinking, citation as search for points of dialogues, practical value of citing to solve problems, citation based on needs)
	• *Foreign citations as "demonstration or show"* (e.g., Other authors have cited foreign journal articles, see "I have reference entries in German", "blind citations" without much thought, "worshipping" attitudes towards foreign language citations)
	• *Citations as dissemination of knowledge*
	• *Facilitations of citing*
	– *Having access to sources* (e.g., asking friends who work at overseas institutions to help forward copies, internet resources, open access journals, having access to library resources, free access to database on campus, top universities having more subscription and access to journal/resource databases than lower-ranked universities, copying/downloading material when studying abroad)
	– *Having sufficient time to read*
	– *Incentives of citing* (e.g., reward of publishing in top journals).
	• *Constraints to citing*
	– *Time constraints* (e.g., no time to read, time-consuming to read, articles are too long to read, unwilling to spend time to read foreign language articles, length of journal articles, time restriction due to journal article length).
	– *Language constraints* (e.g., difficult to understand, seldom finished reading, English is not good enough, painful to read foreign sources).
	– *Constraints due to access* (e.g., limited/no access to foreign language journals and books, no access to original works, online journal databases are too expensive, need to pay a fee to use, limited/no institutional subscription to English journals and other reference databases, library resources are in low priority on university administrators' agenda, very troublesome, inconvenient to use, restricted to internal users only, copyright material).
	– *Publication requirements in Chinese journals* (e.g., lower requirements of publishing, little demand from publishing in Chinese journals, no research incentive).

(Continued)

Table 2. Continued.

Perceptual/Behavioral Categories	Descriptors and Open Codes[a]
	– (of not citing) *Multidisciplinarity as deferments to theoretical advancement, poor theoretical status in tourism.* • ***Other influences*** (e.g., research training, graduate studies, disciplinary traditions, supervisory requirement, norm of scholarship)
Circumstances, Instances, and Contexts of Citing	• ***What are they cited for?*** – *For literature review, critiques, research progress, annotated bibliography, basic/theoretical research.* – *Developing theoretical constructs, developing hypotheses, verifying theories in China contexts, identifying knowledge gaps, replication, adaptation, more citations on rigorous methodology, methodological applications, rigorous methods.* – *For doctoral studies, thesis proposals, dissertation research* (e.g., comprehensive exams, literature review for doctoral research, a requirement of citing 50% foreign literature for doctoral research, supervisor's encouragement and recommendation, "must-cite" for dissertation research) – *Tracing back to original sources* (e.g., beginning with an article on one topic and tracing back to references, tracing further back, tracing back to the first source). • ***Patterns and frequency of citing*** – *Few or fewer citations* (e.g., on well researched Chinese subjects, unique problems in China, applied or problem-based research). – *More citations* (e.g., on innovative or new subjects, on hot topics, of good industry practices in foreign countries). – *Paradoxical patterns of citations for exploratory or challenging topics.* • ***Databases and/for search*** – *Databases* (e.g., scientific databases, foreign reference databases, online/e-journal databases, SCI/SSCI-indexed journals, JSTOR, foreign databases, Elsevier Science Direct, ASP/BSP academic journals full article databases, ProQuest, SpringerLink).

Table 2. Continued.

Perceptual/Behavioral Categories	Descriptors and Open Codes[a]
	– *Web-based search* (e.g., google, by subjects, by topics, by keywords, by themes, most read journals, favorite books, credible sources, authoritative titles, internets, websites). – *Media types* (e.g., influential/international journals, more journals than books). • ***Journals as major sources*** – Annals of Tourism Research, Tourism Management, Journal of Travel Research, Management Information System Quarterly, Information System Research, Tourism Geographies, Geo-Informatics, Journal of China Tourism Research, International Journal of Contemporary Hospitality Management, Management Science, Journal of Management Information Systems, Leisure Studies, Journal of Leisure Research, Journal of Park and Recreation Administration • ***Disciplines, subjects and areas of interests*** – Tourists/Tourism/Tourism Management (e.g., new, multidisciplinary field), Business and Management (including marketing, human resources, industry), Geography/Tourism Geographies, Sociology and Anthropology (including ethnology, cultural studies), Environment and Ecology, Economics/Tourism Economics, Hospitality/Hotel Management, Psychology/Consumer Behavior, Urban Planning/Landscape/Resources, Public Administration/Governance/Politics, Geo-Mathematics/GIS, IT/E-commerce, (Tourism) Education, Festivals/Events, Humanities, Religion, History, Leisure
The Language of Citations	• **(Re)presentation of cited ideas** – *Translation and Interpretation* (e.g., sometimes misleading interpretation, translating abstracts). – *Citation, quotation, and acknowledgement* (e.g., foot notes, end notes, textual citations, direct quotes, using original sentences, indirect quotes, using translated sentences, paraphrasing, in your own words, rendering, presentation quality,

(Continued)

Table 2. Continued.

Perceptual/Behavioral Categories	Descriptors and Open Codes[a]
	rewriting, amendments, reference styles, citation formats, using one's own translation, using well-established translations by other authors).
	– *Deviant behavior of citing* (e.g., plagiarism, citing a title without actually reading it, cut and paste, citing what others have cited without reading a title, distortion and misinterpretation).
	• **Source languages of cited titles**
	– *Primarily from English and occasionally from other languages* (e.g., Japanese, French, German).
	– *Indirect citations from other languages.*
	• **Attitudes towards original versus translated texts**
	– *Predominantly favoring original texts*
	– *Translated texts are largely used as secondary options* (e.g., when there is no other choice; original texts are not available; translated texts are seen as inaccurate/imprecise; too much interpretation or rendering by translators; poor translation; difficult to read and understand; translationese or tones of translation; even more difficult to read than original texts).

[a]Categorical descriptors and open codes are presented in the order of recurrences in the interview transcripts.

clearly outperforms the Chinese counterpart in theoretical richness, methodological sophistication, originality and innovation, and paradigms or ways of thinking. Consequently, conceptual titles and theoretically laden sources are more often cited than empirical ones, where greater similarities are perceived to have existed in the body of literature (despite in different languages). For example, in contrasting English against Chinese tourism literature, Peter noted,

> Readings from English journals almost exclusively follow the structure of a research article and thus represent a kind of rigor or standard, whereas research articles in Chinese journals are often presented as a reflection piece with no methodological processes reported. (Peter, PhD in Hotel and Tourism Management, May 30, 2010 to June 14, 2010)

Motivations and Perceived Benefits of Citing

In addition to quality perceptions, the participants reported that citing foreign language sources helps enhance innovation, creativity, and the usefulness of their research. They admitted that borrowing from foreign literature not only keeps them abreast of cutting-edge research and hence broadens their horizons but also practically helps them solve problems or guide tourism practice in China.

Again, it is often through comparison and contrast with the Chinese research literature that perceived benefits of citing foreign language sources are reported; these include, and are not limited to, the usefulness of foreign literature for review discussions and critiques, preparing annotated bibliographies, developing theoretical constructs and hypotheses, verifying and testing theories in Chinese contexts, identifying knowledge gaps, and replicating models or research designs. As noted by Emily,

> That the Chinese literature is weak in methodology has been an issue of discussion for many years. As a bilingual researcher, the advantages of reading English sources are quite obvious. You learn not only new ideas and perspectives, but are also impressed by the way a research is designed, organized and delivered to its readership. As a result, you got some inspirations for adopting unique approaches to doing your own studies. On the contrary, the Chinese literature is easier to understand and is, relatively speaking, of lower use as a source of reference in my work. (Emily, PhD Candidate in Tourism E-commerce, May 30, 2010 to June 14, 2010)

From a science communication perspective, citations are good examples of dissemination of knowledge across linguistic communities, which was discussed rather philosophically by Mark when he remarked on using East(ern) or West(ern) as prefixes to disciplines or specializations and its consequences on citations by (or dialogues with) authors from the other language community. When probed on the query of whether Chinese tourism researchers citing theories from Western economics could be seen as replication, verification, or falsification of established propositions in an eastern context, Mark responded,

> It will have brought up a very philosophical discussion to address this. I personally do not agree with the term of "Western Economics" [a subject title very often seen in university curricula in China] as this would imply that there is also an "Eastern Economics." In fact, economic theories, including its hypotheses and propositions, are postulated in such a way that they can be of general applications, regardless of the east or the west. I think this has created a concern about citing classic economics sources from English for review discussions in Chinese articles. (Mark, PhD in Resources and Industrial Economics, June 24, 2011)

In this study, a number of factors were found to have exerted an influence over an author's citing foreign language sources in his or her own research. Primarily these include his or her research training or graduate studies, disciplinary traditions, supervisory requirements, as well as norms of scholarship of the scientific community he or she is working in. In particular, the informants see (a) access to library resources and databases, (b) time for academic reading, and (c) foreign language proficiency for reading comprehension as essential or determining factors in understanding the behavior of citing foreign language sources. Notably, as admitted by many of the participants, possession of the above resources or competence would greatly facilitate the instances and frequency of such citations, whereas the lack of which would act as constraints to citing. Mathew, in his recollection of the agony and amount of time consumed by reading research articles in English, shared with us:

> In a great ambition [with a tone of pride], I once searched, downloaded and printed more than thirty articles on tourist souvenirs. However, the reading of them was extremely painful. Most of these articles were 20–30 pages in length, plus embedded ideologies and difficult terms that slowed down the reading and reduced its comprehension. For many articles, I was actually not able to completely read the whole piece. For quite many others, I have never found time to give them a read, not even today. (Mathew, PhD in History, May 30, 2010 to June 14, 2010)

Moreover, a number of other factors were noted either as an incentive/facilitator of citing (e.g., the reward of having research published in a top journal) or as a constraint to citing (e.g., lower requirements or less demand for publishing in Chinese journals, the multidisciplinarity of tourism as deferments to theoretical advancements).

Notably some deviant citing behaviors were reported by the study participants. In this regard, citations from foreign languages were sometimes viewed as a kind of demonstration or show on the part of the author, as Alice (PhD in Tourism Management) cheerfully remarked, "See! I have references in German, French, Japanese, and English." Other such behaviors include Ada's (PhD in Anthropology, May 30, 2010 to June 14, 2010) observation on "citing a title without actually reading it" or "citing indirectly from other authors without actually referencing to the original source" (which, according to this informant, is particularly true of seminal/influential works). Similarly, Carolyn (PhD in Tourism Management, May 30, 2010 to June 14, 2010) variously referred to these as "blind citations without much thought" or "worshipping attitudes towards foreign language citations"; "citing from a translated text without acknowledging the original"; or, worse still, "rendering or interpreting ideas in the authors' own words without due acknowledgements"; and, worst of all, "plagiarism or cut and paste."

Circumstances, Instances, and Contexts of Citing

Much of the interview conversation dealt with the circumstances, instances, or contexts within which the informants themselves or their peers actually cited a foreign language source in writing up their research. In addition to the repeatedly alluded circumstances of usage such as developing review discussions, building theoretical constructs, crafting research hypotheses, etc., citations of foreign language sources are often found to be used for doctoral studies (e.g., in comprehensive exams), thesis/dissertation research, and developing grant proposals. As noted by Steve (PhD candidate) and Mark (doctoral supervisor), some academic institutions have made it part of their programs' foreign language requirement, albeit informally, that their candidates must cite in their overall references about 50% foreign literature for their doctoral research,

> For doctoral studies in this program, we [the candidates] all understand that our references should include half English and half Chinese for doctoral proposal and final thesis. It has almost become a tradition which is passed down from previous years and observed by us all with

no major complaints. (Steve, PhD candidate in Tourism E-commerce, May 30, 2010 to June 14, 2010)

With respect to the circumstances and patterns of usage, the interview results seem to suggest that citations of foreign language sources are associated with the nature of a research subject. For unique problems in China or issues well researched by Chinese academics, fewer citations are borrowed from the outside, whereas a higher frequency of citing foreign language sources is reported in the instances of Chinese research addressing a subject or topic that is hot, cutting-edge, of currency, controversial, or new or innovative. Nevertheless, it is also interesting to note a paradoxical pattern of citations pertaining to exploratory or challenging topics.

Databases used in the search of foreign language sources are typically those of institutional library subscriptions such as e-journals from various international scientific databases. With the widespread use and ever-increasing capacity of personal computers as well as remote access to institutional library e-resources, worldwide webs supported by various search engines and searched in different terms have become the main access to scientific literature published in foreign languages. Henry, in appraising the usefulness of foreign electronic databases such as Elsevier Science Direct, JSTOR, ProQuest, SpringerLink, etc., commented,

> I've learned that my university (and other universities too) are reluctant to spend money on subscription to foreign electronic databases. While I can understand the priority of the administrators, we have to admit the usefulness of having adequate foreign electronic databases for our ongoing research. Indeed they are good complements to the China National Knowledge Infrastructure (CNKI; http://www.cnki.net). (Henry, PhD, professor and director of a tourism school, May 30, 2010 to June 14, 2010)

Notably, as can be seen from Table 2, academic journals, particularly internationally influential periodicals in a specialized field, have been the major sources of such citations. Chinese tourism researchers have cited foreign language publications from a wide range of subject areas by disciplines, subjects, and areas of interests, which is not a surprise in view of the multidisciplinarity of tourism.

The Language of Citations

As narrated by the interview participants, the primary source language of foreign citations by Chinese tourism researchers is English, despite their occasional consultation of literature from other languages such as Japanese, French, or German. In addition, dissemination from foreign languages other than English is made possible through indirect citations such as reading and referencing to translated texts.

The (re)presentation of ideas cited from foreign language sources has resulted in interesting observations in this inductive analysis. In responding to queries pertaining to how (in what ways) citations are used to construct their own research, the informants speak of quotations, interpretations, and/or translations in their citing behavior. Due to the distinctiveness of the two language systems (i.e., Chinese as a Sino-Tibetan versus English as an Indo-European system), the (re)presentation of "borrowed" ideas in a citer's work has taken up a variety of forms such as using original sentences intact through direct quotes and using translated sentences through paraphrasing or rendering in a citer's own words as in the instances of most indirect quotes. However, the former—inserting English quotes directly into a Chinese article—only occurs occasionally due to concerns about reader receptions and publication styles (as in the instance of a central quote or message that may lose its essence through Chinese translations). In recalling her prior attendance of a forum with Chinese editors and publishers, Maggie (PhD candidate in Tourism Management, May 30, 2010 to June 14, 2010) shared her view on publishing a Chinese text with too many foreign language inserts:

> Editors and publishers tend to discourage overuse of English quotes or sentences, as frequent appearances of these may defy the sole purpose of the text as a typical Chinese publication.

With respect to citing original ideas through authors' self-translation, contrasting views were expressed. As noted by John (lecturer, deputy head of a tourism department), "Interpretation or rendering is likely to incorporate the citers' own imaginations or ideas and to result in inaccuracy or poor loyalty to the original text because of distortion, twisting, or misinterpretation." On the contrary, Chris (associate professor, PhD in Tourism Planning and Development, May 30, 2010 to June 14, 2010), in responding to the probe on how he (re)presented ideas originally published in English, suggested,

> Self-interpretation is practically useable and useful with proper acknowl-edgement as it is less acceptable to overuse original/English sentences in a Chinese article.

Nevertheless, he cautioned about excessive use of self-interpretation under the disguise of citations from foreign sources, particularly for quotes from classics or seminal works of which well-established Chinese translations have been in existence.

Another issue of relevance to the (re)presentation of "borrowed" ideas pertains to the citation of China-related research done by foreign scholars and published in other languages. As alluded to by Eric (PhD candidate in Geography, May 30, 2010 to June 14, 2010),

> Research published by foreigners on China issues may well serve as an outsider/complementary perspective, which the insiders, mainland Chinese scholars, may be unaware of if they are not incorporated through citations.

Furthermore, in view of the difficulties and challenges in reading English articles, the participants were solicited for their preferences or opinions on using original versus translated texts in their instances of citing. Most participants reported their preference of original texts to translations; the latter for many will only be used as secondary or optional sources when original texts are not available. In recalling her experience of reading a translated text on governance in the planning and development of protected areas, Helen (assistant professor, MSc in Tourism Policy and Planning, May 30, 2010 to June 14, 2010) joked,

> The translationese or tones of translation makes the Chinese text even more difficult to understand than the original one.

Citation as Science Communication Across Languages

In reflections and prospects, this study reports on the perceptions and behaviors of Chinese tourism researchers citing foreign language sources in (for) their own work. The research adopts a qualitative/inductive approach, through in-depth interviews of 24 active researchers, to the scrutiny of the dynamics, politics, subjectivity, and at times irrationality of citing from foreign languages. Inductive analyses of the interview transcripts shed light on the motivation, perceived benefits, facilitations and constraints, as well as the (re)presentations of borrowed ideas in the observed instances of Chinese tourism researchers citing from foreign languages. The discussion also complements the current measurement-oriented scientometric perspectives on citation impacts.

Results of the study lend to discussions on citation as science communication across languages. A number of observations can be made on the basis of these in-depth interviews with Chinese researchers. Notably, citations from foreign language sources are perceived as an enhancement to the quality of research, yet a citer's decision to cite (or not to cite) often rests upon his or her understanding, often through comparisons and contrasts, of the research literature published in Chinese versus that published in foreign languages. In addition to research preparation and graduate training, a citer's access to foreign language databases or resources, language proficiency or competence, and his or her availability of time for academic reading act as facilitators of (or conversely, as constraints to) citing foreign language sources. Moreover, the (re)presentation of cited ideas in a citer's work and its associated concerns for plagiarism or interpretation with no due acknowledgement conjure up additional issues in the scrutiny of science communication across languages.

As an echo to Xiao et al. (2010), disseminations of knowledge through citations across languages are likely to increase (or expand) in the overall tourism research community worldwide, due to the enhanced status of English as a lingua franca in today's international scientific communication (Ortiz, 2011), the further breakdown of barriers to (or boundaries of) language communities resulting from the entry into the academy by the younger generation of tourism researchers, and the improved access to research information facilitated by Internet. As a result, the fragmented tourism research communities carved out by languages are likely to remain more open to one another through science communication by means of young non-English scholars acquiring research degrees from overseas/English institutions, scholarly visits and exchanges, research collaborations, and, above all, the consultation (or citation) of each other's publications.

Contextually, the call for a scientific community to remain open is not new. Studies in the sociology of knowledge demonstrate that for a research community to remain open is imperative and conducive to productivity, creativity, and innovation because scientific discoveries are more likely to occur in an open (than in a closed) community (Garvey & Griffith, 1967; Hagstrom, 1965; Kulkarni & Simon, 1988; Merton, 1957, 1961; Mulkay, 1977; Tuire & Erno, 2001). In contrast, parochialism, looking inward, or walling-in at the evolution of a research community can be potentially dangerous (Jafari, 2005; Pearce & Butler, 2010; Xiao, 2007), as March (2004) pointed out in the case of organization studies,

> The maintenance of a differentiated structure of beliefs and practices within a small, homogeneous community enforces standards and yields the

elegance of a refined domain of knowledge. However, such cohesion is potentially self-destructive. As a community develops loyalty towards its own members it encourages a conflation of familiarity with quality. The same sense of community that brings refinement and consensus also brings an in-group bias. (p. 15).

As a citation context analysis, this study offers a perspective on the cultural and perceptual–behavioral aspects of citing from foreign languages, which is somehow overlooked in the current scientometric citation impact analysis (Danell, 2012). The study helps understand the dynamics and politics of citing foreign language sources for Chinese tourism research; in the meantime, the study has brought up additional problems that cannot be addressed in a single undertaking.

Though some of the issues pertain to the study's limitations, others may well serve as avenues for future inquiries. First and foremost, the observations reported in this qualitative analysis are context specific and are not intended for generalization. For example, for the sake of operating the term and in view of its sociocultural differences from places such as Hong Kong, Macau, Taiwan, and Singapore, "China tourism research" is rather narrowly defined in this study as the sociolinguistically charted community of tourism researchers who reside in Mainland China and primarily read and write in Chinese. Consequently, narratives and accounts from this induction should only be read as such.

Moreover, the interview participants are largely young and multidisciplinary (tourism-related) researchers; many of them have had international contacts via overseas research/exchange/study experiences. Although it was in our interview plan, we did not succeed in recruiting some senior tourism researchers as informants in the study implementation (due to lack of interest or unavailability). Presumably, contrasting views or different stories on citations from foreign languages could be told by traditional/disciplinary academics or researchers writing at different stages of their publishing careers.

In addition, science communication across languages is typically a two-way interactive and diachronic process of information flow and knowledge exchange. This study nevertheless has only focused on one way of the knowledge traffic from a synchronic perspective. Future research needs to also look at the instances of native English-speaking researchers citing from Chinese and/or other languages in their tourism research, as in the instances documented by Dann and Parrinello (2009) with respect to the origins and developments in the sociological treatments of tourism in several European languages.

In much the same way as variations from language communities, citer behaviors may as well differ from field to field. Future citation context analysis could also look at the instances of citing from foreign languages in the sister fields of hospitality, recreation and leisure studies, and even the emerging fields of convention and event studies. Last but not least, though the (re)presentation of cited ideas in a citer's work is of every relevance to this discussion, the associated concerns about plagiarism and infringements of copyright in science communication across languages are indeed beyond the scope of this scholarly essay.

Acknowledgments

This article is the result of a project funded by a grant from The Hong Kong Polytechnic University (A-PC1Z). We are thankful to the 24 active Chinese tourism researchers, without whose participation this study would not have been completed. The assistance of Liu Wei is also gratefully acknowledged.

References

Beed, C., & Beed, C. (1996). Measuring the quality of academic journals: The case of economics. *Journal of Post Keynesian Economics, 18*(3), 369–396.

Broadus, R. (1971). The literature of the social sciences: A survey of citation studies. *International Social Science Journal, 23*(2), 236–243.

Cronin, B. (1981). The need for a theory of citing. *Journal of Documentation, 37*(1), 16–24.

Cronin, B. (1982). Norms and functions in citation: The view of journal editors and referees in psychology. *Social Science Information Studies, 2*(2), 65–78.

Danell, J. (2012). Representation and negotiation of complementary and alternative medicine: A citation context analysis. *Science Communication, 34*(3), 299–333.

Dann, G. (2005). The theoretical state of the state-of-the-art in the sociology and anthropology of tourism. *Tourism Analysis, 10*(1), 3–15.

Dann, G., & Parrinello, R. (2009). *The sociology of tourism: European origins and developments.* Bingley, England: Emerald.

Garfield, E. (1964). "Science citation index"—A new dimension in indexing. *Science, 144*(3619), 649–654.

Garfield, E. (1979a). *Citation indexing: Its theory and application in science, technology and humanities.* New York, NY: Wiley.

Garfield, E. (1979b). Is citation analysis a legitimate evaluation tool? *Scientometrics, 1*(4), 359–375.

Garvey, W., & Griffith, B. (1967). Scientific communication as a social system. *Science, 157* (3792), 1011–1016.

Glaser, B., & Strauss, A. (1967). *The discovery of grounded theory: Strategies for qualitative research.* Chicago, IL: Aldine.

Hagstrom, W. (1965). *The scientific community.* New York, NY: Basic Books.

Jafari, J. (2005). Bridging out, nesting a field: Powering a new platform. *Journal of Tourism Studies, 16*(2), 1–5.

Kirby, S., & McKenna, K. (1989). *Experience research social change.* Toronto, Canada: Garamond.

Kozak, M. (2011, October 24–25). Trinet discussion: Journal editors' requests for self-citations Retrieved from Honolulu HI: University of Hawaii at Manoa listserv <trinet-1@lists.hawaii.edu>

Kulkarni, D., & Simon, H. (1988). The processes of scientific discovery: The strategy of experimentation. *Cognitive Science, 12*(2), 139–175.

Lofland, J., & Lofland, L. (1995). *Analyzing social settings: A guide to qualitative observations and analysis.* Belmont, CA: Wadsworth.

March, J. (2004). Parochialism in the evolution of a research community: The case of organization studies. *Management and Organization Review, 1*(1), 5–22.

Martyn, J. (1975). Progress in documentation: Citation analysis. *Journal of Documentation, 32*, 390–397.

Merton, R. (1957). Priorities in scientific discoveries: A chapter in the sociology of science. *American Sociological Review, 22*(6), 635–659.

Merton, R. (1961). Singletons and multiples in scientific discovery: A chapter in the sociology of science. *Proceedings of the American Philosophical Society, 105*(5), 470–486.

Mulkay, M. (1977). Sociology of the scientific research community. In I. Spiegel-Rosing & D. Price (Eds.), *Science, technology, and society: A cross-disciplinary perspective* (pp. 93–148). London, England: Sage.

Newton, I. (1676, February 5). A letter to Robert Hooke. In H. W. Turnbull (1959, Ed.), *The correspondence of Isaac Newton,* volume I (p. 416). Chicago, IL: The Royal Society at the University Press.

Ortiz, R. (2011). *The hegemony of the English language and the social sciences.* Retrieved from http://www.isa-sociology.org/global-dialogue/2011/09/the-hegemony-of-the-english-language-and-the-social-sciences/

Pearce, D., & Butler, R. (2010). Conclusions: Trends and advances in tourism research. In D. Pearce & R. Butler (Eds.), *Tourism research: A 20–20 vision* (pp. 229–237). Oxford, England: Goodfellow.

Pechlaner, H., Zehrer, A., Matzler, K., & Abfalter, D. (2004). A ranking of tourism and hospitality journals. *Journal of Travel Research*, *42*(4), 328–332.

Price, D. (1965). Networks of scientific papers. *Science*, *149*(3683), 510–515.

Raju, S. (2006). Production of knowledge: Looking for "theory" in "familiar" faces? *Geoforum*, *37*(2), 155–158.

Rennie, H. (2011, October 24–25). Trinet discussion: Journal editors' requests for self-citations Retrieved from Honolulu HI: University of Hawaii at Manoa listserv <trinet-1@lists.hawaii.edu>

Ryan, C. (2011, October 24–25). Trinet discussion: Journal editors' requests for self-citations Retrieved from Honolulu HI: University of Hawaii at Manoa listserv <trinet-1@lists.hawaii.edu>

Saldaña, J. (2009). *The coding manual for qualitative researchers*. Thousand Oaks, CA: Sage.

Seaton, A. (1996). Blowing the whistle on tourism referees. *Tourism Management*, *17*(6), 397–399.

Strauss, A. (1987). *Qualitative analysis for social scientists*. Thousand Oaks, CA: Sage.

Strauss, A., & Corbin, J. (1998). Grounded theory methodology: An overview. In N. Denzin & Y. Lincoln (Eds.), *Strategies for qualitative enquiry* (pp. 158–183). Thousand Oaks, CA: Sage.

Tuire, P., & Erno, L. (2001). Exploring invisible scientific communities: Studying networking relations within an educational research community. A Finnish case. *Higher Education*, *42*(4), 493–513.

Weinstock, M. (1971). Citation indexes. *Encyclopedia of Library and Information Science*, *5*, 16–40.

Xiao, H. (2007). 旅游科学社区尚需保持开放的格局 [The tourism research community should keep opening up its boundary in its evolution and growth]. *Tourism Tribune*, *22*(1), 8–9.

Xiao, H., & Smith, S. (2008). Knowledge impact: An appraisal of tourism scholarship. *Annals of Tourism Research*, *35*(1), 62–83.

Xiao, H., Su, D., & Li, M. (2010). Diffusion of knowledge across linguistic boundaries: The case of using "foreign" sources for tourism research in China. *Journal of China Tourism Research*, *6*(4), 326–342.

Yuksel, A. (2003). Writing publishable papers. *Tourism Management*, *24*(4), 437–446.

Index

Note: Page numbers in **bold** type refer to figures
Page numbers in *italic* type refer to tables
Page numbers followed by 'n' refer to notes